# Educating
# Shelly

*by*

*Rochelle LaMotte McDonald*

Dedication
This book is dedicated to my children
who have given me a unique education.

Acknowlegements:  I wish to thank all the people who helped me put this project together and believed I had an important message.  Thank you to the friends who allowed me to show their children's experience, my children who I am probably embarrassing totally, the professionals who had the patience to answer my unending questions, and the people who helped me balance my views.

Disclaimer:  The people in this book are real.  This book is a compilation of my experiences, observations, and opinions of the education system and patterns I noticed  in the media.  No malicious intent towards any specific person is intended.  I tried not to mention specific names, but anonymity was sometimes impossible.

# Shelly's ABC's

A. First Impressions
B. Buildings & Grounds
C. Parent-Teacher Entities
D. Fund Raising
E. Differences & Disabilities
F. Programs
G. Transportation & Field Trips
H. Homework
I. Drugs & Weapons
J. Volunteering
K. Curriculum
L. Crimes & Punishment
M. Discrimination, Harassment & Abuse
N. Safety & Security
O. Politics
P. Policies & Procedures
Q. Alternative Education & Getting Credit
R. Reduce, Reuse & Recycle
S. Sickness & Health
T. Technology
U. Celebrations
V. Supplies
W. Sex
X. Summer School
Y. Mobility
Z. Last Impressions

# TABLE OF CONTENTS

## Preface

Recipe for Cooking a Frog

Take one healthy frog
Place it in a pot of cool water.
Gently apply the heat.
By the time the frog realizes the water is getting hot,
the heat will have sapped the strength from his muscles.

Result: One cooked frog

# Introduction

When I embarked upon this endeavor to get my children educated, I didn't realize that I was on a fool's errand. First of all, I didn't consider myself to be a fool, but I did know myself well enough to know that I didn't know everything. Secondly, I didn't think that it would be all that difficult to teach three children who were curious and interested.

A teacher-friend once told me never to trust a teacher. Trusting the teachers was my second mistake. I made my first mistake before any of my children ever set foot in a school. I bought some phonics tapes and allowed my son Jeff, to teach himself to read at the age of four.

Despite these pessimistic statements, I am a strong believer in education. To understand my reasoning and motives, one would have to understand where I came from. My parents believed that we probably wouldn't marry wealthy people when we graduated from high school. Therefore, we would need to be relatively self-sufficient. Boys and girls alike were taught how to cook, clean, tear down a house, and put it back together.

My maternal grandfather told his daughters, if they could learn something for free, that was good, but getting paid to learn something was better. My mother worked for a publishing house from the time she was 16 until she had me, when she was 30. She was one of the people who could figure out how to save time in the workplace, but that wasn't her official job.

My father was within a year of getting his degree in engineering when he was drafted for the Korean War. When he got back, he was never able to return to school. He became a mailman instead. As the oldest of 11 children, he knew how to organize children. He also spent several years as a scoutmaster before we came along. That meant he was a good educator. He always believed in the teachable moment. He and Mom planned several interesting field trips for us, as children.

My parents always allowed us access to whatever information we were interested in. They had encyclopedias and dictionaries in the house. If we wanted to know about a word, we would be told to look it up in the dictionary. Often, the hunt for the word was lengthy. Not because we couldn't find it, but because while we were looking, we might find other interesting words. We also had library cards, and Mom took us to the library regularly.

My parents also encouraged us to have a feasible plan. We would outline our plan and either Mom or Dad would point out only the fatal flaws. Often, a solution could be found to make the plan workable. We learned how to go around obstacles. To this day, we are valuable employees because of this skill. We were expected to do our best and rise to a good challenge. These were the qualities I expected in my own children and their education. Was it too much to expect?

My parents were involved with the PTA. I remember seeing my parents dressed up to go out to a PTA meeting. As an adult, I have something in common with my parents and the PTA meetings: Frustration. Some days, people wonder if the PTA really accomplishes anything of importance. My parents didn't volunteer at the school on a regular basis. If a supply was requested, they sent the required item. Mom baked cookies when they were needed. If my parents had a prop that would help with a subject we were learning about in class, they would send it to the school. Mom did drive for field trips when all four of us were in school for the full day. She would have the most interesting conversations with whichever one of our classmates sat in the front seat with her. She always laughed at the lame jokes elementary school students tell. Mom was also good at short-circuiting disruptive behavior. You can't do that without having some understanding of children.

My parents believed that we should give our teachers a fair chance before judging them. Because our teachers knew that our parents respected them, they listened when Mom and Dad made suggestions about how to deal with us. In my case, I was disruptive during first and second grade when I completed my work. My parents informed the teachers that I wasn't troublesome while reading, so books were offered as an incentive when my work was completed. The teachers learned that a library pass or free reading went a long way toward saving their sanity.

The city I grew up in was small enough, and our family was large enough, that most people in town knew us. There were five elementary schools, a junior high, and a high school. The high school had no specific personal name. It was just THE South Saint Paul High School. My father had attended one of the elementary schools, when he was a child. He was 36 when I was born. It was recently demolished (within the past 10 years) and a new school has been built. There was also an elementary school four blocks from our house. It was built around the time I was born. At the last count, it was a church. The city sold it for a song when the baby boomers from my generation thinned out. Now the city is younger again, and they may have to consider new school construction costs.

Before my children were born, I started buying educational books. We have always had dictionaries and encyclopedias. When my children were little, a book was a book. They saw no difference between a storybook and an encyclopedia. They also have library cards, which they use regularly. Things they have now, that we didn't have then, are the cable and the Internet. One of my daughter's friends teased her about how many books we had in our house. She said we had more than her family did, and her parents were teachers!

I knew that once I had children, I would become part of their education. When they started school, I entered the system, fully intending to be of assistance. My education has been quite interesting. Coming from a family where boredom wasn't tolerated, and the situation had to be pretty extreme to be called "impossible", I tried to pass these ideas on to my children.

Since my older son, Jeff, entered school in 1988, I have dealt with two school districts (California and Alaska), three children (my own), and seven schools. I have experienced: kindergarten school, double-sessions, year-round education, multi-age classrooms, an optional setting, and home schooling. My work experience has included: helping in the classrooms, working in the library, chaperoning field trips, attending and serving at PTA meetings, participating in recycling programs, and attending school board meetings. My children have been labeled "gifted", and "Attention Deficit".

I have seen both the good face and the bad face of education. I don't know what your schools may be like, but I believe school isn't exclusively the teacher's responsibility. It should be a group effort, and we should be challenging our children rather than stifling their gifts.

The following book is the experiences of my friends and I, as we struggled to keep up with the learning curve, while working with our children's teachers to get our children educated. Often, the professional educators would tell us we were responsible for "fixing" our children's educational problems.

Sometimes, we were sure the object of the education system wasn't to teach our children… but to try to teach us.

# Chapter 1
## Kindergarten School 1988-89

A) FIRST IMPRESSIONS: *Location, Location, Location*

When Jeff was three years old, we finally bought our first house. Among the things we considered when making our purchase were; whether the neighborhood was quiet and safe, proximity to shopping and, of course, proximity to a school. With three small children, and only one vehicle in the house, I knew walking long distances could be a problem. The school was only four blocks away from our house. It seemed like a perfect location.

By the time Jeff registered for kindergarten, overcrowding would dictate a shift in the student population. Jeff's school would be miles away, and would be totally populated by kindergärtners With all the new housing being built up in the area, the three elementary schools in our district were filling up fast. The Kindergarten School was being set up in the new construction zone. At the time, it looked like the site was out in the middle of nowhere. It was actually only a few miles away from our house. Yet it took me forty-five minutes to cover the distance, briskly on foot.

B) BUILDINGS & GROUNDS: *The Portable School*

The location for the new Kindergarten School was referred to as, "Future School Site #5". The school was going to be temporary until the new school was completed on "Future School Site #4". It would take about two years to build a new school, from the time the ground was broken. Nobody liked the inconvenience, but there were no alternatives at the time.

The first time we, the parents, saw the nearly completed school, it was about two weeks before school was scheduled to start. There were six "buildings" forming a circle on a dirt lot. Two portable classrooms formed each "building". Two of these classrooms formed the office building. Two of them formed the cafeteria. Two others formed rooms for pull-out classes (gym, music, library). The other three buildings were the regular classrooms.

Two weeks later, water and electricity would be hooked up to the buildings, the area inside the circle would be covered with sod and filled with playground equipment, and most importantly, the area would be surrounded with a chain link fence (to keep curious kindergärtners from straying into construction areas).

The advantage of building a school with portable classrooms is that the portables are rented, so they are a relatively inexpensive alternative for a short-term problem. Building an actual school building would have cost about $5 million. The water and electricity were necessary installations. When the school was dismantled, the utilities could be sealed off until they were needed in the future. The option of a portable school was definitely innovative.

C) PARENT –TEACHER ENTITY: *An Introduction to Parent Teacher Groups*

Soon after school started, Jeff brought home a paper announcing the first parent-teacher meeting for this school. The flier indicated that business covered, during this meeting, would include what the new entity would be called, and fund raising ideas. The objective of the fund raiser was to raise money for some library books for the students to enjoy.

I was bubbly, as I dressed for the meeting. I remember my parents getting dressed up to attend PTA meetings when I was in school. Joining this group would definitely be a way to contribute to my local community. I would be one of many adults, working together for our children's welfare. I thought about all the ideas I knew of for raising money, as I tucked my list into my purse. I even had a new idea to offer that I felt was quite exciting. I put on my rose-colored glasses, kissed my husband and kids goodbye, and drove off to the meeting.

There were several parents in attendance at the meeting. The Principal spoke first. She was a perky blond, who sort of reminded me of Doris Day. She welcomed us and introduced us to the president of our parent-teacher entity.

The president proceeded to talk about what we should call ourselves. She had been a PTA president the previous year. She held up a solitary piece of paper, as evidence of support from the state or national level of PTA. It looked quite insignificant when presented in that manner. Supposedly, our dues would be wasted, if we chose to be PTA members again. We would have to send part of our dues to the state and national levels. Wouldn't it be much better to pay lower dues and keep them in our school?

If we rejected the idea of being a PTA, what were our options? The options were: calling ourselves a PTO (Parent Teacher Organization), or a PTC (Parent Teacher Club). While the dues would stay in the school, the downside was that we wouldn't have any state or national support. Since the president had shown, very clearly, how much support we would get from belonging to a national organization, most of the parents voted to become a PTO.

The meeting closed without any mention of a fund raiser I was somewhat confused. After all, fund raising had been in the biggest type on the flier, yet there was no hint of it at the meeting. No one else seemed to notice that the subject hadn't been brought up. Had I missed something, or had the meeting just run longer than expected?

I decided to drop my fund raising proposal off at the school the next morning. That way, there would probably be more time for the PTO president to consider it.

## D) FUND RAISERS: *Process of Elimination*

As a teenager, I had participated in several fund raising endeavors. I had seen the benefits and drawbacks of several fund raisers. Candy was usually popular because of it's relatively low price, but sometimes it isn't appropriate for diabetics and older people. Gift-wrap also seemed popular, but one can only buy so much gift-wrap in a year. If you sell raffle tickets for a shopping spree, you need to have a value limit for the prize, up front, or you can easily end up in the red.

I sold oranges and grapefruits for a couple years, for a band. The first year, I easily made my quota in my neighborhood. If people didn't know me, they knew my dad, who was the letter carrier. The second year, I was placed on a route that had several older and single person homes. Unfortunately, the quantity of fruit we were offering was more suitable for families. While the people on this route might have been interested in supporting the band, they just couldn't eat that much fruit before it would spoil.

After consulting with my parents, I modified my approach by offering a more manageable quantity at a pro-rated price. I sold fruit to almost every house I visited. I also sold several boxes to my dad's customers, because whoever had been assigned to my previous route wasn't covering it well.

When all was said and done, I had made my quota, but the band director disapproved of my methods. He complained that all of the old and single people would want to buy their fruit that way the next year. He looked at it as lower sales, when, in reality, these people weren't already supporting us. Many of my classmates said they had run into the same difficulty and would have been able to improve their sales if they had known about my strategy. The lesson I had learned was, try to find a way to appeal to as many people as possible with your fund raiser

Since there was no discussion about the fund raiser at the PTO meeting, I decided to submit my idea to the school the next day. I thought I had come up with a decent fund raising plan. The price range fit everyone's budgets, and the products were things almost everyone could use. I think about the only group we couldn't have sold anything to would have been bald men, with sensitive skin. The product line had a price range from 50c to seven dollars. The quality of the products was excellent and the company had a good reputation. There was no sugar content. Best of all, the profit margin was competitive.

I sold Avon products, and I thought it would be great for a fund raiser  Unfortunately, there was no company-approved flier, so I had to make my own.  My fund raiser list included: bars of soap, hand creams, lip balms, shampoo, bubble bath, body lotion, a mini hair brush, and bath oil.  I felt the cause was good enough to waive any personal profit, especially if I got decent help sorting the orders when they came in.

My offer wasn't completely selfless.  A good fund raiser could raise the profit on the rest of my order.  It would have looked like a good increase in sales, which would have translated into a bigger prize from Avon at the end of the year.  I also could have attracted more potential customers.

A week had passed since I had submitted my plan to the school.  The PTO president informed me that they had decided against my offer.  It seemed that a Tupperware mom and I had "canceled each other out".  I wish I could have met with the other mother, because I don't think our fund raisers would have been in competition.  I think we could have had a fantastic fund raiser, if we would have been allowed to combine our offers.  It might have been different if she had been a Mary Kay representative.

The school was looking for something that neither the Tupperware mom, nor I could offer: 50% profit AND a prize for each student who participated.  Supposedly, the school had found such a fund raiser  If they did, Jeff never brought any fund raising paperwork home, except for a flier for a book fair.

## E) DISABILITIES & DIFFERENCES: *Easy Reader*

Jeff taught himself to read when he was four years old.  He used the "Fun with Phonics" set and the "Reader Rabbit" computer program.  We also learned, when he was four, that the computer may not always be our friend.  I assumed, since the computer programs were educational, he could play them to his heart's content.  I was wrong.

Long term exposure to the computer each day caused behavioral problems.  A couple trips to the psychologist helped us solve the problem.  We had owned the computer longer than the child, so we couldn't see the problem right away.  The psychologist advised us to deprive Jeff of something he enjoyed, if he misbehaved so often.  The computer was what he enjoyed most, so that was what we restricted. The computer was allowed as a treat.  We noticed, nearly immediately, that his behavior improved when computer use was restricted.

When Jeff started school, I informed the teacher that he already knew how to read.  She handled it very well.  She told him not to blurt out words that he could read, because everyone needed a turn.  At certain times, he was also allowed free reading time.  He was reading at about second grade level when he entered kindergarten.

An ability that I thought would be a time saving asset for the teacher, would soon become a liability.  Teachers would think that my smart son needed no help.  No child is a perfect student.  There is always a point of weakness.  By the time Jeff's deficiency was recognized, it was the size of the Grand Canyon.

## *Your Son Can Read Cursive!*

While I was dealing with Jeff in a California Kindergarten, Sally was dealing with her son in an Alaskan Kindergarten.

Sally's son had contracted meningitis a few days after receiving a vaccination.  He was nearly two years old.  He had to learn how to walk and talk again at that point.  Sally said he wasn't the same child after the illness.  He would go to school and be diagnosed as Attention Deficit, but that wasn't the whole picture. It was just the easiest label at the time.

When Sally enrolled her son in school, she made a point of telling the teacher what her son could do.  At the time, he had all of his numbers down pretty well, and he could read.  Sally advised the teacher not to write anything down, where he could read it, because he loved to practice his reading and would read everything out loud.  If the teacher didn't want it read out loud, she should keep it out of his sight.  The only thing that Sally hadn't managed to teach her son, was how to use scissors. She hoped the school would have better luck with him on that point.

During the first conference, the teacher exclaimed that Sally's son could read cursive. She also covered all the things the boy was competent in, according to Kindergarten standards. Very little had changed, since Sally brought her son to school. The teacher pointed out that Sally needed to work with her son on using scissors, since that was the point where he was lacking ability.

The teacher effectively took credit for teaching Sally's son all these wonderful skills, that Sally had sent him to school with, but she couldn't teach him how to use scissors. Sally wondered why her son was even in school, if they couldn't teach him the one thing that she had been unsuccessful with.

## G) TRANSPORTATION & FIELD TRIPS: *Bussing the Kindergärtners*
On the first day of school, I stood at the bus stop with two other mothers, as we each put our oldest child on the bus to go to school. To me, it was sort of a scary feeling. It wouldn't be like there were older children on the bus, who Jeff would know. All of the other children would be strangers. The two other children at the bus stop were already friends, so they weren't embarking on this new journey alone. They would probably stick together. Would anyone notice if Jeff were missing?

It is obvious that my fears were unfounded, at the time. The bus ride was always safe, and Jeff always arrived home in good condition. Unfortunately, I would hear about a handful of horror stories of misplaced children over the years.

## W) SEX: *The Birds and the Bees*
Even though Jeff could read already, he still liked it when I read to him. One of our children's favorite books was the encyclopedia. They would pick out one of the encyclopedias, look for interesting pictures, and ask me to read about the picture. One day, I remember the kids asking me to read about a Tasmanian Tiger. It sure looked ferocious in the picture.

One day, Jeff picked up one of the colorful books I had about the human body. As usual, he found a picture that looked interesting, and asked me to read about it. It was an internal depiction of the female reproductive system. Of course, Melissa, who was three years old, and Matthew, who was two, had to hear the story, too. I read what was on the page, as if it was any other story. The kids asked any questions they had, and I answered. Somehow, I hadn't figured I would be having this discussion with my children until they were a little bit older. Finally, the kids lost interest in the picture, and asked if they could go out to play.

I know that five year olds can ask the most interesting questions at the most inconvenient times, so I informed Jeff's teacher, during the parent-teacher conferences, that he was asking questions about sex. If he asked a question during class, he was to be directed back to us. I figured, if she were aware of his curiosity, directing him back to us would keep more kids from asking similar questions in class.

One of my friends had another reason why she would have told her child's teacher about a seemingly precocious interest in sex. Her nephew had been removed from his parents when he displayed knowledge about reproduction that seemed to be beyond his years. Authorities removed him from his parents' custody because they assumed he had been sexually abused. The reality was he had visited a working farm. Animals don't usually go behind locked doors to have sex. When he had questions, his parents answered him. Therefore, he had knowledge.

It would be great if there was an easy way to determine whether a child had been sexually abused. Knowledge of reproductive mechanics shouldn't be the only criteria to remove a child from his family. Jeff never asked his questions at school. He saved them all for me.

Lucky me.

# Chapter 2
## The Neighborhood School 1989-90

### A) FIRST IMPRESSIONS: *Double Sessions*

Jeff was going to be attending the school near our house, but with the building explosion that was going on in our area, the schools were filling up faster than we could generate classrooms. We needed more classrooms, but our options were limited. Basically, our only feasible option was double sessions, until we could install more portable classrooms on any of the school property.

Our school was chosen to receive the portables. If you consider the schools to be labeled A, B, and C (with our school being C), Schools A and B were eliminated due to site problems. School A didn't have any room for installation of portables, and School B had insufficient plumbing and electrical capabilities to accommodate a large influx of students. Therefore, we were left. We had the space and the utility capabilities to accommodate the extra students.

It would take a couple months to get everything installed. Meanwhile, the first and second graders would share the same classroom space and be double-session half a day, as if they were on a kindergarten schedule. This abbreviated schedule would last for two months. During that time, teachers barely had time to teach students the basic reading, writing, and arithmetic. There would be no time for frills like music or art.

### C) THE PARENT-TEACHER ENTITY: *The Parent Teacher Club*

This year, our parent-teacher entity was called the PTC, or the Parent Teacher Club. I went to most of the meetings, but attendance was abysmal. There was a meeting in October that was highly publicized. They were going to discuss school bonds. I remember hearing that California had a "Triple A" bond rating. If California were a person; "Triple A" would indicate an excellent credit rating. Overcrowded schools was a major concern, and bringing in more money was one way to alleviate the problem.

I arrived at the meeting and was surprised to find that I was the only non-board member who was in attendance. The guest speaker was well prepared, and gave a wonderful speech. Too bad more people didn't feel it was worth their time to find out what was happening. It would be May before any more interest was generated on this subject.

The speaker discussed the condition of schools in California. Money was needed to build new schools and upgrade aging schools. Unfortunately, the estimate for everything that needed to be done "at this minute" was conservatively $17 BILLION. This was unfortunate because the track record for California voters, voting on bond measures, showed that as soon as the word 'billion' shows up on the ballot, it was voted down. In other words, the most money the state could ask for on a bond issue was $999,999,999.99. I'm not sure if there was any way that they could have put educational bonds on local ballots in local elections. At the current acceptance rate of state voters, it would take eighteen elections to raise the money that was needed at that minute. Realistically, the work that was needed on the school system couldn't be accomplished in a year, but the timetable for raising the money was unbelievable.

Because raising the necessary money was truly an impossible dream, the state had devised some guidelines to determine which school districts would get more funding, as far as new buildings went. The school districts would be prioritized depending on how many avenues they had exhausted. Before a school district could ask for more money for new buildings, they had to exhaust: double-seasoning, portable classrooms, and converting existing schools to year-round education (YRE) programs. A school district could get money for upgrading a school if the school was going to be converted to YRE. The school district would also have to agree to this condition: any new schools in their district would be designated YRE. These measures were the only way to bridge the fiscal gap, no matter how many people objected to them.

I could see the logic of these measures. If they were having trouble trying to get the money to maintain existing schools, building more schools might just compound the maintenance problem. Converting the traditional school to a YRE school could accommodate 33% more students without having the overcrowding problem.

This was the first time I heard that the new school would be YRE, and the prospect intrigued me. This was also the first time that I heard the price of an elementary school. At the time, an elementary school cost $5 million to build. I wish I had asked whether that was just for the building, or if the price included the furniture.

### D) FUND RAISING: *Timing is Everything*

As I mentioned in the previous chapter, I thought I had an extremely good fund raising idea, and I offered it to the school. It had a good price range, could be used by nearly everyone, wouldn't spoil very quickly, and wouldn't derail your diet or affect your diabetes. Again, I was enthusiastic as I made my pitch. Again, I was shot down. I don't know if the school even thought my idea was good. I was only told that my timing was off. They chose fund raisers in the spring for the fall. I was too late for this year.

The fund raiser that had been chosen was gift-wrap. The letter that accompanied the fund raising packet suggested that students sell to their neighbors and relatives. It was also suggested that parents take the materials to their work. Almost all the avenues for raising the money were difficult for our family. Neighbors said they already knew a child they would be buying from, our relatives were all far away, and my business already involved sales. If I sold the fund raiser to my customers, it could decrease my regular income. My husband had a good reason not to take the materials to work. He worked for the government, and no soliciting was allowed on government property. Living near a military base, I wonder how many other parents had that restriction, too.

We did manage to buy enough of the products from the fund raiser to qualify for the prize Jeff wanted. Unfortunately, they were short on that item and he was given an alternate prize.

### *Santa's Secret Shop*

This was the first year that I had ever heard of the concept referred to as, "Santa's Secret Shop". The concept involved parents donating "white elephants" or craft items to the cause. The donations would then be priced reasonably for a child's budget. The children would choose what they wanted for their parents, within their allowance, and they could surprise their parents.

I painted about a dozen inexpensive plaster ornaments, and donated them. I heard that they sold really fast. This was quite different than the traditional school art projects that we had made growing up. I guess it's because so many children currently have multiple sets of parents, and there is rarely enough time (during the school day) to duplicate projects. With cutbacks, the schools don't have the funding to have several projects that are suitable as gifts. While we had easily made the paperweight/impaler from plaster, a nail, and some paint. Projects like that are frowned upon these days.

### E) DIFFERENCES & DISABILITIES: *Let Her Read to the Class*

Laurel's daughter was curious. Like Jeff, she showed interest in reading at an early age. Laurel's family always had books around, so her daughter was exposed to reading. Everyone read to her. She begged Laurel to teach her how to read, so Laurel taught her.

In Kindergarten, Laurel's daughter was reading at a second grade level. Laurel spoke with the teacher and the principal about her daughter's ability, and how to deal with it. Everyone was in agreement. Her daughter should be allowed to read at her own speed.

Everything seemed to be going well at school, until report card time. Laurel's daughter received low marks in behavior from the school's librarian. If the librarian was reading a book to the class that Laurel's daughter had already read, she quietly got up, went to the nearest bookshelf, and chose a book that interested her.  As her mother instructed her, when in a library situation, she replaced the book from the shelf with a "marker".  She wasn't being disruptive, just disinterested.

Laurel went to speak with the school librarian.  The librarian thought the idea of a child reading at that age was ludicrous.  Obviously, there was something wrong with Laurel, if she believed her daughter could actually read.  Laurel suggested, when her daughter showed signs of losing interest, the librarian should offer her the chance to read the story to the class.

Laurel asked the librarian if she had spoken to her daughter's teacher, the principal, her daughter, or her husband about the situation.  The answer was, "No".  The librarian refused to budge. Laurel said that the librarian acted as if her daughter had been extremely disruptive as she went to the bookshelf, picking out massive quantities of books, and juggling with them.

The principal and the teacher intervened to straighten the librarian out, by giving her a demonstration of the girl's reading ability.  After that, she was allowed to choose whichever book she wanted for quiet reading.

## F) PROGRAMS: *D.E.A.R. B.E.A.R.*

The school had a really good reading program.  It was called DEAR BEAR.  That stood for Drop Everything And Read (and) Be Enthusiastic About Reading.  It required that a certain amount of reading be done by each child, according to their age and reading ability.  Younger students usually had to read a certain amount of books.  Older students read by the page.

The program required that the reading be recorded.  It was sort of like the practice time sheets that one fills out for playing a musical instrument.  The students are supposed to record which books or how many pages of a certain book they read that day.  The parents are supposed to encourage the reading, and sign the bottom of the paper at the end of the month.

Each month a child participated, they got a prize.  As the year progressed, the prizes got bigger.  Buttons, pencils, an age appropriate paperback book, and a T-shirt were among the prizes given.  The T-shirt was given to those students who had participated consistently for the whole year.  Each year, the T-shirt was different because different people designed them.

Jeff had no trouble with the reading program.  Even though he was only a first grader, he was a voracious reader, and was reading books that are referred to as "three letter fiction" (because of the way they are shelved), or chapter books.

## H) HOMEWORK: *Writer's Block?*

As a first grader, Jeff was given basic spelling words.  To be exact, each week they would be given a dozen words.  Jeff's teacher gave the class a weekly assignment, where they were supposed to come up with a sentence for each of their words.  I remember clearly that the word 'bird' was on one list.  We went around in circles trying to get that list done.  It wasn't that Jeff couldn't spell the word.  He just couldn't/wouldn't come up with a sentence for these words.  In high school, he would have to do the same activity with more difficult words, that I even found difficult to use in a sentence.

I think I spent nearly an hour trying to get him to write his twelve sentences, before I gave up.  I remember asking him to describe a bird.  He countered with, "What bird?"  I made several suggestions of birds.  He wasn't interested.  I suggested basic, age appropriate sentences, which he also rejected.  I couldn't get inside his head.  I knew that his vocabulary wasn't limited.  I'm sure he could have described a specific bird in detail, if he was interested enough. What was wrong with my son?

After trying to work with him for a while, I decided he was just being stubborn, so I told him that he would be grounded to his room until the homework was done.  I checked in on him several times that evening, but he still had no sentences done. I kept him home from school the next day and fought with him over his assignment. It was an easy assignment, yet I couldn't motivate him with praise or force.

I sent him to school the following day, with his completed homework and a note of explanation for his teacher. I should have realized by his slow and meticulous writing, that I was dealing with either a perfectionist or someone who was having difficulty holding his pencil. Looking back, I might have been more successful if we had had a pencil grip in his pencil, right away. An implement that was so inexpensive might have saved us a lot of friction. Homework would continue to be a battle for the rest of the year.

## J) VOLUNTEERING: *Testing the Water*

Even though I wanted to help at school, I still had two preschoolers to deal with at home, so my volunteer activity would be limited. This year, I donated things for Santa's Secret Shop and baked cookies whenever the need arose. I also helped the PTC by cutting out cute graphics for their newsletters. I felt the people I worked with appreciated my contributions. Not everyone can contribute to the education process the same way, but I feel we all have something to contribute. It's just a matter of finding our niche.

## Q) ALTERNATIVE EDUCATION & GETTING CREDIT: *Don't Shoot the Messenger!*

It was almost the end of the school year. The new school was going to be opening up. It was a time to rejoice. Soon, the overcrowding would end. Celebration time lasted about a nanosecond. The school district sent out a paper that announced a meeting about zoning for the new school. If zoning was the only topic, the meeting might have been more peaceful. Besides zoning changes, the new school was, according to the state's requirements, designated as a YRE school.

We walked into the meeting, and were lucky to get a seat. I had pulled some muscles in my back and standing was extremely uncomfortable, but I was interested in what was going to be said about the rezoning. My interest in the information was stronger than my physical discomfort. The meeting soon turned into "Standing Room Only". I was intrigued by the concept of YRE, and I had friends whose children were blossoming in that type of school.

I felt sorry for the man who was chairing the meeting. I believe he was the Superintendent. The packed room soon turned into an angry mob. This man had probably been dealing with how to present this information to these parents for the better part of a year. Supposedly, these parents were intelligent, yet they claimed to be surprised by this situation. I wondered how the whole room full of people could be so ignorant.

Transparencies were displayed showing the current boundaries for the existing three schools. Our school had a relatively central location. New houses had been built on the east and west sides of our school zone. The kindergarten school was in the area to the west. The year-round school was located in the east. Basically, the new zoning would affect students who were currently going to our neighborhood school. Students who lived in the new neighborhoods on the west side would be transported to the new school. The kindergarten school would be dismantled. If students who lived near our school wanted to attend the year-round school, they had to have their own transportation. I had figured it out. The new school was eight and a half blocks from our house. If I wanted to send my children there, I would be doing a lot of walking.

The floor was open to comments, and there was a lectern set up at the back of the room for that purpose. In the forty-five minutes I stood in line to present testimony, I thought that I had never heard so much whining and hostility in my life. Parents objected to the multi-track system. The schedule was nine weeks in school and three weeks out, with four tracks.

Three groups of students (tracks) would be in school at any given time. The first track would start July 2. Three weeks later, the next track would start. By the time the fourth track started, the first track would be ready for their break. One mom claimed she couldn't get twelve weeks off to deal with her child's erratic vacation schedule. I wondered what she did with her child when there were twelve weeks of vacation in a block, during the summer. Parents came up to speak with (what seemed like) reams of notes to prove their objections. The only valid objection that I could see was the custody issue. Sharing custody with an out-of-state parent can be both tricky and costly, if there are no YRE schools in your ex's location.

Parents were irate. How dare the school district dictate where their children could go to school! This was the first time I heard the term "zone exemption". Parents could possibly get a zone exemption to put their children in one of the traditional schools. Of course, there would be limited space and special requirements for receiving the zone exemption.

I finally got up to the lectern. I'm sure there was fire in my eyes when I addressed the gathering. I chastised them for trying to shoot the messenger. He had to work within the boundaries he was allowed. I told them that there had been at least one meeting earlier in the year, which discussed these problems, yet nobody bothered to attend. I loudly proclaimed that I was going to get a zone exemption for my children to be able to attend this new school, even though it would cause some hardship as far as transportation went.

After I said my piece, we left the meeting. I don't know how many other parents actually felt the same way I did. I know the teachers had been polled as to who wanted to teach at the new school. Some of them went voluntarily. Others were volunteered military style.

# Chapter 3
## Year Round Education 1990-91

### A) FIRST IMPRESSIONS: *The New School*

Jeff was starting the second grade and Melissa was starting Kindergarten. We were accepted for the first track, which started on July 2. That was only two weeks after the traditional school let out. We had arranged our vacation for three weeks as soon as Jeff got out of school, so the kids had almost a week to catch up on, when we got back.

This school was set up as individual buildings for each grade level. Each little building had four rooms in it, except the kindergarten. The Kindergarten only needed two rooms. The four rooms in the other grades consisted of three classrooms, and a storage room that was accessible from each classroom. The storage room had storage space for all four teachers. There was also a main building, which housed the office, gym, library, and music room.

The Kindergarten School had been dismantled, and our kindergärtners benefited by receiving the playground equipment. I thought both of the teachers I had to deal with were nice. Of course, I introduced myself and offered to make cookies, if any were needed. Jeff's first grade teacher was at the new school. Both she and the second grade teacher came to the new school voluntarily.

### B) BUILDINGS & GROUNDS: *The Garden*

The new school had a garden. One of the teachers worked with some of the students to get it ready. It covered a decent area and had a fence around it. In the springtime, they planted some vegetables and flowers. It was growing pretty decently by the time our school year ended.

*Tall Grass and Union Labor*

Because the school was new when school started, they had to keep watering the sod to make sure it would get good roots. Being summertime, I wondered why people watered their grass in the afternoon. It seemed like a waste of water. Half of it would probably evaporate before it reached the ground. The water in California was metered, and I don't know how much difference watering our grounds made in the whole scheme of things. One thing was sure though, the grass was definitely growing.

Several of the parents noticed that the grass was getting quite tall and we asked why it wasn't getting cut. The answer was simple. They couldn't afford to pay the people who cut the grass for the school district to come as often as we might have thought the grass needed to be cut. Some of the parents offered to come and cut the grass. Their offers were met with the response of, "Thank you, but no thanks". Volunteers cutting the grass could cause a myriad of problems. The first problem was, people who kept up the grounds were union workers. Volunteers couldn't be allowed to take their places (jobs). The second reason the school said "No" was because of insurance reasons. If a volunteer got injured because he hit a rock or a sprinkler head, the school district would be liable. They couldn't afford the liability.

The watering was reduced at one point. Then, people who were qualified to do it cut the grass about once a month.

### C) PARENT -TEACHER ENTITY: *Nice Enough*

The school chose the PTC for this year. I tried to attend the meetings. It would be one of the first times I would feel like an outsider at the schools. I asked questions and made suggestions, but I got strange looks. One of the reasons, probably, was the way I think. The other reason probably had more to do with my economic status. I lived in a house that was only about a third of the value of the new houses that were being built in the area. The women in the PTC, who seemed to fit in, all lived in the more expensive houses. It seemed a little bit like a closed society. The kids had friends in school, but they rarely saw them outside of the school setting.

The people around me acted nice enough, but I felt like I wasn't really wanted there. It was probably the only time I have felt like a minority. Their group might have accomplished a lot, but I felt what I could offer wasn't of much value to this group.

## D) FUND RAISING: *Geography Smart*

I offered my fund raiser again. I figured, since this was a new school, they might not have had a chance to choose one yet. Obviously, I wasn't hanging around with the proper people to get the information I needed. I was late again.

One of the fund raisers for this year was called "Geography Smart". I liked the idea because the kids would be earning money for learning something. Kindergärtners and first graders were expected to learn the names of as many states as possible. (My sister had learned a song, in elementary school, called "Fifty Nifty United States", which could have possibly helped this group.) Second, third, and fourth graders had to label the states on a map. The fifth and sixth graders were given the most difficult task. They had to label both the states and capitals, on the map.

Students set out to get pledges for their efforts. A child could get a pledge per state, or a flat pledge of at least $2.00. The company who ran the fund raiser promised to paint a map of the United States on the concrete section of the playground, at the end of the fund raiser. Each child who got a certain amount of pledges got a key ring with a globe on it.

I was among the parents who helped check the papers when the fund raiser was over. Considering we nearly lived on top of Sacramento, the capital of California, there were a lot of students who missed the easy point. I was also amazed at how poorly the majority of sixth graders did. It was almost as if they put no effort into it. Looking back, they might just have been laughing at the process, because some of them had country names instead of state names, all over their maps.

The company did paint a very colorful map on the playground. I don't know how much money we raised, because I never asked. I also don't know how the company who arranged it "profited". The concept could be done in a variety of imaginative ways, without the aid of an outside company. I thought the idea was great because this put some value on what the students were learning. Isn't that the most important thing about education? Placing some value on learning.

## F) PROGRAMS: *S.T.A.R.*

This school had a new acronym for their reading program. It was STAR, which stood for, Sit There And Read. Like the program at the other school, reading records were kept and prizes were awarded for achievement. This program had a slight twist. At the end of the year, every child who had participated for the whole year got to participate in the school sleepover.

The school had enough parental involvement to have an activity like this. Parents volunteered to supervise entertainment, stand watch over the kids as they slept, and make breakfast in the morning. The sleepover was scheduled for a Friday night. My husband volunteered for this activity because he usually couldn't volunteer during the regular school day. There was some horsing around, but there was no malicious activity. There were only two casualties that night. One child got sick during the sleepover. Another student jammed the door into his toe on his way into the bathroom. The adults thought he might have broken it. The sleepover took place in the gym, with boys on one side of the room, and girls on the other side. Both Jeff and Melissa completed the requirements to participate in the sleepover.

## G) TRANSPORTATION & FIELD TRIPS: *The Long Walk*

My husband and my children had to be at their respective work at approximately the same time, but at opposite ends of town. Since we only had one car, driving everyone to his or her destinations in the morning wasn't an option. I would have to walk the kids to school. The route was eight and a half blocks each way. Matthew, who was four, and I would make the round trip three times a day. Melissa would walk it twice a day, and Jeff would make only one round trip.

The school bus passed us every day, and we would wave to the driver. She wasn't allowed to stop to pick us up because it was against the rules. She could lose her job if she made an extra stop. We used the bus to tell time. If the bus passed us when we were closer to the house, we knew we were late.

In the summertime, the walk sometimes seemed so long and hot. Fortunately for us, we passed several sprinklers as we got close to home. We would run through every sprinkler we passed. Most of the time the walk would go quickly, because the kids were always talking to me. I remember Jeff telling me that the teacher had played "The 1812 Overture" for them, in music class. I asked him if he wanted to learn some words for it. He responded, "An overture has no words". By the time we got home, all three of the kids were singing a song to the tune of the 1812 Overture. I felt that was definitely time well spent.

When third quarter came around, I had to buy some new walking shoes, so I decided to buy some shoes that would support my ankles. Two weeks before the quarter ended, I started having some trouble with my knees and walking became excruciating. I asked the school if there was any way I could get Jeff and Melissa on the bus, but nothing could be done.

Jeff had a friend whose mom could drive Jeff and Melissa to school, and bring Jeff home. The school nurse said that she could bring Melissa home, when she went home for lunch. The problem was temporarily solved, and I gave the drivers something for doing this favor. I wondered how we would make it through the fourth quarter. I really didn't want to be dependent on other people for another nine weeks.

Luckily, I had only used my new shoes for walking to school. My knee problem went away and only appeared when I was wearing those shoes. While we were on break, I bought a new pair of shoes, in a less restrictive style. We were back in business and finished out the year walking. As much as we liked the school, transportation was our biggest problem. If something major would happen to me, the kids couldn't walk that far, by themselves.

## J) VOLUNTEERING: *Sugar Cookies and Avon Boxes*

My volunteering was pretty minimal. If sugar cookies were needed, I would whip up a batch. Melissa's class was studying letters of the alphabet. I asked the teacher when they would be studying the letter "R". I would send a treat that fit the lesson. I sent round, red, raspberry sugar cookies.

At the end of the school year, the teacher had to pack all of her classroom into a fourth of the storage room. My kids and I helped Jeff's teacher pack up her room. Usually, boxes from the copier paper were coveted packing boxes. They were the right size for lifting. Avon boxes are a similar size. Both boxes have a fitted lid. On the way to school, I would transport a few boxes on my luggage carrier, these boxes were for Jeff's teacher. I managed to get rid of a few more boxes to other teachers who were also getting ready to pack up.

The classrooms needed a minor stripping. Anything that personally belonged to the teacher had to be removed and stored. Textbooks, and anything else that was school property pretty much stayed in their own places. Jeff's teacher had a rolling shelf to store her reading books on. It was specially built to fit almost snuggly under the counter in the storage room.

I think it took the teacher two or three days to get everything cleared out. The incoming teacher had the weekend to move her things into the classroom. When our teacher came back, she would be in a different classroom.

## K) CURRICULUM: *Minute Math*

One of the things that I thought was great in Jeff's class was "Minute Math". The teacher gave students a worksheet every few days. It consisted of problems in addition, subtraction, or a mixture of both. Students had one minute to complete as many problems as possible. The repetition improved their math skills and represented a competition between students and against their own last score. The students glowed as they watched their scores go up. This was something measurable.

Ironically, Jeff was usually at the end of the group. While he and one of the girls in the class were gifted in math and could solve multiplication and division problems easily, they struggled with addition and subtraction.

### *Silkworms and Mulberry Leaves*

Jeff's class had silkworms. These little creatures were voracious. They just ate so fast. The teacher was trying to find enough food to keep their project fed. The diet of a silkworm consists of mulberry leaves. No other leaf will do. Mulberry trees were plentiful in the area, but I didn't know what one looked like. I looked carefully at the leaves the teacher needed, and realized we passed a very annoying mulberry tree on the way to school every day. We could probably bring in a good supply of fresh leaves.

The next day, when we walked to school, I was carrying a pair of scissors. The tree we passed had branches hanging down so far over the fence that they nearly obstructed the sidewalk. An adult had to either duck under the branch or walk in the street. We could have asked the owner to remove the branch, or we could deal with it in a definitely positive way. Without defacing the tree, we cut a few of the offending groups of leaves off each day, until there was a clear path for walking. By that time, the silk worms were done eating.

## Q) ALTERNATIVE EDUCATION & GETTING CREDIT: *A Legitimate Downside*

One of Jeff's classmates was having some trouble in school. She was a really bright girl. In fact, she was Jeff's closest academic competitor. While Jeff was excelling with the teacher, his classmate was having problems with the teacher. There seemed to be no way to resolve the personality conflict within the school. Since we were in the first track of this multi-track system, the only option was to drop her back to the next track, which was three weeks behind us. Her parents chose the other option available. They moved her back into one of the traditional schools to finish out the year. In this case, I think their choice was determined by getting orders to a new base for the next school year. If there hadn't been a personality conflict, the schedule they had been on still would have fit in with the moving plans. Being on another track might not have worked.

# Chapter 4
## Back to the Neighborhood School - Fall 1991

### A) FIRST IMPRESSIONS: *Meeting the Teachers*

Matthew started school this year. He hadn't had much opportunity to be among other children. There were few children on our street. In order to play with someone in our neighborhood, my kids usually had to walk around the block, because of the high redwood "privacy" fences that separated all of us. I barely knew my neighbors behind us, so I didn't allow the kids to roam. The only other time Matthew had other children to play with was when he was in the nursery at church. He played well by himself, but he was interested in going to school. His teacher was a very pleasant young woman.

Melissa was starting first grade. She was looking forward to learning how to read. She also had a female teacher.

Jeff had his first male teacher. I had met this teacher in a recycling meeting the previous spring. At first, he had looked intimidating. He was a big man with a beard and mustache. I liked the way he thought, though. I was sure he would understand Jeff just fine.

### D) FUND RAISING: *Boycotting the Fund Raiser*

I didn't try offering my fund raiser this year. We had found out in April that my husband's job was going to disappear. In military or government terms, it was referred to as a reduction in forces or "RIF". We didn't know how long we would be in the area for the next school year. I couldn't start up a fund raiser if he found a new job in June and we were in transit by September.

The kids brought home the fund raising packets with the hopes of getting the cheap prizes. There was no way any of them would get the top prize: the bicycle. I looked at the prizes they wanted, and bought them locally. Then, I gave each of them a check to take to school, for the amount I had decided I would have spent on fund raising products I didn't need. The previous reasons for our family being unsuccessful with a fund raiser still applied, and I wasn't interested in packing things I didn't really need.

### E) DISABILITIES & DIFFERENCES: *Congratulations, You have a Gifted Child!*

I was first asked to have Jeff tested for the Gifted class, by his teacher. After he completed his testing, he was labeled as being gifted across the board: Math, Science, and English. He was still having some trouble with his writing, so he would be pulled from his regular classes of Science and Math to be placed in the GATE (Gifted And Talented Education) classes for these subjects.

Jeff's teacher suggested the testing because Jeff's interest and knowledge far outstripped the regular class. Whenever the teacher asked questions, Jeff seemed to be a bottomless pit of knowledge. He always had his hand in the air, ready for the answer. Unfortunately, the teacher couldn't explore Jeff's depths during class time. Sometimes, he reached the point where Jeff was the only one raising his hand for the answers. Jeff obviously needed more to challenge him.

### *I Think There's Something Wrong With Your Son*

Matthew's teacher complained about Matthew's lack of attention to his projects. He was constantly moving and always visiting. If this were the Kindergarten of my childhood, maybe the kids would have been visiting, but this was considered to be serious. I chalked the visiting up to the fact that Matthew was now exposed to more new children than he had ever seen gathered together before. I was sure he would settle down eventually.

The teacher complained that he either wasn't listening to the instructions, or he chose not to finish his work. The work I was shown were things that showed repeated sequencing. Matthew stopped after doing two sequences. The lesson might have required three or four sequences. Was he possibly bored?

My husband and a male friend had to repeat kindergarten because they were actually above the thinking that went on in the class. Because they were bored, it was perceived that they were slow.

Both of these men were summertime babies, born in July. Like them, Matthew was born in the summer. The teacher suggested maybe Matthew might have been too young (immature) to enter kindergarten. Since he had the desire to go to school, I hadn't seen any good reason to hold him back. Would his actions be any different if I had held him back? Wouldn't he still be overly social a year from now, in a group that had already been "socialized" by childcare and preschools?

F) PROGRAMS: *I Want to Read NOW!*

Melissa wanted to learn how to read, but she refused to play the word games with me or look at the materials Jeff had used. She wanted me to teach her how to recognize the words as whole entities. She didn't want to waste time learning how to sound them out.

Melissa's teacher introduced a set of books to the class. While there were multiple copies of each book, there weren't enough copies in the set for each child to take a copy of the same book home every night. The first story had very simple words that were repeated. The next book built on the vocabulary of the previous book. The book set was through SRA. I believe that means the Scholastic Reading Association, but I may be wrong. There were 40 titles in each box, and two different boxes of books.

Once Melissa started on these books, her reading took off. She wanted to read more of them and go faster. The first week, we took home one book per night. By the weekend, she complained that she wished she could bring some books home for the weekend. The following Monday, we asked the teacher if it was possible for us to bring home two books per night, and two for the weekend. The teacher allowed it. She might have known that mobility is one of the things that can really slow down education, and she knew we would be leaving the school at Christmas time to move to Alaska, so she supported Melissa's interest in developing a good reading base.

By the time we left the school, Melissa managed to read 60 out of the 80 booklets in the reading program. I think I might have managed to sneak a little bit of phonics into her reading. Whatever method she used to learn how to read, once she got started, there was no stopping her. I'm thankful that the teacher allowed her to work at her own pace. It probably helped her to be a more successful person.

J) VOLUNTEERING: *Flexing My Muscles*

My volunteering was relatively limited this year. I baked cookies again. This year, Matthew's class got the round, red, raspberry cookies. I also made play dough for Matthew's class. He was so proud, because his mom was the only one who could make root beer scented play dough. I made it using a package of unsweetened drink mix for the coloring and fragrance.

M) DISCRIMINATION, HARASSMENT & ABUSE: *Living in a Poor Neighborhood*

I heard some of my neighbors talking about the school. It seemed that our school was undesirable in some ways. I couldn't figure out what all the fuss was about. As far as I could see, our school seemed fine. Then, I heard a term I didn't understand. The term was "Title I". Supposedly, attending a Title I school had some sort of stigma attached to it. About all I could glean from the conversation was that we lived in a "poor" neighborhood.

It would be years before I would understand that being labeled "Title I" meant that there was more funding for the school because there was a higher percentage of low income families. Compared to some of the people, who lived in the new $250,000 houses that were being built around us, we were poor. Our house wasn't even worth $100,000. Unlike some of our neighbors, we weren't on welfare and we had things like decent health insurance. I never considered us as a poor family, and I didn't feel that we were anywhere near the poverty level. My perception of being poor meant that you couldn't feed your family and provide the necessities. We weren't anywhere near that.

I wonder if the families who were so shocked by the label were actually shocked enough to move away from the school.

R) REDUCE, REUSE & RECYCLE: *Baby Steps*

Recycling was starting to grow in the Sacramento area. They had a recycling center, so the kids and I actively picked up recyclable glass and aluminum on the way to school. Glass was paying about 2 cents per pound, and aluminum was nearing a dollar a pound. The city was gearing up to do curbside recycling in a quarter of Sacramento. Of course, it wouldn't be our quarter.

Our school district was interested in getting involved with the recycling program. A meeting was scheduled for any interested parties who wanted to attend. Since I had been participating in recycling programs since I had been a teenager, I was definitely interested.

I had attended the meeting the previous spring. Only about a dozen people showed up, but I understood that any teachers who attended were ready to take any information back to their schools. There were lots of ideas, but implementing them would be difficult. We discussed methods like two-sided copying and half sheet fliers. This required minimal training to implement. The next method we discussed was collecting paper at the school, for recycling. This was going to be more difficult. A representative from the local waste management company was at the meeting, to answer any of our questions.

This meeting was where I first met Jeff's teacher. He said that he sent home folders full of corrected homework, newsletters, and advertisements, each week with each student. Parents were asked to sign and date the inside of the folder, to show they had seen the homework. Then, they were to return the emptied folder to the school for the next week. Jeff's teacher suggested they could send the folder home as usual, but the parents could return any papers they didn't want to keep. All the school needed was an efficient collection system.

The waste management representative said they could deliver a handful of large barrels for paper collection. The major training point would be separating the white paper from the colored paper, because they paid different rates. While the waste management company couldn't pay the school for the paper, they offered to pick up the filled barrels for free. Each barrel came up to about my waist. Even though we wouldn't be getting the money for the paper, we would have the satisfaction that our paper wasn't going to make it to the local landfills.

We had three choices for disposing of our paper. They were: 1) Throw the paper in the trash; 2) Transport small amounts of paper to the recycling center and collect a penny per pound; or 3) Accept the free transport. We chose option 3.

The barrels were installed in the fall, and by the time we left the school, at Christmastime, the barrels were being well used.

# Chapter 5
## North to Alaska -Spring 1992

A)  FIRST IMPRESSIONS: *New State, New Teachers, New School*

By the time the kids and I got to Alaska, my husband had picked out a house in a neighborhood like the one we lived in while we were in California.  He enrolled the kids in school before Christmas break, so when school started again, they were all ready to go.

Jeff had a male teacher again. I thought this was probably a good way to continue the year. Melissa had a teacher with a last name that was difficult to spell, so she used it on spelling tests as extra credit. Matthew's teacher was very young, and from the first day, I heard a lot of criticism about her.  I wondered if the criticism was really based on fact, or if it was only jealousy.

I offered to volunteer in all of my children's classes.  Matthew and Melissa's teachers readily accepted my offer.  Jeff's teacher never rejected the offer outright.  He just never completely accepted it.

I seemed to have a problem fitting in at first, because the other adults had decided I was something that I really wasn't.  It was assumed that I was a Californian, just because we had moved to Alaska from California.  Considering we were living in the shadow of two military bases, and the population of the school was highly military and mobile, I wondered why I was labeled.  Maybe it was because my husband no longer had a military label.

I knew when we moved that Alaskans were supposed to be different.  I was looking forward to new experiences.  Who knows, maybe I could learn something new, too.

B) BUILDINGS & GROUNDS: *Inside the School*

Our school was quite full.  There were three kindergarten classes.  The Art teacher used one Kindergarten room in the afternoons.  Each of the other grades had two standard classes, except Modified Primary.  The Music teacher had no classroom.  I would see her rolling her piano up and down the hallway, as she visited each classroom.  Our school was running at capacity, at least.

C) PARENT-TEACHER ENTITY: *You're Not in California Anymore*

I found out that this school had a PTA, and I was interested in attending the next meeting.  Like the meeting I attended in California, I believe I was the only one to show up to this meeting who wasn't on the board.

The main topic of discussion was overcrowding.  It was amazing how universal certain topics were.  The options they discussed to alleviate the overcrowding were: portable buildings or double sessions.  Our school was at capacity.  There wasn't much room for portable classrooms, and double sessions were considered very undesirable.  If the whole school went for double sessions, one group would start at 6 AM and attend school until noon.  The next group would start at noon and attend until 6 PM, in order to comply with educational time requirements.  Supposedly, that would cut into a lot of families' schedules.

I suggested that they look at year round education. I mentioned that building new schools was expensive.  The last I had heard, the price tag was $5 million. You should have seen the horrified looks I received for my nave comment. I was informed, in no uncertain terms, that I was no longer in California. Supposedly, schools didn't cost $5 million in Alaska, but no one seemed interested in enlightening me on what Alaskan schools did cost.  The only information I got about the price of building supplies was, until recently, it cost less to send building materials to Alaska brick by brick, through the mail.

A survey was being sent out to parents, to find out how they felt about the different options.  Year Round Education would be discouraged at all costs, and for the flimsiest reasons.

## D) FUND RAISING: *We Can't Play Favorites*

I offered my fund raiser again at the new school. For some reason, I thought that helping the school raise money was important. Silly me. After I made my offer, the PTA President looked at me, and said, "If we choose your fund raiser, we would have to consider all the parents who want to sell something. We can't play favorites."

I couldn't see any problem with the involvement of other parents. My plan was a one-shot fund raiser, where I wouldn't personally profit from the actual fund raiser My goal was building my customer base, and this might help me find customers in the neighborhood. If another parent wanted to make the same offer I did, the only thing that I could think was, "Wow, what great community involvement and support!" Why did all the fund raisers have to come from outside the state?

### *Gift-wrap and School Pictures*

By the time the pitchmen came in from the gift-wrap and photography companies, I was PTA Secretary. The position was somewhat of a challenge considering I couldn't actually type or take shorthand, and I had a hearing problem that a hearing aid wouldn't help. I took notes about what the pitchmen said.

First came the men from the photography studios. One offered pre-made packages. The school would receive a standard package for each student. There would be an 8 x 10 portrait, a couple 5 x 7 pictures, a few 3 x 5 pictures, and a sheet of wallet sizes. A price list would be included. Parents could pay for any pictures they wanted, and return the rest. They could also order more of the sizes they wanted. We rarely purchased an 8 x 10, unless it was a picture of the family. If it didn't fit in a wallet, most of our relatives wouldn't display it. In my opinion, packages like this were just a waste of materials. Of course, I understand the reasoning behind this offer. Once the parents see the wonderful pictures of their children, they will want to buy the whole package. The photographer is betting on the impulse buy.

The second photographer offered a proof concept. Parents could see the proofs, and order packages before the retake time. I liked this concept better. There have been a few times when I haven't been happy with my proofs and had to get a retake. One such instance was my graduation picture.

Of course, my opinion didn't amount to much. The first photographer's company was chosen. It hadn't occurred to me at this point that school pictures were a fund raiser The school makes money off them. The decision was motivated by greed.

The annual fund raiser was a choice of gift-wrap companies. One supposedly had better paper. Both took about six weeks for turnaround. Turnaround is the time it takes between turning in the orders and receiving the products. The company with (supposedly) the better quality paper didn't send a representative to speak to us. They only sent a package for our consideration. Without a representative, they had no chance against their competitor.

The competition sent a representative. He was definitely a fast talker. If he were trying to deal with me, personally, he would have been out of luck. I wanted to leave the room. He claimed that his fund raiser would provide certain "extras" if we chose them for our fall fund raiser, Santa's Secret Shop, and possibly, a spring fund raiser The extras included free knick-knacks for the fall carnival. He was a smooth talker, and the Board voted for his fund raiser I was sort of tired of overpriced gift-wrap and poor quality merchandise, but that seemed to be the only game in town.

## E) DIFFERENCES & DISABILITIES: *The Gifted Program in Anchorage*

Jeff's status as a "gifted" student carried over to the new school. Instead of having pullouts within the school, students at different grade levels would leave the school for half a day between Tuesday and Thursday, to attend the gifted classes at another school. At this time, five different schools had their gifted students feeding into one school. I don't know if this was due to lack of qualified teachers, lack of funding, low number of gifted students in each school or if that was just the way it was.

Jeff went to the other school with a few of his classmates. He liked his gifted class teacher, but she would have problems with him on certain projects. He always wanted to know how an experiment was supposed to turn out. The students were supposed to give their hypothesis of how things might turn out, but Jeff didn't want to play that game. This is my son who doesn't like surprises. It's just his nature.

The curriculum for this gifted class was different than the class in California. Rather than building on the strengths of each gifted child, this class dealt more with exploration. Besides classroom activities, there were field trips. Was this program good or bad? I don't know, because I didn't attend this class as a volunteer, at this point.

I would learn something else about the special education classes much later. Special education students usually lost time in their core classes for their special attention classes. They weren't allowed to be removed from gym class, music class, library, or art class. Jeff would lose valuable time in his English classes.

## Holding Matthew Back

At the end of the school year, several of the other parents and I were approached by the Kindergarten teacher and the Modified Primary teacher, about our children. While the new kindergarten teacher had cited Matthew's activity level, I still chalked it up to his personality and new surroundings. I didn't want to put Matthew on drugs, because I didn't think he had Attention Deficit Disorder. I had seen him play quietly by himself. He wasn't overly active.

At this meeting, I was told that Matthew was immature and either he needed to be held back in kindergarten or moved up half a step, into Modified Primary. The Modified Primary teacher had interacted with children who were considered to be good candidates for this program. The first thing they looked at was the child's birth date. If a child was born in the summer, like Matthew, or just before the fall cutoff, they were considered young and were therefore potentially immature.

This was a case of two more teachers saying that my son wasn't up to the standard. There was something wrong with him, and they had the answer. Given the choice of holding him back completely, or moving him forward some, I chose to move him forward. I was told that students would be evaluated again, after Modified Primary, to decide whether they were ready for second grade or if they should be placed in first grade.

At the time, I didn't realize how much power I actually had as a parent, and I didn't understand the system very well. I would learn the consequences of not flexing my parental muscles much later. I could have demanded that Matthew be placed in the first grade. If the school didn't believe it was acceptable, I could have gone to Elementary Education, at the school district level, and requested a placement test. But I decided to trust the experience of the teachers rather than my own maternal instinct. Matthew was signed up for Modified Primary for the next year.

Betty's son was also signed up for Modified Primary. He was also a summer baby. In his case, there were vision and hearing problems, which had slowed his progress. Betty hoped gaining an extra year would help her son make up lost ground.

## F) PROGRAMS: *The Green Team*

Melissa's teacher had a large piece of cardboard with 25 pockets glued onto it. The pockets were like the ones in the back of library books, before computerized checkout became popular. Each pocket had a student's name on it. Inside each pocket were five colored cards. They were in this order: green, yellow, orange, red, and blue. If the green card was still showing at the end of the day, you behaved well during class. A yellow or orange card showed you had some difficulty trying to behave. A red card meant that you had been bad enough to visit the principal. A blue card meant that your parents had been called.

When a student misbehaved, they were instructed to pull a card and put it in the back of the pocket, revealing the next card. The goal of the program was for students to "stay on the Green Team". Supposedly, the visual and tactile parts of this activity were to help the students self-monitor their behavior. Melissa had little difficulty with this program.

*Buddy Classes*

Students in older classes were paired up with students from younger classes, for projects and reading. A younger child could read to an older child, and be given a little bit of individual attention. Sometimes, smaller children would feel more comfortable reading to another student, than to an adult. The program also taught a little bit of responsibility to the older students.

I) DRUGS & WEAPONS: *Chasing Melissa*

Melissa had developed strep and we had seen the doctor. He prescribed an antibiotic and required her to stay home from school for a couple days. The day she returned to school, she had a field trip. I saw the teacher in the office, and asked her if she could carry Melissa's medicine on the field trip, making sure Melissa took it at lunchtime. The teacher told me it would be too difficult for her to remember to give Melissa her medicine.

According to school policy, a child couldn't carry any medicine on them, except maybe an asthma inhaler. I would have tucked it in her lunch, if I thought she would notice it and the teacher wouldn't. She hadn't been on the medicine long enough to remember to take it with her lunch. Since having Melissa carry the medicine was against the rules and the teacher couldn't be held responsible for administering it, there was only one option left. I had to ask where they would be at lunchtime, so I could take the medicine to her.

One would have thought I was asking for a state secret, by the reaction I got from the principal and the teacher. Finally, I was told they would be at the children's museum downtown, at lunchtime. I drove downtown, paid a dollar for the parking space, arrived at the museum as the bus pulled up, intercepted Melissa as she got off the bus, made sure she took the pill, and ran off. I saw the look on the face of the parent who was in charge of Melissa. My actions definitely looked suspicious. I might have looked a little more suspicious if I wasn't dragging a kindergärtner along. We arrived back at the school just before the bell rang for Matthew's class.

It seems like there should have been an easier way to do this.

J) VOLUNTEERING: *Acceptance in the Workroom*

This year, when I started volunteering in the school, I met a group of moms who had children Matthew's age. Mary and Betty were first-time kindergarten moms. Susie had a daughter Jeff's age. The diversity of this group was both racial and economic. The following year, Linda would join our group. Her son was also Matthew's age. Sally would round out my friends from this time period. Her son was Jeff's age. I consider myself lucky to be associated with these women. At the time of this writing, we have been friends for over fourteen years!

As a group, we probably could have moved mountains. We were energetic, enthusiastic, and intelligent. We all believed in a better education for our children and honestly thought our participation might help eliminate some of the stress for the overworked teachers.

I saw Mary the most during the first year. You could say that we latched onto the teacher's aide for Modified Primary. She explained to us how the various machines in the workroom worked. The first machine I remember being fascinated by was the mimeograph (ditto) machine. If your master copy was weak, you could put a piece of paper behind it to make a better impression. There was also a machine in the workroom that allowed a person to make new masters from regularly printed paper. I was able to get a lot of use out of this machine. Certain teachers loved us because we could run these machines. If the Xerox machine was down, and the project wasn't too detailed, we would just make a master and run it through the mimeograph machine.

With the financial cutbacks in the schools, our teachers were allowed 2000 copies from the copy machine each month. For classes of about 30-35 students, that averaged out to about three one-sided copies per day. Part of the allowance was due to the wear and tear on the machine. The rest was to conserve paper. The copier had accounts set up for each teacher. When they entered their code, it added to (or subtracted from, depending on your viewpoint) their account total. A teacher could check to see how many copies had been made, periodically. Supposedly, 2000 copies per month is plenty. But then again, plenty is a subjective term.

One of the things I found interesting between different teachers was how they did their copying. I dealt with some teachers who color-coded their worksheets for each subject. The office ran its newsletter on goldenrod paper. It was easy to find the newsletters among other papers, because no one else in the school was allowed to use that color. PTA also had a designated color. I understand that in some classrooms, permission slips were printed on a specific color.

Our workroom was pretty well equipped for volunteers. We had two guillotine-type paper cutters, alphabet die cutters, the mimeograph machine, the Thermofax machine, a computer, a laminator, and a dry mount press. There was only one shortcoming of the workroom. The only work surface was a single, long table for everyone to work at. There wasn't any more space for additional work surfaces.

As a parent–volunteer in a group like this, I felt like I was part of a well-oiled machine. If we found new and better ways to do things, we passed the information on. If a new parent volunteered, we tried to make them feel welcome. Our group was productive, friendly, and efficient.

With a group of parent-volunteers like us, one would have thought we would be a teacher's dream. The teachers were currently in contract negotiations. By the time they were ready for their next contract negotiations, a sinister light would be shined on us, and the teachers would perceive us as a threat to their jobs.

## K) CURRICULUM: *Group Projects*

Jeff's teacher advocated working in groups. The concept wasn't popular with many of the parents I knew. The most undesirable part of the concept was the fact that your grade was dependent on how well your group performed. Some students may have been able to do the assignment alone, with one hand tied behind their back, and get a better grade than they could working with their assigned group. The only alternative for this student might be to do the bulk of the work and carry the rest of the group. This solution means that some members of the group might get a great grade with little or no input.

If the students must work in a group, the work should be divided up fairly, in my opinion. This way, the teacher can monitor individual progress. Otherwise, it can turn into a bigger problem later. While cooperation is important, learning basic skills at this age is crucial. Elementary school is where they should catch the academic problems before they become nearly crippling. By Junior High or High School, the teachers don't have the time and resources to retrain the students who fell through the cracks in elementary school.

### The Whole Word Method

Melissa's teacher taught the whole word method for reading, also known as sight-reading. While this was the method Melissa wanted to learn with originally, I was concerned these students might not be able to sound out more difficult words later. Students were given a list of sight words to learn. Parent volunteers would quiz the students individually with a deck of flash cards. I volunteered for this activity often. There was only one student who couldn't use the flash cards. She read the list with a green transparency over it. That was the first time I had ever heard of color being used in the treatment of dyslexia.

When I worked with most of the students, I wondered if they had learned the list in alphabetical order. Like their list, my stack of cards was alphabetized. I decided to shuffle the deck. At first, the students seemed to be shocked that the words weren't in order.

If a student got a word wrong, I placed that card in a separate pile. They would have a second chance at the rejects. If the word was incorrect a second time, I put it on a list for more practice. As a parent, this was a job I could do. Each student took about 5-10 minutes to quiz. This would have been very time consuming for a teacher to do, without an aide. The teacher had an activity going on in the classroom that wasn't disrupted by students going in and out of the room. I think the time was managed very well.

*Sidewalk Art*

In the springtime, the art teacher took the students outside to paint on the sidewalk around the school. Each square in the sidewalk was divided into sections. Each student was assigned a section, and allowed to design their own pictures. The teacher got the sidewalk wet, and the students used large brushes and tempera paint.

By the end of the week, the sidewalk was completely decorated. You might think that painting a sidewalk would be a short-lived project, but it lasted through the summer and fall. Winter covered it up, and by spring, the sidewalk was ready for the next group. It stayed so long because the teacher got the sidewalk wet before the students applied their paint.

L) CRIMES & PUNISHMENT: *No Farting Allowed*

One morning, before we left California, Matthew had been riding in the car with me, and we were listening to the radio. The disc jockeys were discussing the "greenhouse effect". There was some news story about the problem of methane production by cows. As I understood it, cows were producing too much methane. Since a cow's diet consists mostly of plant materials, the disc jockeys contemplated the effect of methane production by another group of plant eaters. The plant eaters in question were the dinosaurs. Being much bigger animals, they had to produce much more methane than our modern day cows. Maybe the comet didn't cause the extinction of the dinosaurs. Maybe, they produced too much methane, causing the greenhouse effect, which could possibly mean that they literally farted themselves out of existence. Matthew and I both laughed when the DJ used the phrase, "farted themselves out of existence".

Matthew retained the information from the radio show, and about six months later, he had a chance to use it. Matthew's teacher asked if any of the students knew how the dinosaurs died. At this point, Matthew probably raised his hand enthusiastically. When he was chosen, he informed the teacher that they farted themselves out of existence. Of course, the rest of the class laughed. The teacher didn't. Without asking for any explanation of his answer, he was directed to sit in the corner for 15 minutes for using the word "fart" in her classroom.

When I came to pick the kids up, Matthew's teacher informed me of his crime. She told me that I was to impress upon him that he was never to use the word again in her classroom. I asked her how it had been used. When she told me, I said that I would have to teach him how to say "flatulate", for future farting references. She was very adamant that the concept wouldn't come up in her class again, no matter how fancy the word.

The teacher didn't apologize to Matthew, after understanding his answer. In fact, she wasn't particularly interested in how he had come up with an idea that was so different. Sometimes, I think if teachers would ask more questions of students who give different answers, they might find out how smart, and sometimes creative, these students really are.

An interesting postscript to this section: the next year, there was a book on the children's best sellers list. The teacher actually read it to her whole class. It was called, "The Fart Book". I wondered what happened to her policy against using that word in her class. I'm also sure she could have found something more educational to read to her class than that book.

## M) DISCRIMINATION, HARASSMENT & ABUSE: *The Blond Trio*

Jeff attracted a lot of negative attention just by being himself. As far as some of his classmates were concerned, he had three strikes against him. He was a new kid, he spoke differently, and he was a stickler for rules. I tried to see if I could help him pick up social cues, such as when to keep his mouth shut about the rules, but I had been the same way as a kid. He was having difficulty making friends. That may or may not have bothered him very much. He liked to read and was comfortable being alone.

Unfortunately, at school they were expected to go out for recess and play with the other children. When Jeff tried to fit into a group, everyone except Jeff was invited to play with a certain group. This happened every time. None of the other kids who were invited to join the popular group gave a noticeable second thought to Jeff. They just left. Students weren't allowed to sit around on the playground. You were supposed to be moving. With nothing to do, Jeff basically stood around for the duration of the time he had to be outside.

At conference time, Jeff's teacher spoke to me about the problem. It concerned him, but he couldn't see any way to deal with the problem. The activity seemed to be instigated by a trio of blond girls in Jeff's class. There wasn't much I could do about the problem, but be aware of it. I hadn't seen the girls in action, so I couldn't offer a solution. It would have been great if the teacher could have found Jeff a job like working in the library for some lunch periods. Anything productive would have been more acceptable. The problem persisted for the rest of the year.

## N) SAFETY & SECURITY: *You're Not in California Anymore (Again)*

I walked the kids back and forth from school. I had started doing it as soon as we arrived in Alaska, due to the limited daylight. On the shortest day of the year, there might be only four hours of daylight between 10 AM and 2 PM. There was also the possibility of running into moose.

The first time I saw a moose up close, I was walking back from school with Matthew. We had to stand still until the moose looked away. I could have sworn that the moose looked like a Volkswagen Beetle on stilts. That can give you an idea of the height and the bulk.

For some reason, one day I told the kids they could walk home alone. It was spring, and there was more light. Matthew came running into the house screaming that a boy was trying to suffocate Melissa, down the street. I ran out the door after him. A sixth grade boy was pushing my first grade daughter's face into a snow bank, while my third grade son was trying to get the boy off her. When the boy saw me, he let go of Melissa and ran home. Melissa's face was scratched by ice crystals and she was shaken up, but otherwise she didn't need any medical attention. Jeff identified the boy as the brother of one of the blonds in his class.

I took the kids home and waited for a parent to show up at the boy's house. When I saw a car, I went over to talk to the boy's parents. His father answered the door. I explained the situation, and asked if he could please keep his son away from Melissa. I explained that I wanted the situation stopped, before it become more serious. The father didn't think there was anything wrong with his son's behavior. I wondered how he would have reacted if Melissa would have been seriously injured or killed by his son, and we were suing him. Would he have been so complacent if someone had been attacking his daughter? This man told me, "Kids will be kids. You aren't living in California anymore." I was hearing that phrase a lot, and always wondered what it meant. Was Alaska supposed to be a place that promoted bad behavior and bad judgment?

I chose to walk the kids to school from that time on. I told them, if their classmates teased them about it, they were just to tell them that they were exercising me.

O) POLITICS: *Keep Your Mouth Shut*

Around February, the teachers were discussing contract negotiations. I understand they wanted more money. I didn't know a whole lot about the teaching situation, but I did understand something about tact and etiquette. By this time, I had become invisible as I volunteered.

I was sitting in the classroom cutting out sheep bodies (for March goes out like a lamb), the kindergärtners were in gym class, and the teacher was talking to her aide. I realized I was considered a non-entity because of their discussion. Most of the teachers I knew were married, and had children. This teacher was single, and it was her first year of teaching. Her comment to her aide was, "I don't see why the other teachers are asking for more money. I'm making plenty of money at this job." I could have slapped her. You know, one of those slaps that says, "Come to your senses, woman!" If I were politically correct enough to have been heard by any of the other parents, and this was the only exposure I had to a teacher, I could have told everyone that my son's teacher said, "Teachers make plenty of money." Luckily for her, who would have listened to me anyhow? I believe the teachers should be paid what they are worth. If the system required them to negotiate their contracts every three years, who was I to say that shouldn't/couldn't be done?

(Fast Forward three years: This same teacher is complaining that she isn't making enough money, and decides to quit teaching to go into law, where there's more money. Only time has passed. She's still single without dependents.)

S) SICKNESS & HEALTH: *Matthew's Emergency Pouch*

Wetting the bed and wetting your pants can be considered health problems. We had both of these problems with Matthew at this age. At night, he wouldn't wake up at the right time. We dealt with this problem in a variety of ways at home. Being at school was a different matter.

When we were in California, Matthew had a traumatic experience that kept him away from school bathrooms for a long time. It's customary when you complete your business to flush. Matthew did as he was told, and the toilet overflowed. I don't know if he was made to feel the incident was his fault, but he thought it was. He didn't want to be blamed for another overflow, so he stayed away from the bathrooms.

Sometimes, he couldn't hold it until he got home, so he had an accident. I decided to put together a set of clothes for him, in case it happened again. I put a pair of pants, new underwear, and a large zippered plastic bag in a large manila envelope. It was labeled "Matthew's Emergency Pouch". That way, if I couldn't get to him in a timely manner, he could take care of himself. I think the teacher only needed it once. By the end of the first grade, he had overcome his fear of the school bathroom.

# Chapter 6
## Modified Primary 1992-93

### A) FIRST IMPRESSIONS: *Another Opening…*

As I started my second year of school in Alaska, I was involved with the PTA and liked all my children's teachers. We had a new principal. The last principal had decided to move to a school closer to her home. As the PTA, we had been able to have some say in the choice of the new principal. The process that was used was referred to as, "site-based management". I remember that I thought this principal seemed friendly and approachable.

I started out by helping the teachers put together bulletin boards and assembling homework packets. These were things that the teachers could do, but their time was needed to do more important things. The first couple weeks of getting organized and decorated made me think of the song "Another Opening, Another Show" from the musical "Kiss Me Kate".

Melissa had a teacher who was new to teaching and to the school. She was closer to my age than Matthew's Kindergarten teacher had been. She seemed so fresh and optimistic.

### B) BUILDINGS & GROUNDS: *Portable Classrooms*

This year, two portable classrooms were installed on site. One of them went to the Music teacher. Now, she had a classroom. I forget who got the second one, but it was definitely needed. The portable classrooms were set alongside the school, near a door. That way, students wouldn't have very far to walk between the school and the portable.

### *The Playground Grant*

I'm not sure exactly when we got the playground grant. I know it was in place by the beginning of this school year, because there was a discussion about what we should spend the money on. We also had to decide which type of ground cover to put around any new equipment we got. Sand might have been cheaper, but it can pack down after a while. It can also be scattered very easily. Pea gravel compacts less easily, but it can still be scattered. Bark chips can provide the most cushioning, but they can rot. They might have been the most ecological option. We finally decided on the pea gravel.

Some of the current playground equipment had asphalt under it. Melissa broke her wrist when someone pushed her while she was crossing some monkey bars that were set in asphalt. The school district advocates a three-point hold on a jungle gym, but a three-point hold didn't apply to the activity she was doing. When she was pushed, she was moving from one bar to the next, so she only had a one-point hold.

We had to decide what equipment we wanted to spend the money on. Some people wanted more swings. The gym teacher requested a strip of track. Some people wanted to consider leveling out the floor of the hockey rink area. It dipped in the middle for drainage purposes during the rest of the year. Our school was always the first one to "get ice", so why tamper with success? I had heard a rumor that the current "big toy" was rotting at the base. Besides, it didn't fit current safety codes. It was too high. If we modified it any, we could void any warranties on it.

We made our wish list for the equipment we wanted, in the order of preference. Then, we submitted our request to the school district. By the next fall, we would probably have our new playground.

### C) PARENT-TEACHER ENTITY: *Crucifying the President*

I had started getting involved in the school by becoming a parent volunteer, and then I had tried my hand at the secretary position for a couple months. I hadn't officially been the secretary, but another person had been taking the minutes in the absence of a secretary. I took minutes just to see if I could do it. My minutes were considered quite comprehensive. This was the first year I felt confident enough to actually try out for a position on the PTA Board.

I really didn't know the woman who was the new PTA President. Our first meeting was scheduled to take place in August, before school started. The PTA president had called me, to tell me the date of the meeting. She also requested that we not bring our children, since it was going to be at her house. I figured that was fair enough. I repeated the date and time to her, as I was writing it down on my calendar.

On the day of the meeting, I drove over to her house, only to find her doing yard work. She told me that I had the day wrong. It was the next day. I went home and rescheduled my childcare. The actual meeting seemed to go well enough, when it did happen.

When we had the second meeting, I noticed something wrong with the president. She was nearly militaristic and expected absolute order. I could understand why she wanted a paper trail for all spending, and insisted on at least two signatures on all checks. Our Board had inherited a financial nightmare. There were serious inconsistencies in the money from the previous PTA. The biggest problem involved checks that the previous PTA President had written out for cash, with only her signature. They averaged out to about $600 per month. There was no way to contact this woman because she had left the state. (The statute of limitations for stealing money from the PTA, is two years. This woman would be outside Alaska for two years.)

The problem I had with the current president had to do with her expecting us to attend all meetings, and to be on time. Absences or tardiness wouldn't be tolerated. I questioned her humanity. She had given me the wrong information about the first meeting, and it was considered my fault. I wondered if she had an emergency, would she excuse herself for being human? How could we recruit new volunteers with such a strident attitude? I felt she definitely needed a firmer stance on the finances, but a gentler touch with the volunteers. As a parent who had finally gained enough confidence to get more involved, I knew how others, who were steps behind me, felt. I felt if a potential volunteer stuck their toe in the water and had it bitten off, they would be less likely to try the water again, in the near future. I felt that the path to greater membership involvement was encouragement.

The assembled Board Members heavily chastised me. The president was in tears because of my criticism. She told me how she was the twelfth choice for president. Eleven others had been approached, and had rejected the nomination. She made some allusion to her religion and community service requirements. In other words, she felt serving on the PTA Board was a mission from God. One would have thought that I was trying to crucify the president, by suggesting that she might have a more "Christian" attitude towards the volunteers she was supposed to be leading. I know I wasn't politically correct, but I had to try. I felt it was *my* Christian duty.


D) FUND RAISING: *Impossible Dreams*

At the Back to School Night, the fund raising line was displayed. The fund raising packets had been handed out that morning. I wasn't thrilled with the quality of the chocolate that was offered. There were several tins, novelty items, and of course, the gift-wrap.

I had three children who all wanted the bicycle, which was the top prize. That would never happen in their lifetime, unless I won some sort of lottery. In that case, I would have been able to buy them each a bicycle outright. The student who sold the most would win the bicycle, and I had to treat three children equally. The limitations still held as far as my husband's and my employment. We sold things to a few of our neighbors, and bought a little for ourselves. When I delivered the products that year, I was so embarrassed. Some of the products looked so junky. I decided not to sell anything like that to my neighbors again.

The kids each got a Level 1 prize, and I got an idea about recycling from the fund raiser.

*The Book Fair*

I volunteered for the book fair this year. The room we normally used for art was converted into a bookstore. A nice, little, local bookstore delivered a variety of suitable books for the children to choose from. As with the Santa's Secret Shop, children were allowed to go to the Book Fair twice. The first time, they were expected to make a "wish list" for their parents to choose from. The second time they showed up, it was to buy books. The book fair usually took place during conference time, and volunteers were available to sell books during the conference time.

There were two things I disliked about the book fair. First, the children didn't seem to respect the books. Many books were damaged in the process, and I'm sure someone had to pay for those. Secondly, I watched some of the teachers with children who couldn't write. We were supposed to help them fill out their lists. One child only looked at the paperback books. When his teacher saw the list, she told him he had to put at least one hardcover (more expensive) book on the list. To me, this just looked like excessive greed on the part of the teacher.

I happened to know the boy's family. Their finances might have allowed a couple paperback books, but the hardcover would just be considered a luxury. I'm sure many other families had the same financial restrictions. I'm sure we made some money for the school despite the damages. I thought, "There must be a better way to do this."

If buying new books for the library was the goal, the librarian could have assembled a wish list for books the library wanted, and parents could adopt (buy) a book their child was interested in, it could have been affixed with a book plate noting the child who had donated it, and that child would have the chance to be the first to check it out. The concept of tax-deductions works really well for some parents. If the books are purchased through a school program, the money goes farther.

## E) DIFFERENCES & DISABILITIES: *Distribution of Time*

I made the copies for the teachers. Jeff's teacher had three sets of worksheets for me to copy for her math class. The first set had an "R" before the lesson number. The second set had a "P", and the third set had an "A". The majority of copies were P. That was the middle range of the students. R was for remedial, and A stood for advanced. The teacher gave the lesson with worksheets that suited each student's needs.

I spoke with the teacher at conference time. She said she was frustrated. Jeff was definitely ahead of his class on some subjects, but she felt she wasn't giving his group enough attention. Her main goal was to reach the middle group of students. Once she reached them, she needed to spend time with the stragglers. By the time she finished with them, she barely had any time to deal with the students who seemed to be ahead of the game. Maybe they needed help, but there wasn't enough time.

This teacher decided to get certified for Gifted Education. A year after her certification, she retired from teaching. Was it too little, too late?

## F) PROGRAMS: *B.A.R.K.*

We had an absolutely fantastic librarian. She was a little bit older than I was, and she absolutely loved kids. She was very creative. The reading program that she developed at our school was fantastic. The students had a monthly reading requirement, the same way our past schools had, but the prizes were different. We also had an acronym for our program. It was B.A.R.K., or "Be A Reading Kid".

Any student who fulfilled the reading requirement was able to attend a special assembly. The assembly took place once every month or two, depending on scheduling and supplies. One month, students were supposed to dress like they were on a tropical vacation. They got candy leis and tropical treats. Another month, we had someone from the railroad as a guest speaker. The treat was a train, made out of candy, for each participant. (I helped assemble 200 of them!) In April, the theme was, "April in Paris". They had croissants and marmalade, did sidewalk art, and got perfume samples. (I know the teachers loved me for that contribution.)

The librarian asked local businesses for donations for her program. The students just loved the assemblies. At the end of the year, if you had participated in the reading program every month, you got a T-shirt. Local artists designed them. The shirt this year was designed by one of Mary's siblings.

*Pencil Full of Stars*

Melissa's teacher encouraged her class to participate in a poetry contest through the school district. It was called, "Pencil Full of Stars". The competition was open to all elementary students in the Anchorage area.

Winners got their poems published in a slim softbound booklet. The poetry was grouped by grade level. I don't know if there were any big prizes for participation. One of Melissa's poems was published in the booklet this year. For her efforts, she received a copy of the booklet for herself, and another one for her teacher.

Melissa participated in the contest again the following year, and got published again. After that, either there was no more competition (very unlikely), or there was no emphasis in our school to participate in the contest. Melissa's teacher had moved to another school.

G) TRANSPORTATION & FIELD TRIPS: *Insurance and Five to One*

With all three children in school, I could help chaperon on the field trips. I really enjoyed going on the field trips with the kids. They were always so interesting. I'm sure I was able to see a lot of things in town that I might not have seen otherwise. For elementary students, the student to parent ratio was five to one. This was relatively manageable.

Matthew's teacher had some buttons with our school name on them. These buttons were color coded for small groups. She would write names on the buttons with a permanent marker. If a student's parent was the chaperon, the student could choose which classmates they wanted in their group. The buttons were erasable with some alcohol, so the names could be changed. Once a student was assigned to a parent, they were given a badge that matched the adult. The adult was given their list of students. It worked very nicely.

Sometimes, we took the school bus for field trips. Other times, we had to use privately owned vehicles. There was a form to fill out at the school for parents who drove students on field trips. It only had to be filled out once. Then it was put on file for the rest of the year.

The insurance requirements on the form were more than what many people normally carried. Our insurance was at least the minimum requirement for the school district. I kept the insurance at that level until we stopped driving for field trips.

H) HOMEWORK: *The Interactive Journal & Personal Dictionaries*

Melissa's teacher had the students put together a folder that was called, "The Interactive Journal". The students were allowed to personalize their journal cover with artwork. It was one of those folders that are like a notebook, so the paper is held in place.

Students would write a letter to one of the adults in their life. In our case, Melissa could write her letter to her dad, or to me. Some children had grandparents who lived nearby. The adult had to be someone who would be willing to write a response letter. The teacher also required the student to ask at least one question for the adult's response. In one of Melissa's letters, she asked if we could have a puppy.

The letters didn't have to be long, and the topic wasn't criticized. Spelling and writing were the goals of this exercise. On any of the writing projects, the teacher would look at the spelling. If a word was spelled incorrectly, the student would enter the word into their "dictionary". Each child was required to have a small notebook. Only their personal misspellings were entered into the book. By writing it down properly, they might remember the correct spelling later. Each child had different words in their dictionary. Some had more difficulty with simple words, and others were stretching their vocabulary. Melissa didn't have too many words in her dictionary. I think it was because she was reading at such a high level already, so she recognized the words from sight more often.

*The Reading Race*

In Matthew's class, his teacher had a set of books for the children to read. Once they were able to read, she gave them the first book. Like Melissa's first grade class, there were a limited number of these books. There were either two or three of each title. Matthew was able to bring one home per night. At first, he was ahead in the class. A couple times he forgot to bring a book home, so one of his classmates got ahead of him. It was pretty much a competition between these two boys to see who could finish the set first. I think it ended in a tie. By the end of Modified Primary, Matthew was reading at a third grade level.

*Quad Paper*

The Friday before class was supposed to start, the class lists were posted. The school also posted a supply list for each grade level. Jeff's teacher required a quadrille paper on her supply list. It was supposed to be four squares per inch. This was a requirement for showing their work, on their math problems. With multiplication and division being a big part of fourth grade math, it was easier to line the columns of numbers up, neatly, on this paper. I think it was a big help.

J) VOLUNTEERING: *Organizational Efforts*

This year, the volunteer pool was at its strongest. Most of the core volunteers came in at this time. We shared ideas we had for doing different projects. If we were waiting for the copier, and another parent had a project going, we helped each other. Our timing was good. Even though we only had the one table to work on, we managed to get all of our work done in an efficient manner.

One of the things we noticed about the projects was, teachers assembled lamination projects and brought them to the workroom during their planning period, to laminate. That meant preheating the laminator. Sometimes, the laminator was on all day. Many people don't realize that electrical appliances that produce heat also draw a lot of energy. The laminator was doing a good job of heating up the room, and we had to be careful not to bump into it while it was hot. We tried to see if we could organize the teachers, so that we could get all the lamination done at one time during the day, rather than having the machine running all day. If a teacher had a laminating project, they had to have it done right away. No matter how much heat or waste it produced. I wonder if the teachers felt we weren't qualified to run the laminator, or if they were just so disorganized.

*Bookworm*

I was volunteering in the library at least half a day a week. If I walked the kids to school on a cold day, and I wasn't scheduled to stay that day, I usually spent 5 or 10 minutes warming up in the library, before walking home. The librarian usually had a cart full of books that needed to be shelved. I would arrange the books so they could be shelved faster, for a few minutes then head home.

When I was actually spending time in the library, I tried shelving the books without organizing them first. I got dizzy looking at the numbers. I decided that there had to be an easier way. I sorted the books into three different categories on the cart. There were the numbered books, the three letter fiction books, and the "everybody" or easy reader books. As I pulled them out of the crowd, I put them in the order they would be on the shelves. Once they were in a decent order, they could be shelved very quickly by anyone.

There was another mother besides me who spent a good deal of time shelving books. The librarian commented on how fast we were when it came to shelving the books. We never did have a competition to see who could shelf books faster, but we kept the librarian happy.

I liked helping in the library because I got to see all the new titles that were coming in. Sometimes, I would check out a book from the school library that I thought would interest my kids.

The only time I didn't like helping in the library was when it involved taking stacks of books to a bunch of classrooms. The librarian had pulled books on a variety of subjects that the teachers wanted. She had the stacks on her desk with each teacher's name. I told her I would run them to the classrooms, since it was lunchtime. I didn't think I would disturb anyone.

All of the classrooms were unlit, and the doors were closed. That was a signal that the room was unoccupied. One room wasn't empty, though. I opened the door to put the books on the table near the door, without looking around. As I set the books down, I heard a noise. The teacher was sitting in the relative dark, crying. She gave me a hostile look. I was confused, and left the room as quickly as possible, but the damage was done. I had seen a teacher being human, and she obviously didn't like it. I would have cried in her position, too. I found out her child had recently died. Her job required her to be surrounded by children, daily. I don't know why she couldn't have taken some time off.

She would have Betty's son in her class the next year.

*The Volunteer Recognition Social*

I had attended the Volunteer Recognition Social the previous year. The teachers were given invitations to distribute to their parent-volunteers. This spring, I got four of them. The Volunteer Social had really nice hors d'oeuvres to nibble on. After a period of mingling with volunteers from other schools, we sat at tables and waited for the awards to be given. There were four awards given to each school. I saw the results of the awards the previous year. This year, I hoped to earn one. I had put in a lot of volunteer time.

The award ceremony took a couple hours. Our school district had 55 schools. At four awards each, that meant that there were at least 220 awards to be given out. There were two special awards that were given out at the end. They were called, "The Gold Pan Awards". One of these was given to a boy whose Eagle Scout project affected one of the schools. He did something to improve a playground. I thought that was wonderful. It was great to see a student being recognized for community service.

I didn't get an award that night. Like the previous year, the award that I would have qualified for went to the PTA President. I figured the award was rigged. I really tried for that award, and decided to put less time into my volunteering for the next year. Why try for an unreachable goal?

K) CURRICULUM: *Team Teaching*

This was the first year I noticed the concept of team teaching. Jeff's teacher split the curriculum with the other fourth grade teacher. One of the teachers put together the Science lessons, while the other teacher did the lesson plan for Social Studies. It cut their planning time in half, and they got to teach the same subject twice, instead of two subjects once. This way, both teachers had a chance to know all of the students, too. If I remember correctly, they shuffled the students a little bit also, so there would be a little more social variety with this grouping. Team teaching allowed more standardization on certain subjects. These students would be going into the next grade having more of the same reference points. Their next teacher would be spending less time filling in common knowledge gaps.

I heard that one of the teachers at the school was going to be fired if he didn't teach a subject that he felt weak in. He didn't make much effort to teach the students the subject he disliked. Conversely, when you asked the students about the subject he had a passion for, they could give great answers. Firing him would have been one solution, but a great resource would be lost in the subject he loved to teach. He got involved with the team teaching concept, and didn't lose his job.

It seems to work best when each of the teachers in the grade level is strong in a different subject. I saw this during the next year, when there were three classes in one grade. The students loved the variety of teachers.

## N) SAFETY & SECURITY: *The Volunteer Log and a Pager*

My husband had a very erratic schedule. He only had weekends off once a month, because of the rotation. His schedule also rotated around the clock. On his days off, we would try to get any errands done. We had provided the school with an emergency number, but the number wasn't ever needed. Twice, we happened to stop in at the school just as Matthew had shown up at the Nurse's office, with an illness or injury. The secretary was surprised to see us, because she was just getting ready to call us both times.

We knew we couldn't be lucky enough to be in the school every time we were needed, and it was getting harder to have an emergency number, so we invested in a pager. Over the next five years, the pager was rarely needed. The one time our presence was definitely required, a message was left on our answering machine at home.

The school had a record book in the office. Visitors to the school were expected to sign in. I was told it was a volunteer book. Besides tracking the volunteer hours, this book could be used to keep track of who was in the building, because we were expected to sign in and out with a notation of the time. We were also supposed to note our destination.

I went to the school early in the afternoon, one day, to do some library work. On this day, I didn't check in with the office. There wasn't any library work at the time. Someone else had dispensed with the mountain of books I had noticed that morning. I saw one of the other teachers I knew. She was replacing a bulletin board while her class was out of the room. I stopped in to help her and we chatted. The next thing I knew, my pager was going off. Melissa was sick, and the school had called my husband because they couldn't reach me. Since I hadn't checked in at the office they were unaware I was at the school. In the future, I made sure to sign in.

## R) REDUCE, REUSE & RECYCLE: *The Green Star Program*

I was volunteering two days per week. Each teacher got half a day, and the librarian got half a day. We were looking at ways to cut down the waste in our workroom. As parent volunteers, we did what we could. One of the things I noticed during fund raising time was the samples of gift-wrap were the same width as the dies used in our die cutters.

For anyone who doesn't know, a die is a block of wood with an extremely sharp metal "cookie cutter" embedded in it. The sharp edge sticks out from the wood. In this case, it is surrounded by a thick foam rubber. A person would have to make an effort to cut their finger on one. The block of wood is placed face down, on top of 1-3 pieces of paper, inside a small press. When pressure is applied, the die cuts through the papers, producing the desired shape.

Our school had a set of alphabet dies for making bulletin boards. These dies were in the D'Nealean style. They were skinny.

We traditionally used two contrasting colors of construction paper to make our letters. If we glued them together in an offset manner, they looked like they had shading or depth. I realized that the gift wrap samples were just the right size for these projects. If we collected up all the samples from the fund raiser, we could make spectacular bulletin boards with interesting designs. Our letters could have polka dots or stripes on them. They could be holographic silver or plaid. Some of the samples were two sided.

There were so many choices. I collected up as many samples as I could from the catalogs that had been returned, separated them, and put them in a box near the die cutter. These samples cost us nothing!

Trying to get regular paper to fit through the die cutter was also a matter of waste. I saw other parents try to use the huge paper cutter to cut the papers to the right size. If you had too thick a stack of paper, we would end up with varying sizes. This caused more waste. The average size piece of construction paper is divisible by 4 and 6. A die cutter is 4 x 6 inches. If a paper is folded properly into columns, you can cleanly rip the paper and feed the strip through the die cutter.

It was late November, when I found out about an actual program that could be run by the school to reduce waste. It was called "Green Star". If I contacted the Green Star Program, they could provide me with a packet about ways to save money in our school. They also provided me with some waste receptacles to collect recyclable paper. I thought this was really great.

Since I was the one showing interest, I would be the Green Star Chair. One of Matthew's classmates had a mom who taught at another school. She was heavily involved with the Green Star Program. Their school did everything the packet outlined. If a school was in total compliance, there was the possibility of some grant money for the school. I doubted that I could get that much cooperation from my school. It didn't seem that I was important enough to attract much positive attention. People still looked at me as if I was from another planet whenever I opened my mouth.

*The Aluminum Can Round-Up*

This was my first year experiencing this phenomenon. Students were asked to bring aluminum cans to the school, for recycling. The student who brought in the most cans would get a prize. I can't remember what the prize was, but I do remember that there were ribbons to award the children. This seemed to be run under the PTA umbrella. I guess the money that was made from recycling the cans would go into the PTA fund.

There were no guidelines for the condition of the cans. My children collected up cans that were rinsed out and crushed before they were taken to school. Many other children neither rinsed nor crushed their cans. I thought it was quite ironic. The Aluminum Can Round Up took place right around Red Ribbon Week, which is the week the students are advised to stay away from drugs and alcohol. For the duration of the recycling drive, one hallway was filled with bags of beer cans, causing the school to smell like a brewery.

S) SICKNESS & HEALTH: *When Will Your Son Be Well?*

Betty's son had the flu that everyone was getting. He was so lucky to get it in February. The first day of the flu, Betty received a call from his teacher. She wanted to know if the boy would be back in school the next day. Betty told her he had the flu and, at this time, she didn't know when he would be back.

The next day, the call came again. The teacher wanted to know when Betty's son would be back to school. Betty told her, "As soon as he gets well enough to send." Betty suspected that the teacher thought she was keeping him home on purpose. I knew other children had been sick in his class. The germs were probably still in the room, because I had seen one student trying to make a run for the door. He wasn't fast enough, and vomited on the carpet in the classroom. The janitor came in to clean it up as well as he could.

The problem with Betty's son being ill wasn't really his illness. It was his timing. In Alaska, according to the statute, a student count is done for the months of October and February, to determine funding for the next school year. All of the teachers were told to make sure that everyone was in attendance these months, no matter what.

*Home Testing*

Jeff was ill most of the month of February. The first week, he missed a few days due to the flu. The second week, he was diagnosed with bronchitis and sinusitis, and put on antibiotics, so he missed a couple days there. The third week was the flu again. The fourth week, the doctor changed his antibiotics. Out of twenty possible school days, Jeff missed ten days this month. I wondered as much as the teacher did, if he would ever be able to put in a full week at school again.

During either Week 2 or Week 4, he had to take a test. He wasn't able to be in school, because the doctor had advised a few days of bed rest. By Day 2, he was getting bored, so I went to the school to ask the teacher if I could administer the test at home. She gave me the test, and told me how long she was allowing for completion. When Jeff was ready, I pulled out the test, set the timer, and read my book for the duration of the test time. I took his test back to the teacher. He had completed it before the timer went off.

## T) TECHNOLOGY: *The Technology Learning Center*

When the students arrived at school this year, there was a new computer lab. It was called the Technology Learning Center, or TLC. There were three printers, and several computers. Students sat at hexagonal tables. There were either five or six computers at each table. We got all this wonderful technology through a grant from Apple Computers. It was absolutely fantastic. Unfortunately, several of the teachers weren't computer literate, yet.

Matthew's teacher was the computer whiz who wrote out the grant request for our school. Supposedly, each teacher was to choose a program to learn, and teach the other teachers. That way, everyone would learn how to do the programs the students would be working with.

I wasn't very computer literate. The school was looking for parent volunteers to help in the computer lab. The school advertised in the newsletter that parents were welcome on Wednesdays, to attend the computer classes, so they would learn how to work with the computers. I decided to attend these before school classes. About six other parents decided to attend also.

The computer training took place during the second half of the staff meetings on Wednesday mornings. The teachers were being trained how to use ClarisWorks. I had never used that program, so I started taking notes.

I attended six of these meetings before stopping. I was the last parent to drop out. Each lesson, everyone had to go through all the steps that we had covered previously. I think I was only adding two steps on for each half-hour class I attended. It was a waste of my time. Besides that, the teachers didn't seem to particularly want the parents to see them before their morning coffee. I couldn't believe that we had these nice computers, and teachers were walking into the lab with coffee and sticky fingers.

I tried to help with the computer lab, in Jeff's class. Jeff ended up answering a lot of the students' questions because the teacher wasn't up to speed on the program they were using. I did what I could to help, but most of the students were more interested in wasting time. Computer lab was two half hours per week, and it was considered to be the writing class. Jeff spent more time solving computer problems for other students than he did working on his own assignments. He was so smart, and so helpful that the teacher didn't realize he was avoiding the writing assignments. He was failing writing, and no one really knew why.

## U) CELEBRATIONS: *The Price of Sugar Cookies*

In the school, the students were allowed to decide which three holidays they wanted to celebrate. Usually, they would pick Halloween, Christmas, and Valentine's Day. This year, Melissa's class made these choices. Her teacher had a great way to bring a lesson into the party. She made some sugar cookies that were a shape suitable for the holiday. She brought in frosting and a variety of toppings for the students to choose from. The frosting on the cookie was "free", but the other toppings had a price. Students were allowed 25 cents. They could get as many toppings as they could afford. They couldn't afford all the toppings, so they had to choose.

Each student came up to the table with their list. Chocolate chips, peanuts, and raisins were sold individually. Some of the sprinkles were sold by the spoonful, or by the shake. I was one of the parents who helped dispense the toppings. The students decorated their cookies and learned a lesson. Obviously, this lesson may not be for every class. I know there are children out there who are diabetic or allergic to peanuts. All of our students were able to participate.

*Holiday Traditions*

One of the positive things our school did during the holiday season involved a school assembly, which lasted about an hour. I happened to be volunteering this day, so I went to the assembly, too.

Some of the students sang holiday songs. They sang "The Dreidel Song" and a couple other Christmassy ones. A few of the teachers told standard holiday short stories, and a few of the other teachers told about their childhood holiday memories as children of immigrants. At the end, all of the students were invited to sing along to more secular holiday songs. The teachers displayed the words on an overhead projector, for anyone who didn't know them. It was quite cheerful, and I don't think it could have offended anyone.

# Chapter 7
## Total Involvement 1993-94

### A)  FIRST IMPRESSIONS: *Paranoia?*

For some reason, there seemed to be something wrong about the school. I couldn't put my finger on it. I liked many of the teachers enough, but I was having nightmares and other difficulties sleeping the nights before I volunteered. What was bothering me?

Jeff was in a multi-age 5/6 classroom. I had hoped he would have a different teacher, because I thought this teacher was very abrupt. I would have two years to get to know her. Melissa had Jeff's third grade teacher. It seemed OK. Matthew had the option of being put into the first or second grade. Without my input, he was arbitrarily put into the first grade. I tried to see if I could get him placed in the first-second grade combo class that Melissa's first grade teacher was now teaching, but I didn't have any luck. Several parents told me that the teacher we had was very nice. In fact, Mary's daughter had her the previous year. The woman seemed almost grandmotherly. What on Earth was nagging at me?

### B) BUILDINGS & GROUNDS: *Disaster Preparedness 101*

As you can tell, people didn't seem to notice me very much while I was at the school. Hearing things was a mixed blessing. On this day, I was in the teachers' lounge reading the newspaper. I was slated to be in the school the whole day, but I had finished my morning projects early. By the time the teachers came into the room for lunch, I would probably be shelving books in the library. For now, I was listening to the janitor talking with some other men about making the rooms in the school earthquake resistant. I tried to look like I wasn't listening, because I was interested in hearing more.

There were some difficulties in making a building like our school earthquake resistant. The first problem was the walls. They weren't reinforced with anything. The space between the walls didn't have any "I" beams in them for support. The beams were much smaller on certain walls. The idea of chaining the television carts to the walls so they wouldn't tip over in an earthquake was ridiculous for our school. There was nothing to anchor a chain in. We couldn't put brackets on the walls either to keep cabinets and shelving units from falling over, for the same reason.

The tall cabinet in the teacher's lounge was opened up. The higher shelves were filled with heavier materials. In an earthquake, it would topple or fly open because of the weight distribution. How many teachers were filling their cabinets the same way?

Our building had been built to last 30 years. We were coming up on the 25th anniversary in about a year's time, yet there were no plans to upgrade the school any. I wondered how long our school would actually stand in a respectable earthquake.

### C) PARENT-TEACHER ENTITY: *Just Say "No"*

I had done a fantastic job as PTA secretary the previous year. My minutes were very easy to read and reference. The PTA President from the previous year was re-elected for a second term. I chose not to work with her. She asked me several times to be the secretary, but I was expecting my first book to come out, and I wanted to leave my calendar open. I still disliked this woman's attitude towards volunteers. She was like a dog guarding the door of the school. She was nearly blatant with her prejudices, yet she claimed to be "Christian".

I did promise to help train any new secretary they managed to get. I tried training my first replacement, but she didn't last long. She didn't care much for the discrimination in the school, so she moved her child to a more tolerant school.

## D) FUND RAISERS: *The Home Business Fair -Part I*

One of the major concerns every school year is fund raising  Everybody wants to get the most return for his or her investment of time.  This year, my parents gave me an interesting idea.  It wasn't original, but it was fresh and exciting.  It was a relatively new concept called, "The Home Business Fair".

My parents said they had attended a fund raiser at a local school.  It had featured local vendors who usually sold door-to-door or in a party setting.  Several businesses were able to participate, and each business was assigned to a classroom, where they were able to display their products in a shop-like setting.  All profits from the evening's sales went to the school, who acted as the host. The businesses profited from this event by getting the exposure, and attracting new potential customers.

The fact that these businesses were local people was a very positive point.  They weren't some nameless, faceless entity from another state.  Also, the fund raising activity only took one day, children weren't used as sales people, and there was minimal inconvenience for the teachers.  Delivery of products might have taken up to six weeks, but that's what we usually had from the other fund raisers

I assembled my proposal and offered it to the next year's PTA, as a fund raising idea.  In contrast, I also offered Avon as a solitary fund raiser  I reasoned that the PTA would be more inclined to choose the more community involved fund raiser

I was unable to attend the meeting personally due to a previous engagement, but I sent the proposal with a friend, who brought it up at the meeting.  The president referenced her copy and presented it as a fund raiser that I would personally profit from.  The PTA Board voted against the idea unanimously.  No one heard the other option.

The next day, the president saw me in the hallway.  Without breaking stride, she told me that my idea had been rejected.  She sounded as if I had been trying to sell manure as a fund raiser  The community school was interested in my idea, and I was asked to present it to their group.  They thought it would be a good idea to incorporate it with the spring craft fair.

Advertisements were sent out to attract vendors  There were 18 classrooms to use as store space, and we filled every one of them.  The event was supposed to take place the first Saturday in May.  I requested a copy of each company's logo, so I could make some uniform signs to display in front of each "store".  I also requested door prizes.  Each business offered something, which we displayed in a case by the front door.  Each shopper would be given a ticket that had every participating business.  If the card was initialed by every business, it could be entered into the drawing for the door prizes.  The initials had to be in the color of the pen I provided for all the businesses.

I displayed signs inside each shop, that stated (in large print) the shipping fees and delivery schedules.

The event was a successful failure.  For the amount of money that was brought in, it would be considered a failure by PTA standards.  We didn't break $200.  We had asked for a percentage of the profits.  After all, it was a trial run.  The day was wrong, too.  It was the first day of fishing season, and it was gorgeous outside.

On the successful side, the vendors thought I had done quite a good job. Especially since it was done almost single-handedly.  I had hand painted the signs, which looked quite professional.  Many of the vendors said that they would participate again, if it were a fall or wintertime fund raiser  If imitation is the sincerest form of flattery, several other schools threw together the same idea between the time it was presented (January) and the time we actually had our fund raiser  The idea must have had some merit. I'm personally biased, though.  I think my Fair showcased each vendor better than any of the other schools I had seen.  I decided to try again in the fall.

E) DISABILITIES & DIFFERENCES: *Mature in Math*

Jeff and our neighbor's son were both advanced in their Math abilities. The neighbor's boy was placed in the second grade after having been home schooled since kindergarten. I think his mom hoped he would make friends in their new area. When she saw the Math homework that was coming home, she was a little disappointed. Her son was quite proficient in addition and subtraction. He was already into multiplying complex numbers. The teacher had spoken to her about her son being disruptive in class. Mom knew her son was bored, and offered an easy solution. She had some Math workbooks around the house. The teacher could supplement the Math assignments with the more difficult worksheets. She only had to pass them out and collect them. Mom would corrected the extra work. This couldn't be done. The next year, the neighbor's boy was put back into home schooling, where he was challenged.

Jeff was much luckier. His teacher had a couple sixth graders who were advanced in Math, so she had seventh grade Math books to challenge them. Since Jeff was a fifth grader, it was even easier to deal with him. He was just added to the sixth grade Math group. When he reached the sixth grade, he would be given the opportunity to work on seventh grade Math. As far as challenging students in Math went, Jeff's teacher was no idiot. She kept them interested.

*Your Son Needs Drugs*

From the time Matthew started school, the teachers had been telling me something was wrong with him. Both the Modified Primary teacher and his First Grade teacher insisted that he was "Attention Deficit". I tried to fight it. I had failed to get him placed in a more age appropriate classroom where he might be challenged more. I thought it might have been boredom. These two women were experienced teachers. Did they know something I didn't know? There's a commercial out there that says, 'if your child has a learning disability, sometimes it takes a year or more before parents realize there's a problem.' My parents and my husband didn't seem to be much help either. They seemed to think that I had to get Matthew under control also. (I didn't realize it at the time, but I was gradually slipping into a moderate depression. I would be diagnosed in the springtime.)

I allowed testing to be set up with the school Psychologist. I also made an appointment with a "good" child psychologist. Our appointment was about a month away. It was about a week before Halloween. I had to go to the Psychologist's office to pick up some papers. There was a questionnaire for the teacher to fill out, and one for me to fill out. I returned them to the Doctor's office when we had our appointment.

My sister-in-law had warned me about Ritalin. Supposedly, it could damage your blood cells. That was all we needed with the specter of leukemia in our family medical history. She said that Matthew's blood should be tested every month, if he was put on medicine. I told the Doctor about my concerns. She saw Matthew for about half an hour, prescribed Methylphenidate, and gave us a flier with 15 behavior modification points on it. The medicine had to be taken at lunchtime, so we had to ask for a bottle for the school, when we got the prescription filled.

Matthew's behavior "improved". He faithfully took his medicine for two months. Despite my best efforts to make another appointment with the Doctor, I had no luck during those two months. His medicine could be refilled without any problem, though. Around Christmas time, Matthew got the flu, so he couldn't keep his medicine down. I decided not to give it to him again until he was well.

Matthew had always been a cuddly kid, so when he was sick he curled up with me to watch TV. I realized how slow his heart was beating, compared to the week before. His heart wasn't beating abnormally slow. It was beating about the same as his siblings. This was my first concrete clue that something was definitely wrong. I decided not to give him the medicine again.

After Christmas vacation, we got the results of the annual standardized tests back. He had taken them before he was put on the medicine. The results were in the upper 80 and 90 percentile range. These tests are so time intensive. If he was hyperactive, how could he sit still so long to complete these tests? I also got the results of the tests back from the school Psychologist. When I saw the test dates, I was angry. These "important" tests were given after Matthew was already on medicine. I couldn't see how these test results proved he needed the medicine.

Matthew was in school for about a week without the medicine. His teacher pulled him aside and complimented him on how well he was doing with the medicine. Being a proud little 7-year-old, he told her that he hadn't been on the medicine for a long time. Suddenly, I was getting calls about behavior problems again.

Supposedly, Attention Deficit Disorder affects about 2-8% of the US population. In Matthew's class, 30% of the students were on the medicine. Most of them were boys. (Can we say 'profiling'?) Why was the percentage in his class so high? Was the whole school this high?

The medicine that is prescribed to balance the child is amphetamines, also known as "Speed". In the ADD brain, an upper, like caffeine, actually has a calming effect. A downer, like a decongestant, that will normally put one to sleep, will actually invigorate the same person. How many kids were being prescribed Methylphenidate (Ritalin) just because the teacher couldn't control a student? If a person doesn't need the addictive medicine, it can become a gateway drug.

Diagnosis for Attention Deficit was subjective at best, even by a "qualified" doctor. If the teachers couldn't handle the jobs they were trained for, how could they be considered experts in this arena? If you took a child off ADD medicine, a teacher could turn you in for negligence, and your child could be taken away from you. I was glad I didn't know this while we went through this process. Someone (up there) was watching out for me.

F) PROGRAMS: *Red Ribbon Week*

Red Ribbon Week happens just before Halloween. The teachers all discuss the evils of using drugs and alcohol. They try to promote the differences between candies and pills. Often, they can look almost the same, so children were told not to eat any "candy" they found without asking an adult. Children were also told that medicines your doctor gave you were acceptable. If a doctor didn't give it to you, you shouldn't be taking it. Sally's son had latched onto this idea when he was in a lower grade. When he saw her taking an aspirin, he labeled it as a drug that she shouldn't be taking. After all, he hadn't seen a doctor give her the pill.

In Matthew's class, he asked if the non-alcohol champagne that we drank was OK. The teacher looked at Matthew with open-mouthed disbelief, and said that anything that was meant to represent alcohol was bad for children. I wondered if she ever had sparkling cider for a celebration. This woman was so against any hint of drugs that pushing "speed" was the last thing you might think she would do. But then, again, aren't the worst alcoholics the ones who preach temperance the loudest?

*The Green Team*

This year, the Green Team became the model for the whole school. I would be volunteering in the workroom, and several teachers handed me stacks of colored cards to run through the laminator. It finally got to the point where I realized I was wasting so much lamination trying to get these pieces of paper coated, so I put full-sized sheets of construction paper through, and cut them down to the right size.

For Kindergärtners, the Green Team system is the easiest way to make them hate the colors red and blue. For fifth and sixth graders, the Green Team was a laughing matter. "You're misbehaving, so you must pull a card." I'm sure it really made an impact on them. If you stayed on green for the whole quarter, you got an award. Hooray!

I) DRUGS & WEAPONS: *Detention for a Knife*

I tried to make sure my children didn't bring any contraband to school. According to the school rules, knives (of any kind) were not allowed on school property. Even if a Kindergärtner wore a cardboard sword on his pirate costume for the Halloween parade, it had to be removed.

Cold weather meant winter coats. Each of my children had only one winter coat. They used this for play, school, and church. Matthew had been playing with a friend the night before. His friend had a plastic, retractable, Peter Pan type dagger that was three inches from end to end. On impact, the inch and a half blade retracted into the handle. It was Matthew's misfortune to have put it in his coat pocket after they were done playing. It fell out of his pocket at school the next day. He was given detention for the offense. It's unfortunate that he had the detention, but he did break the rule.

*My Classmate's Going to Bring a Gun to School*

One of Melissa's classmates told her he was going to bring a gun from his father's house to school, to shoot me when I volunteered next. Melissa rightfully felt alarmed. The boy who had made the threat had been picking on her, intermittently, for a long time. This time, she felt she needed to tell someone. So she told the principal.

After telling the principal about this boy's plans to bring a gun to school, the principal called the boy into the office. The boy brought up an incident where Melissa had splashed some water on him during Easter vacation. Mentioning Easter vacation watered down the incident. Since the incident obviously took place outside of the school's jurisdiction, Melissa must be tattling. The principal offered Melissa detention if she was caught tattling again.

Melissa was quite upset when we picked them up from school that day. We were heading home as she told us what the problem was. My husband turned the car around and we headed back to the school. He went into the school and demanded to see the principal. If a student threatened to bring a weapon to the school to shoot his wife and daughter, why was the principal offering Melissa detention? How far away did the boy's father live? Did he have weapons that the boy had access to? Had the principal even contacted the boy's parents about the threat? The principal answered all of these questions unsatisfactorily.

She hadn't considered the concept of a student bringing a gun into her school. Two years later, a school shooting in a Bush village called Bethel would shake Alaska. Supposedly, several students knew the boy was bringing a gun to school, but nobody said anything. The student in Bethel managed to kill the principal, and injure two students. Columbine would shake the nation.

J) VOLUNTEERING: *What's an Award Worth?*

I received invitations to the Volunteer Recognition Social again. I had pretty much decided I wasn't going to attend. While the food was good, I didn't enjoy the company. Award ceremonies can be so boring without good company. Then they become an endurance test.

At the school, I was asked if I was going to the Social. I said that I didn't think so. There wasn't much point. The people in the room looked shocked. They told me I needed to attend, because I had won an award. I knew at least three other people who were more deserving of the award, so why was it given to me? Personally, I think the people who voted were trying to soothe me, but I'm not sure why.

I collected the award and, literally, put it away in my closet. The previous year, I had perceived the award as an accomplishment that might look good on a future resume. This year, I realized it didn't matter how fantastic a volunteer you were. The award was given to the person who, they thought, "needed" the recognition. A little bit of genuine respect would have meant so much more to me than any paper.

K) CURRICULUM: *Knitting Helps Writing*

Jeff's teacher was known for her knitting projects. Each child learned how to knit and was expected to make at least one project. They were basically taught how to knit a cap. The finished products were fitted on balloons with faces, and displayed for everyone to see. Jeff's teacher mentioned that the knitting helped with writing, but I didn't ask how and she never explained. I should have asked.

When conference time came around, the teacher commented that Jeff wasn't completing his writing projects. What was his problem? I told her that we had always had problems getting him to write. She said we needed to work on his writing with him. I had no clue how to get my son to write. I asked for suggestions on dealing with the problem, but the teacher couldn't provide any.

Seven years would pass before we figured out why Jeff didn't write. Meanwhile, teachers would complain to me at conferences, and no one had anything constructive to offer me on the subject. If this teacher would have requested Jeff to do more knitting projects, we might have been given the key to unlocking his problem years sooner.

*Gingerbread Houses*

Jeff's teacher had one of the two food permits in the school. The other teacher was the Modified Primary teacher. This meant, the teachers were allowed to do food preparation projects in their classrooms. Every year, Jeff's teacher allowed time during art classes to make gingerbread houses.

Parents were asked to donate mixing bowls, spatulas, rolling pins, and cookie sheets. The students were assigned an ingredient to bring in, and everyone brought in materials for decorating the houses.
The students were divided up into groups of four to make the dough. This meant that there had to be teamwork. The dough was divided up, and the students were shown how thin they needed to roll it out. Each group used some cardboard patterns to cut out their parts. The cutting tool of choice was a plastic knife. This meant that the edges weren't too even. I brought a pizza wheel in, because I figured it couldn't be considered a weapon. It also cut neater and faster than the plastic knife. It saved a lot of time.

As the pieces were cut out, they were placed on cookie sheets, and each student initialed their pieces. Parent volunteers manned the ovens during school time, and the teacher completed any baking after school that day. Each student's pieces were put in large zippered plastic bags, for the next step. The next class period, frosting was made to cement the houses together and everyone was decorating. It was great fun.

*Self Publishing*

One of the projects that Matthew's teacher had was publishing their own books. She was one of the few teachers who really understood the computers in the school. Students were asked to write stories. Then, they were to submit them to the teacher, who would format the story into pages that could be illustrated. After illustrations were added, the student presented it to the class.

I saw some of these presentations. The stories seemed simple enough. They were relatively short, and there were about two or three sentences per page. Matthew didn't present any books. I wondered why. It would be nearly spring before I found out why.

We thought Matthew had an organizational problem, so I went to the school and helped him clean out his desk, at the end of the quarter. Way in the back of his desk, I found lots of papers that were covered with writing. This wasn't the newsprint that first graders usually use. It was regular notebook paper that was covered front and back with writing. These were his stories. Even as a first grader, he knew they didn't fit the model. He would have needed thirty pages of drawings to accompany his words. Who had that much time? Besides, the teacher wanted age appropriate output. He was writing at a higher level. She refused to publish these wonderful stories. The lesson Matthew learned was: Don't write so much.

M) DISCRIMINATION, HARASSMENT & ABUSE: *Walking Backwards*

At our school, there were two bells to start the school day. The first one indicated that the students should line up for their teachers to bring them into the school. The second bell rang ten minutes later, to signal the start of the actual school day. Students were advised to arrive at the school as close to the first bell, as possible. Being on the playground earlier was dangerous in numerous ways. Besides potential injuries from several children congregating on an unsupervised (and often dark) playground, we had to contend with the problem of wild animals. If there was a moose on that playground, no amount of begging or pleading could get a child into the school any earlier than the first bell.

If a student came in (even a second) after the second bell, they had to report to the office and pick up a tardy slip. This process could take fifteen minutes, depending on the amount of students ahead of you. Several days, I happened to be in the hallway during the space between the bells, and I noticed an interesting phenomenon. Betty dropped her son off at the front door, because they were running late. The front door was closest to her son's classroom, but it wasn't the one he was supposed to be entering through. He was supposed to be going around to the back of the building, to come in that door. By coming through the front door, Betty's son had to walk past the office.

With other students milling around, several teachers and the school's secretary singled out Betty's son. I heard the message loud and clear. Each adult had to stop him and tell him he was late. He was directed to the office to pick up a late slip. I saw him go into the office just as the second bell rang.

I don't know why these adults all had to pick on a child who was very mild-mannered. As time went on, I watched him walk slower and slower towards the building. If he were going any slower, he would have been walking backwards.

I also noticed something as I passed by his classroom. I heard his teacher yelling and screaming at him, specifically. The boy had just lost his grandfather and a favorite pet. He had also gone through some surgery that wasn't covered under his parents' insurance because it was considered a "pre-existing condition". His mother was working two jobs. If she passed the trial period on the second job, she would be getting better pay, and could quit the other job. Between the two parents, they were working hard just to cover this medical bill. The teacher was only aggravating the stress at home.

One day, I confronted the teacher. Her students were in a pullout class, so I felt I could talk to her with relative privacy. I asked her if she couldn't say anything positive to Betty's son. The teacher was offended by my suggestion. She raised her voice and told me that she needed parental permission to give the boy any words of encouragement. I couldn't believe what I was hearing. Obviously, she didn't need any parental consent to verbally beat a student into the ground. She also told me if Betty was as involved in the school as I was; maybe she would treat the boy better.

I asked the teacher if she was aware of the stress this family was under. She looked me straight in the eye, and asked what I meant. When I went through the list of recent difficulties, she said, "Oh, that. I thought you meant they had something else happen." I wondered what else it would take for this woman to have some sensitivity.

While I was speaking with this teacher, the Modified Primary teacher walked by, and asked what the problem was. When I explained, she told me if his parents wanted to make a complaint, they should talk to the teacher directly. The teacher didn't have to answer to me. The only problem with this situation was that I was the one who was seeing the child being abused, and it was making ME nauseous. His parents could file a complaint, but they would still have me as their witness.

Betty's son was pulled out of the classroom, and had a visit with the school's Psychologist. They were suspecting he was being abused, and were investigating his parents. Betty's son had told her that his teacher hated him, but she thought he was exaggerating. Who could hate her son? Pieces started coming together. Betty and her husband confronted the teacher. As in my case, they were unable to get him moved out of the classroom. Things improved a little and he survived the rest of the school year. No child should have been required to endure the abuse this child went through. Shame on the school for allowing it.

*The Negative Attention Monster*

Once Matthew's teacher found out that Matthew wasn't on the Ritalin anymore, everything changed in the classroom. I was constantly being told that Matthew was on the blue card. It wasn't just the teacher telling me this, either. Like many other parents, I waited outside my son's classroom after school, so we could walk home. As his classmates streamed out the door, they all had to announce to me, "Matthew got a blue card today." This was unacceptable. I asked the teacher to try to impress on the children that they shouldn't announce things like that, especially with so much glee. The teacher saw nothing wrong with this behavior. I suspect she even promoted it.

I tried to get Matthew moved out of this school and into the neighboring school. The only way I could do that was by entering him into a lottery for May. The neighboring school wasn't accepting anymore zone-exemptions otherwise.

I tried to see if I could figure out what was going on in Matthew's class. I told the teacher, if he got a blue card again, I would come to class to observe. I wanted to see how he got these cards. The day after he got his next blue card, I woke up with a headache and a major sore throat, but I went to school anyhow. I was sure that the teacher would view my absence as a weakness, otherwise. I sat way in the back of the classroom with a book. Every once in a while, I looked down at the book. It seemed that any time I looked down at the book, the teacher complained about Matthew. The children all had their backs to me, and I only lowered my eyes to see the book. The only person who could see that was the teacher.

I noticed something else. The teacher seemed to be losing control of the class while she was trying to discipline Matthew. I wondered if Matthew was misbehaving because it was so much fun to watch the teacher lose control. I also knew that Matthew hadn't pulled any blue cards as long as the teacher thought he was on the medicine. After this day, I should have told the teacher she was right, and give her the lip service that I would put Matthew back on his medicine. Instead, I focused on the negative attention. I suggested to the teacher that she should withhold the negative attention for about a week, and see what happened. Of course, she couldn't go without disciplining him for any length of time, so the problem continued. After seeing her losing control some, while I was in the room, I was sure she was feeding the "Negative Attention Monster". If she could only stop playing the game with Matthew, her life would have been a lot easier.

After sitting in class for the morning, I went off to the doctor's office, and was diagnosed with strep. Too bad I hadn't hugged the teacher.

*Physical Violence Isn't Tolerated*

Mary's son was in Kindergarten. The children sat around tables, and he was assigned to sit next to a little girl who didn't like him. Not liking another child might be considered a minor offense, but constantly leaning over and whispering racial slurs into your neighbor's ear is more sinister.

The school had rules spelled out in the student handbook. Supposedly, racial intolerance wasn't tolerated in the School District. This school, being part of the School District, should have adhered to this rule. Of course, it has to be proven that a student was offensive. No one had heard what the girl whispered, except Mary's son, and he pushed her away from him. The teacher saw him push her and his parents were called to the school.

Mary and her husband showed up at the school together. They were told that their son had pushed another student. Physical violence wasn't tolerated at this school. Mary and her husband explained that something needed to be done about the original problem. Their son had been taught that he didn't have to take the racial slurs. Wasn't there a school policy about that? The teacher squirmed for a while.

Mary and her husband suggested that the teacher change the situation, so their son wouldn't have to push someone away. The teacher hadn't considered separating the students. At the time, she was focusing on the shoving. It hadn't occurred to her to talk to the little girl, or the class, about how words can hurt people. The teacher wanted the parents to fix a situation where she was responsible. Mary and her husband made it quite clear that their son shouldn't be subjected to any more harassment. If he was harassed, he would be instructed to call them. If the school couldn't solve the problem, they would look for authority higher up. The situation was solved quite rapidly.

## N) SAFETY & SECURITY: *Take Better Care of Your Supplies*

Melissa had been absent for a day. When she came back, they were supposed to be doing an art project that involved crayons. I had marked my children's crayons specially. One wouldn't have noticed the markings unless the crayons were outside the box. I had run a line of nail polish over the paper and the end of the crayon. It would be hard to remove this marking without scraping and peeling.

Melissa wasn't able to find her crayons. Since she hadn't taken them home, someone must have taken them. The teacher criticized her for not taking care of her supplies. I happened to be in the room at the time. I asked the teacher if he would ask the other students to dump their crayons on their desks. If they were still in the classroom, I could identify them. He refused. Melissa had to borrow crayons for the project, and we had to buy her a new set. We wondered how she was supposed to secure her supplies when she wasn't in the classroom and her desk wasn't lockable. Hmm.

## *We Can't Locate Your Son*

I received the call from the school secretary at about 1:30 in the afternoon. I hadn't been feeling well, so I thought I would take a nap before the kids were ready to come home. When the secretary asked if Jeff was home, I became fully alert. I had walked to school with them that morning, and Jeff wasn't the type to be skipping school. If he wasn't at the school, where was he?

The secretary said that the janitor had looked into the classroom he was supposed to have been in for his after lunch class, but he wasn't there. He also wasn't in the lavatories. She thought, since he had been bullied on the playground often, maybe he had been beaten up and had just decided to walk home. I became frantic. It was an hour past lunchtime, and it takes about 15 minutes for us to walk home at a leisurely pace. My husband drove me to the school, and I vaulted out of the car as soon as he stopped. I raced into the school just as the secretary was paging my son over the intercom. Jeff's teacher came down one hallway, and Jeff came down another hallway. Both of them had confused looks on their faces as they walked towards the office and saw my frantic appearance.

Jeff was in a 5/6-grade combination class. Since there were only about 8 fifth graders in the class, they took their Science and Social Studies classes with the fifth graders. There weren't any extra chairs in the fifth grade classrooms, so his classmates sat on the floor along the wall, near the door. When the janitor looked into the room, Jeff was sitting below the level of the window the janitor was looking through. No one inside the classroom had any clue he was looking for Jeff.

The things that upset me most about this situation are: (1) The secretary knew my child was being bullied, yet nothing was being done, and (2) The secretary hadn't paged Jeff before alerting me.

## O) POLITICS: *Golden Parachutes*

The School District was looking for ways to cut back on their operating costs. Contract negotiations were starting again. This year, they were offering the more experienced (higher salaried) teachers early retirement packages. To me, the offer sounded a lot like "golden parachutes". It didn't make any sense to me. Why get rid of all the experienced teachers who knew how to deal with students, and replace them with inexperienced teachers? Who would provide the continuity? New teachers without seasoned advice would have to spend valuable time reinventing the wheel. I also wondered what impact this tactic would have on student test scores in the future. After all, isn't the quality of the education measured by those test scores?

I was around the school and overheard at least a few teachers grappling with the prospect. These were teachers who were good with children, but some of the older students were disrespectful. These teachers loved their jobs. But was there enough harassment to make them want to leave?

The teachers in question ended up taking the early retirement package. They found other jobs elsewhere, where they were more appreciated. Some of the teachers came back to the schools as substitute teachers. Since people from the substitute pool filled their previous jobs, there was now a shortage of substitute teachers. I wonder how much money was really saved in this maneuver.

Almost as important as the money issue is, the student proficiency rating. Did all this shuffling improve test scores? If the scores went down, the School District should get a failing mark on their report card.

*Substitute Teacher Pool*

I was in the workroom one day, when I heard some teachers discussing substitutes. The School District has a substitute pool. When a teacher needs a substitute, they put in their request, and a substitute is chosen for them. Our School District is about 40 miles from end to end. From the way the teachers spoke, it didn't seem like the substitutes were assigned to small groups of schools. It seemed like they could be sent anywhere. Other than accepting or declining the offered job for the day, the substitutes didn't seem to have much of a choice.

Two of the teachers were discussing needing a substitute in the near future. A third teacher recommended a substitute that she usually requested when she had advance notice of absence. If the substitute wasn't already engaged for the date, the requesting teacher might have a good chance of getting her. Illness and family emergencies weren't the only reasons a teacher would be absent. There were various classes and seminars which teachers were required to take, during school hours. With the variety of reasons a teacher might not be in school, teacher absences could be as high as 10%. If the School District's substitute pool equaled less than 10% of the School District's teacher population, the District ran the risk of having classrooms without teachers.

To me, it seemed like the substitutes should be assigned to small clusters of schools, with an option to sub outside the area, if necessary. By being assigned to a small group of schools, the chances that the substitute looking like "fresh meat" to the classes she's subbing for are lessened. It's harder to sink a sub who knows you (and maybe your parents). The substitutes would be able to pick up on the lesson plans faster, and be part of the schools' teaching teams, rather than an outsider.

R) REDUCE, REUSE & RECYCLE: *Green Star in Full Swing*

I was learning more about the workroom. We were implementing processes within the workroom that would probably never leave the room, but could be passed on easily. There were two trashcans to collect white and colored bond paper. They were labeled as such, but sometimes, it seemed like the teachers couldn't read.

At the mimeograph machine, we realized how much paper was being used to check for a good impression. If we only used one side of the paper, it was definitely a waste. Why use a new piece of paper to make a test impression, if there were rejected copies around. I had a box of one-sided "reject" copies on the shelf below the mimeograph machine. Parents who used the machine were trained to go there first. Teachers had no clue.

Rejected copies also made good scratch paper. The local copy shop padded them for us for free. If we wanted pads that were smaller than 8½" x 11", we had to pay a dollar per cut (on pads of 100 sheets or less).

This year, I also learned something about the dry mount press. It was a machine with a scissors-type hinge on it. I knew it heated up, and I knew it closed, but I didn't know how to close it, so I asked someone. I had noticed that the rolls of lamination were discarded when they reached a certain point. After that, it was hard to run it through the machine, but there was still plenty of usable lamination. With the dry mount press, I could laminate single items by folding the leftover lamination around the project. Supposedly, this lamination was so expensive, and I wanted to keep from wasting as much of it as possible. Whatever the waste was, it was the same for two rolls at a time. We went through at least two rolls of lamination per week. I wondered how long it took us to waste one complete roll.

I collected recyclable paper from the classrooms once a week. It seemed like the lower grades made more of an effort to keep the paper clean. The older grades threw garbage in their recycling container. I often found candy wrappers among the papers. I rejected any wadded up papers, because they usually hid gum.

At the end of the school year, I noticed some of the teachers getting rid of a lot of papers. They were filling huge garbage bags to drop into the dumpster. When I asked why they weren't putting them into the recycling, I was told that they were student progress reports, and the information on them was very sensitive. They didn't want the papers to get into the wrong hands. I thought this was sort of silly. When I recycled the papers, they went directly from the school to the processing area at the recycling center. The bags that the teachers were filling would sit in the dumpster, at least overnight.

A better way to have dealt with the security issue was to cut the top and bottom of the papers off. That is usually where the personal information is. The middle could have been recycled, and the ends could have been shredded, if necessary.

I spent three hours a week collecting up the recyclable paper. I think we averaged 40 pounds per week. The school had an account at the recycling center. We got a penny per pound for clean white paper, and half a penny for mixed colored bond paper. The school secretary once asked how much we had made. I told her that I never knew. When I tried to find out how much we had recycled over the school year, I was told that they couldn't give me that information, because my name wasn't on the account. The PTA President's name was on the account, so she had collected the money in December, along with the report.

*Paper Maché Dinosaurs*

Matthew's class made paper maché dinosaurs using the colorful butcher paper that is used as the background of the bulletin boards. They tore huge chunks of this paper off the rolls, and ripped it into small pieces to fit over their dinosaur forms. The dinosaurs were cute, but it was a waste of paper.

Towards the end of the year, I would realize how much butcher paper was thrown in the trash after it had been removed from a bulletin board. Instead of throwing the paper away, it should have been cut or rolled into more manageable sizes to be more easily stored for projects like this. If teachers planned ahead a little bit, the used paper could have been recycled into another project like this, or used to cover tables in the Art room, for a messy project.

S) SICKNESS & HEALTH: *Awards R Us*

At the end of each quarter, there was an award ceremony in every classroom. Teachers would flood the workroom to assemble these awards. There would be a run on the copier and the laminator. The awards were always on a full sheet of paper, usually mounted on a sheet of construction paper. Sometimes they had a gold seal on them, and they were usually laminated.

Awards were given for perfect attendance, staying on the "Green Team", and a variety of academic achievements. I often wondered how many of the students who got the "perfect attendance" award really came to school healthy for the whole quarter. Teachers applied pressure on parents about the importance of good attendance. The school may say, "Don't send a child to school sick.." But they will harass you if your child stays home.

Besides the waste of supplies, I objected to the fact that teachers seemed to think every student needed to have some award, no matter how feeble the achievement. Matthew had awards on handwriting, knowing his letters, reading, and math. What a waste of paper!

In Jeff's class, there was a girl with a weight problem. Three of her classmates were given awards for exercising her at recess. Everyone assumed that the girl's problem was too much food, and not enough exercise. It seemed that the three girls had taken on the task as a community service.

The awards were given publicly, and the girls accepted them proudly. I think I was the only one who might have been embarrassed about the whole situation, besides the overweight girl. A couple weeks later, I overheard the "fat" girl's mother telling another mother, "The doctors have finally figured out what's causing our daughter's weight problem. She's got trouble with her thyroid."

The girl moved to a different school for her last year in elementary school. I wonder if public humiliation had anything to do with the move.

## T) TECHNOLOGY: *Computerizing the Library*

When we arrived at this school, the card catalog was on microfiche. Two huge reels of film on two viewing machines. You had to run through the whole reel if what you were looking for was on the opposite end of the reel. I wanted the card catalogs back, but what I wanted wasn't important. The traditional card catalog took up a lot of space. The microfiche took up less space, but might have still been considered somewhat time consuming to use. We were moving up to the next step. Putting the card catalog on the computer. This meant, putting bar codes on the books. It would end up taking much less time at the end of the year to do the inventory.

Putting our library's books on computer might not have taken much time, but it was part of a much bigger process. It was a school district-wide plan. With about 55 schools to connect to the network, it was going to take some time. I'm not sure, but I think the University was also on the same system. I know their books were cataloged to interact with the main library, which was a separate system from the School District's system. The whole cataloging effort took two years to complete.

## U) CELEBRATIONS: *The Christmas Concert*

This was the first school Linda had ever seen that didn't have a Christmas program where children sang and parents watched proudly. I hadn't really considered the fact that the music teacher was teaching the students holiday songs, but there wouldn't be any place for them to perform. Linda's older son was in the second grade. She asked the principal when they were going to be having the Christmas program. She was shocked to find out that there would be no such thing in the school. Having a program that the parents could attend, after school hours, wasn't feasible. You couldn't ask the Music teacher to do more than her scheduled time.

Linda did ask the Music teacher about a program. At first, the teacher was reluctant, but Linda reminded the teacher that it would only take a few hours out of her precious personal time. Once the Music teacher was involved, they scheduled an evening for the performance.

The night of the Christmas program, six of us were supposed to set things up. Santa's Shop was taking place in one of the classrooms. Parents were bringing cookies for refreshments, so we had to set them out on plates. One of the volunteers ended up getting sick, and another became an emergency babysitter.

About an hour before the program, parents started dropping children off for the program. We had small children running around under our feet without any parental supervision. The program was meant to be a family activity, not childcare. When we couldn't find the big cooler to mix up lemonade, I offered to run out to get some ready-made drinks. We were running out of time and options.

The program was quite successful. I ended up getting back with enough time to see my children sing, in spite of being delayed by a moose.

W) SEX: *Sex Education (for Parents)*

In the fifth grade, they start teaching a class called, "Human Growth and Development". Before our children took this class, the school had to arrange for parents to be able to view the study materials. I was one of a handful of parents who showed up to see what they intended to teach my son.

They handed out a syllabus. We were able to view some of the films and books the students would reference. If a parent didn't want their child to learn about any portion of the material, arrangements would be made for the student to visit the library to do an alternate activity. The big catch was it was all or nothing. If you objected to anything being taught, your child would get none of the information directly from the teacher. The library would be the student's option for the duration of the course.

I thought the objection the other parents had seemed quite petty. They said the drawings of the human body seemed too realistic. That had nothing to do with the educational content. My main objection was to the amount of time they spent discussing some words, but I didn't voice my opinion. Maybe some people needed more explanation, but I doubted these kids did. As far as I could see, the curriculum was pretty accurate.

They were supposed to discuss homosexuality, too. I don't know if that was age appropriate, and I'm still not sure how much is nature, and how much is nurture. Who knows what we are doing to our population with the garbage we produce? It might actually be in the water.

*A Blind Eye*

Joan's daughter was in the sixth grade, and she thought something was wrong. What does a 12-year-old know? She told Joan that her teacher seemed to like the boys better than the girls. The boys were called in from recess sooner, and the classroom was often locked when the girls came back into the school.

Joan mentioned her concern to the principal, but the principal wasn't interested in what she considered to be a vague "feeling" that something was wrong. Several other parents voiced a concern, but they had all done it individually, so it was easily ignored.

The class was to go out on a field trip to the pool, and Joan invited Mary to come as a chaperon, since Mary was impartial. Mary watched the activity in the pool. The teacher was wearing a bikini, which could have been considered inappropriate for a school function. She played water games with the boys, which seemed suggestive to Mary. Joan asked Mary what she should do, since this seemed to be a bigger problem than just her imagination. Mary advised Joan that the parents should confront the principal as a group. There was strength in numbers. When they got back to the school, Mary went to speak to the principal. She told the principal to listen to what the parents had to say, because they had a valid concern.

The principal didn't show much concern, until a couple teachers voiced concern that this teacher was acting way out of character. By this time, the year was nearly over. The teacher was transferred to another school for the next two years.

She was finally removed from the system when two male students accused her of having sex or kissing them, during the year she taught Joan's daughter. She was indicted on four felony counts of first degree child sexual abuse and one misdemeanor count, of harassment.

My concern with this situation may not be whether or not she had sex with her students. Some cases can be "he said - she said", and it can be very difficult to prove anything. Having sex with a student is always a serious problem. My major concern about this particular situation is that parents voiced their concerns and were completely ignored. Isn't the principal supposed to be in charge, and know what's going on in her school?  If the principal isn't aware of, and responsible for, what happens in their school, is it really safe to send our children to the schools?

# Chapter 8
## The Strike Zone Fall 1994

A) FIRST IMPRESSIONS: *Musical Teachers and Contract Negotiations*

Matthew was finally going into the second grade. I had hoped he would get Melissa's teacher, but she moved to a school that was closer to home. The Kindergarten teacher moved into a second grade space. Luckily, Matthew got didn't have to serve more time with his Kindergarten teacher. Melissa moved into the fourth grade and got the teacher that Jeff hadn't had. Jeff stayed with the teacher he had from the year before. By this time, I was sort of understanding what made this woman tick, and could work with her a lot more easily. I was back on the PTA Board, as secretary.

Things looked like they might get better, especially if the teachers were able to get their contract ironed out. I was in the workroom one day, and heard two teachers talking about a paper that had been sent out during summer vacation. It stated that health benefits were going to be arbitrarily cut. One teacher said, "If I had known my orthodontic benefits would be cut, I wouldn't have put my daughter in braces."

This was a professional woman who was married to a professional man, and she was fussing about one child's braces. We had no coverage, and I was looking at three children in braces over the next three years. I had very little sympathy. We hoped contract negotiations would be settled soon, and dug into the year.

B) BUILDINGS & GROUNDS: *The Invisible Playground*

The big toy had been partially dismantled by the former PTA President before the end of the last school year. Basically, all that was left was a low bridge and several tall upright pieces of wood. It wasn't much to play on. The remaining equipment couldn't be removed by parent-volunteers, without making the situation more dangerous.

During the summer, our new playground equipment was supposed to have been installed. All summer, the neighbors had watched for signs of activity in vain. When our PTA Board arrived on the scene, we asked when they were going to complete our playground. Schools around us, who had been behind us on the list, were already completed, while we were still waiting.

Buildings and Grounds for the School District said according to their records it had already been done. We asked to speak with the man who was handling our order. He had quit his job and moved out of state. I guess he took all of our plans with him, because no one could find them. We had to resubmit the plans. We also challenged the people who said the project was complete, by inviting them to come over to look at our "new" playground equipment.

We finally got our new playground equipment installed the following summer.

C) PARENT-TEACHER ENTITY: *A Brief History of PTA*

This was the first year that I actually understood what the PTA stood for. We had basically been dealing with funding issues. Sometimes, we funded cultural assemblies for the students. There was lots of discussion about buildings and grounds and technology, but little emphasis was placed on the true mission. I was fascinated by how different our school's focus was from the ideal.

According to National PTA pamphlets, The PTA was founded in 1897 as the National Congress of Mothers. Their first convention recommended public kindergartens. In 1924, the organization's name changed to the National Congress of Parents and Teachers. In 1926, a separate but equal entity was needed for states that had legal segregation, so the National Congress of Colored Parents and Teachers was born. These two groups worked together closely until 1970 when they merged to become the National Parent Teacher Association.

In 1899, the convention petitioned Congress for a national health bureau. Fourteen years later, the US Public Health Service was created. PTA currently deals with issues on parenting, drug and alcohol abuse, child safety, cultural arts, and education. They have accumulated a wealth of information that is accessible by its members. PTA membership isn't limited to parents and teachers, and it doesn't have to be attached to a school. The PTA can promote ideas, but cannot promote candidates. Part of the PTA's goal is to encourage parental involvement in schools, and promote cooperative relations between home and school for more productive education.

This is the barest thumbnail sketch of the PTA. For more specific information, you might want to get involved.

*Phase 1: Enthusiasm*

They say there are six phases for a project. 1) Enthusiasm; 2) Disillusionment; 3) Panic; 4) Search for the Guilty; 5) Punishment of the Innocent; and 6) Praise and Honors for the Non-Participants.

Our PTA Board this year was what some would consider a "dream team". Of course, I am biased, by including myself. The president had training in "Total Quality Management". I viewed him as being a principled person, so I agreed to be secretary. Our first vice president was the only one among us who had no outstanding quality. She could have been considered the token black person, if we didn't already have a diverse board. Our second vice president and treasurer had been a married couple who moved out of the area, so those positions were temporarily open.

As far as "minor officers", we still had big league players. We had two people in the position of Programs Chair. He could acquire things for prizes or supplies. He knew how to ask businesses for donations. She was able to attract and motivate volunteers. The reason we had co-chairs on this position was because his work took him out of town on short notice. We had to have someone in place to implement plans. This year, the female co-chair wanted to form a new chair called, "Volunteer Liaison". We also had a Disaster Preparedness Chair who had put together a comprehensive Disaster Plan for the school district she worked for in California.

Before the meeting, we tried to add two new people to the board. I had a great idea. The president's wife had a background as a loan officer. Who would be more qualified to be our treasurer? I didn't see any legal conflict with this arrangement, since two of our original slate of officers had been married. The bigger question was, "Did she want to work with her husband?" She decided the project was worth it.

The "Volunteer Liaison" and I were walking down the hall. As we passed by the old Modified Primary classroom, we both commented on how we missed the teacher there. Her class had been discontinued and she had retired. She had been a great Technology Chair, and her input would really be missed. At that moment, we both realized that we had a new teacher in the building who was very technology savvy. He was one of the new Gifted teachers. We approached him about the position, and he agreed to attend the meeting. He wasn't interested in joining our PTA, since he dealt with several schools. He said he didn't want to show favoritism. We knew his input could impact his classroom's supplies though, and his students from the various schools. Maybe he would join later.

We voted in the new treasurer, and voted to create the new position of "Volunteer Liaison". During this meeting, we covered the concepts of the Safe Home Program, Child Watch, building up our Disaster Preparedness Program, the fund raiser, and attracting more volunteers. My job was made a little bit easier this year. I actually had a tape recorder to tape the information at the meeting. Something bothered me at this meeting though, the principal requested that I turn off the tape recorder, and she proceeded to whisper something into the president's ear. What did she think I was going to catch on my tape?

With our enthusiasm intact, we were ready to go out and make our little corner of the world safe for our children.

*Phase 2- Disillusionment*

Back to School Night has been traditionally a night where parents are briefly introduced to the new PTA, and they get to find out what their children's teachers' plans are for the year. We had come up with several ideas about safety and parent involvement in the school, and we hoped to outline these ideas briefly at the Back to School Night. Just before the event, we were told that we wouldn't be allowed to speak to the parents, unless we were sitting at a PTA membership table. There would be no customary PTA presentation. We wondered why we were being gagged.

*The Legislative Chair*

Before the October PTA meeting, the original PTA President moved back to the state. Upon her return to our school, she requested the Legislative Chair. The duties of this position included attending assembly and school board meetings, and taking notes about legislation that could affect our school. She was accepted onto our team, but she wouldn't be authorized to sign checks or be given a vote.
As secretary, my minutes would reflect legislative activities done by our representatives. We had some pretty powerful advocates working for us. Unfortunately, when I had a chance to meet these women in person, I was signing each of them in to vote. I never really got a chance to say what a great job I thought they had done.

*Phase 3- Panic*

The PTA treasurer started noticing little things about the books and her job that weren't quite right. One of the first things she noticed was the intricate bookkeeping by "the last treasurer". She said that it was definitely a work of art, in accounting terms. She could see how someone could possibly have two sets of books with this type of ability. The intricacy made it confusing to comprehend at first glance. The last two years, the PTA had designated accounts under its umbrella for all the teachers. The teachers kept asking her how much money was in their accounts. It was almost as if it were the PTA ATM. Designated accounts through PTA is illegal.

Another thing she noticed was money for lost books went through the PTA fund instead of going to the School District or library accounts. That looked like money laundering. The more questions she asked, the more hostile the school officials acted towards her.

We came into the PTA with a beginning balance of $6000, but the ending balance on the previous year's audit was $10,000. Everyone wanted to know what our board did with the other $4000. The audit was done before the bills came in for the end of the year field trips, so the former PTA President disbursed $4000 after the audit.

The treasurer asked for outside help from the State PTA. They sent a representative who was also running for School Board. She was often seen in our school, after hours, with the original PTA President. Who knows exactly what that was about?

The treasurer wanted to get clarification about her job. Was status quo acceptable, or was she supposed to go by the book? She was justifiably concerned that the status quo was illegal, and action could be taken against her. The State PTA's representative was no help. The treasurer requested another audit, but no permission would be given for an impartial outside audit. The only other option was the three-person audit team, but who would pick out the team? The previous year's audit had been done by the former PTA President's husband and the couple we had lost from our Board. They couldn't exactly be considered impartial auditors.

Without any visible support for her position from the State PTA, the treasurer decided to pay for an audit out of her own pocket, to end all of the rumor and conjecture about her job. An audit would be considered legal proof of her innocence.

D) FUND RAISING: *The Gift-Wrap Gridlock*

We were having a great deal of difficulty reaching the salesman for the fund raiser directly. He returned any of our communications through the previous PTA President. She had signed the contract with the fund raising company, so the salesman would only work with her. The samples came to the school in her name, and she would have been within her rights to walk off with them. The contracted date for our fund raiser was rapidly approaching, and we hadn't had any contact from the salesman, nor received any sales materials.

The salesman arrived at the meeting late, with samples of catalogs. He was an extremely fast talker. The fund raiser was scheduled to start the following week. The company would print up fliers to accompany the catalogs. These fliers would outline the purpose of the fund raiser, and indicate when payment was due. The salesman said that if we advertised payment was due when the orders arrived, we could sell 33% more products. I watched the teachers' eyes light up.
According to my tape, we had decided collecting at the time the order was placed was best. Having the option to collect before or after would cause a bookkeeping nightmare.

The day after our PTA meeting, two things happened. The first was we received a note from the principal who said that "several teachers had complained about the noise our children made during our (after school) meeting." The sound hadn't been coming from our children. They were quietly lying around the hall doing their homework. The sound had been coming from the gym, where there had been an after school basketball program. The second incident involved me, personally. I was called into the principal's office and asked what was the exact day the fund raiser was due to start. Because the fund raiser was going to be so "disruptive" to the teachers' activities, we had to give them plenty of advanced warning. I'm sure we could have canceled the fund raiser if it was viewed as such an inconvenience. I'm sure the parents wouldn't have minded.

The materials for the fund raiser arrived exactly on the day the fund raiser was due to start. Starting our fund raiser on time was very important, because we would be competing against all of the neighboring schools for sales. It was sort of a "gift wrap gridlock". Three of us emptied the boxes of supplies in the teachers' lounge. That was the only area big enough to assemble the packets. Morning Kindergarten was getting ready to leave for the day, so we hurried to get the supplies to that teacher. The principal came in to tell us that we had to have all of our "junk" cleared out by the time the teachers started their lunches. It would have progressed a lot faster without the extra interruptions. We assembled nearly four hundred packets by lunchtime. Unfortunately, the paper said that payment could be accepted before or after delivery of the items. We didn't have enough time to cross out, "or after".

The packets were distributed and collected by the teachers. While we were waiting for the products to return, teachers could be heard in the hallways, comparing how much money they were going to be getting from their students' sales. So much for the inconvenience aspect of fund raising, It was more like "Greed Incorporated."

The products arrived. When we tried to collect the money that was due to the PTA upon arrival of the products, buyers refused to pay until the products were in their hands. The treasurer was forbidden, by the principal, from getting signatures before releasing partially paid orders. Some people never even came to pick up their orders, and the PTA was ordered to remove the products from the school. The treasurer ended up driving around in a near blizzard, just before Christmas, to try to deliver the orders. Because of the "printing error", it cost our PTA dearly.

*Home Business Fair-Part 2*

I attended the Community School meeting to decide when to schedule the next Home Business Fair. I was hoping for a date in October, but most of the people on the board complained that the Community

School calendar was filled every weekend in October, except one. It would be better to have the Fair in November. The weekend of the 12th would be assigned for my project.

The other reason I was at this meeting was to form a committee to help me accomplish my task. I think it was the first time in my adult life that I had seen "civilized" women look like wolves. One woman in particular seemed to bare her teeth at me. I don't know why she was angry with me, but the sentiment caught on with the group. The Community School Coordinator wasn't in the room at this point. She had been called away for a phone call. While she was supportive of my project, no one else seemed to be.

The short dating before Christmas would cause some problems with which vendors I could attract. I sent letters out to my previous clients, and most of them were able to return. The lady for Longaberger said she would be there, too. She had the longest turnaround time. Her products might not arrive before Christmas. I searched for the signs I had made the year before, and was informed they had been considered garbage and were destroyed. I had to make new signs as the climate inside the school was becoming more hostile. I got the tag board from Community School, and covertly traced the outlines for my signs by the glow of the overhead projector in the darkened Art room.

The next obstacle I had to overcome was the Public Service Announcement in the paper. For six weeks, they announced the Fair for the week before the actual scheduled date. For six weeks, we tried to get the announcement changed.

The day before the Fair, we asked the teachers to form the desks in their classrooms into a counter area. I was hoping for some help from the Community School. Basically, the help I got was from a teenage boy who needed to do some community service, and my own family. Teachers were informed that any disruption of their classrooms would be repaired by "my team" after the fair, if a seating plan was provided. Friday, after school, I set up half of the rooms with display areas. Most of the teachers had placed four desks in a semicircle, just inside the door, for a display area. I lined up all the desks in a double row, so the open part of the desks faced each other. This arrangement provided both a decent sized display area, and a barricade to keep customers from disturbing the rest of the classroom.

I was very weak by Saturday morning. The doctor had just prescribed Cipro for a respiratory problem and recommended bed rest. There was no one else to run the Fair in my absence. The teenager helped me set up the rest of the classrooms. We had to move a heavy cabinet in one class. It would have been inside the display area.

The people arrived. Many customers complained that they had come the week before, when the Fair was advertised, and accused me of false advertising. Three vendors didn't show. Shaklee thought I was supposed to confirm their space again, even though the paper I sent them said a space was reserved. Longaberger had scheduled for a show that had more prestige than we did. The Discovery Toys representative was ill, and couldn't make it. I heard complaints from customers that they had come because these companies were advertised. When anything went wrong, I was called to straighten it out. We made more money than the first time, but I decided I didn't have the strength or the clout to run it again. I went home and slept through Sunday.

I dragged myself out of bed early on Monday morning. I took the kids to school early, in case any of the teachers needed their rooms changed back, as promised by the Community School. One teacher needed her room changed back and had provided a seating chart. I think it took us five minutes to change her room back. A few other teachers I checked with said that they were planning on changing the seating anyhow, so their students could hunt for their own desks and move them accordingly. The first bell had just rung when I got to the last teacher. She stood in the hall and (literally) screamed at me for not putting her classroom back in order. She said that the Community School promised that my team would straighten everything out. I wanted to yell back at her, "You are looking at my team, and I'm moving as fast as I can for someone who's supposed to be in bed!" Besides, she hadn't provided a seating chart. The students were streaming into her room. I asked the students to help me find their desks, and see if they could move them back to the right places. It took five minutes, and I helped the teacher move the heavy cabinet back into position.

This accounting may sound like a "whine fest", but here's what I learned from my experience:

1) It's better to have one of these fund raisers around October. It will bring in more money.
2) The way I had the classrooms set up was more professional than my imitators were.
3) There should be at least two people representing each company, so space won't be wasted, or customers disappointed.
4) Don't run the fund raiser and be a vendor too, unless you have a strong team behind you.
5) The newspaper can say, "Better luck next time", after the fact.
6) Don't do it in a year where there are heavy teacher contract negotiations.

*Santa's Secret Shop*

This year was particularly troubling in Santa's Secret Shop. Sally volunteered to work the shop during the time that was allowed for the fifth and sixth graders to preview the products. Sally couldn't understand why the students were so interested in a wrench that was on display, until they left and she had a chance to look at it more closely. The handle had a knife blade in it. The students were looking at it as a weapon that was permitted by the school.

As soon as her shift was over, she looked for the principal. The principal was in the workroom with the former PTA President. Sally brought up her concern, and both women looked at her as if she had lost her mind. She was complaining about weapons being provided by the fund raising organization and sold by the school. Wasn't that considered to be grounds for concern? Neither woman seemed very concerned at all, so Sally took matters into her own hands, and removed the handful of offensive merchandise from the display table. She placed the wrenches in a box, taped it shut, and labeled it "Returns".

When she told me about this situation, I considered the fact that Matthew had been given detention for the plastic knife the year before, yet in Santa's Secret Shop they sold weapons that were more damaging besides the wrenches in question. They sold small screwdriver sets and long letter openers. One would think possession of these items might be grounds for detention also.

The other thing that bothered me about Santa's Secret Shop involved a comment a teacher made. One of the parents who had volunteered to open the shop one morning was late. The class that was scheduled to visit didn't have a whole lot of time. If nobody was watching the shop, the class would lose their spot. I wasn't particularly busy at the moment, so I was asked if I would watch the shop. When I said that I would, one of the teachers made some comment about me being "easy" and doing anything anyone asked. I guess she never understood the real reason I was volunteering at the school. I thought I could make the teacher's job easier, and maybe even help make the school a better place.

I couldn't see any reason I couldn't help out, and was relieved about half an hour later by the original volunteer, who had been late due to an emergency.

F) PROGRAMS: *Homework Hot Line*

I don't remember who sponsored the homework hot line, but the PTA was allowed a voice mail account through the same system. The PTA treasurer figured out how to use the hot line and update messages. I don't know if anyone else called it, but her messages were upbeat and informative.

As I said, the teachers had the same access to the service, but few of them utilized the option. Many said it was too difficult to use. My children's teachers rarely upgraded the homework messages, so parents stopped checking them. The tool was free, yet it seemed to be of no value. If parents and teachers had trouble communicating directly, this was definitely a viable communications option, but it fell along the wayside. Teachers had too much else on their minds besides the actual education process.

I) DRUGS & WEAPONS: *Gunshots and Safety Issues*

The first class in the K-3$^{rd}$ grades and the 4-6$^{th}$ grades that turned in their fund raising materials got Popsicles. One of the fifth grade classes had won, and they were on the playground. The PTA President and I were taking the Popsicles outside when we saw two cars race through the school parking lot. About a minute later, we heard a couple popping noises. We didn't know if they were gunshots or backfires.

We peeked around the building. The kids with the cars were parked on the street in front of the school and standing around their cars. Two more pops punctuated the air, and the entire group dove for cover behind their cars. Then, both cars drove off in a hurry.

When we got back into the school, the principal was already on the phone to the police. She was trying to explain to the police what had happened. About half a dozen of us had seen what happened at different angles. We all heard her request a police car be visible around the school when we sent our students home in the afternoon. No police officer appeared at the school for the remainder of the day. As I walked home with my kids, about half an hour after school had let out, I saw a police car cruise towards the school.

Within the week, my husband had reason to visit the police station. He asked about the incident at the school and why they hadn't sent a police car. The officer at the desk looked up the report and said that the principal hadn't made any request. A neighbor had asked for a police car to come out after the incident, but no one had been dispatched to the school.

J) VOLUNTEERING: *Overstepping My Boundaries*

At the beginning of the school year, the PTA had been enthusiastic and full of ideas. The principal had made it crystal clear that we wouldn't be allowed to voice our ideas. On the other hand, the principal lamented about our diminishing volunteer population, which had steadily decreased over the past two years. She was supposedly concerned about burnout among the core volunteers.

The previous year, the principal had asked me to write up some slogans to promote parental involvement. They were quite cute.

"Volunteer and Help Us Grow, Find Out What Your Children Know."

"The More Our Children Know, The Farther They Can Go. Share Your Experience"

"Give By the Hour, or Give By the Day, Volunteering Can Really Pay."

and

"Come to Class and Give Some Aide, Help Our Children Make the Grade"

This year, I came up with a different idea. I designed an appeal requesting parent involvement to help make the school more successful. The projects were all fund raisers Things like the book fair, school pictures, the carnival, Santa's Shop, and the actual annual "fund raiser". Without parent volunteers to run these, they don't succeed.

Being somewhat passionate about the education system, I was impatient and impulsive with my actions. I put my large, index card sized, goldenrod notes on all of the doors into the school. It seemed like the only way to reach the parents, but it reached the teachers instead. My attempt to alleviate some of the pressure on the stressed out teachers only intensified it. I had made a major detour around protocol.

I should have submitted my suggestion to the PTA President, who would have passed any good ideas onto the principal. The principal would have OK'd or vetoed the idea. The intent of my idea didn't matter, because I was viewed as having taken a dishonorable route to achieve results.

*Celebrate Diversity*

I was very enthusiastic at the beginning of the year about an idea I had to utilize all the resources our school had to their fullest potential. There was one resource that we were barely tapping: our diversity. The cultural mix in our school was respectable. Besides that, we had a lot of military parents, who had probably traveled all over the world. Between these two groups, we could have had a Social Studies program that would have been the envy of anyone. We wouldn't have been limited to books, because we had people in our school who had actually been to these places. They could have brought life to the curriculum with stories and props.

I had made some presentations at elementary schools when I returned from being an exchange student in Colombia. I grossed the kids out by talking about eating ants. It may have been gross, but would it be in a textbook?

We had parents who were artisans with a variety of crafts. They could have helped the Art teacher for a class on their specialty. I'm sure most of the hobbies parents had could be used as resource material.

The Community School had handed out a form the first year we were there, which asked about a variety of office skills and any other skills that could be used in the classroom. I don't think many people filled it out. The paper seemed relatively unimportant. We needed a paper that was more involved. Especially about what subjects parents could supplement. I wanted our school to celebrate its diversity, and demonstrate that everyone had something to offer the community. If it takes a village to raise a child, we had a village with a lot of knowledge to pass on.

I think this is why our PTA was gagged. Too many new ideas that might threaten the teachers.

K) Curriculum: *Music Lessons*

Sixth graders were encouraged to join the band or orchestra to the point that they were expected to pick up an instrument. Jeff chose to play the flute. He chose it for the same reason I did. He had braces. It didn't hurt matters that we had my well-used flute around the house, either. Jeff progressed well with his lessons. His timing was perfect. That was something that always seemed to elude me.

Susie's daughter chose the violin. They rented it because they didn't know if she would like it. Susie's daughter had been taking lessons for about a month when Melissa and I went over for a visit. The violin fascinated Melissa, so Susie's daughter showed her what she had learned about playing it. Melissa was an avid student. After her second impromptu lesson, Melissa asked for a violin.

We found one for a reasonable price at a pawnshop. It needed a minor repair. Melissa took off with the violin. Two years would pass before she would be allowed to play in the orchestra. There was no allowance for students who already played an instrument to be in the school's music groups before the sixth grade.

*Moving Ahead in Math*

This year Jeff's teacher had a more difficult task than the previous year. Her class was a 4/5/6 class. That meant, besides the fifth and sixth grade curriculum she had the previous year, she also had to allow for fourth graders. In the previous year, the fifth graders would join their peers for Social Studies and Science classes, and she would deal with the Math and English in her room. Logistics of the new group would involve schedule coordination with two additional teachers.

The teacher continued to teach Math at the students' ability level. In order to be in this class, you had to be at the top of your grade. Therefore, she had a lot of students who could be challenged by the next grade level Math. While she had three grade levels in her classroom, she had four Math levels. Jeff and a couple other sixth grade students were allowed to use the seventh grade Math book. It made her job slightly more difficult, but these students required only minimal guidance. Often, they had figured out the lesson, together, without any assistance from her. They only asked for help when none of them could figure the problems out.

## M) DISRIMINATION, HARASSMENT & ABUSE: *Sinking the Sub*

In November, Jeff's teacher's husband became seriously ill. She would have to take an extended leave of absence to deal with the medical problem. I believe it required leaving the state for treatment. The teacher had a favorite substitute teacher, so she requested her for the time she would be gone. The substitute was a sturdy, grandmotherly, German woman. She could be very pleasant, but she was firm when crossed.

I don't know why Jeff's class developed such bad manners, but Jeff would come home and tell me how his class was making life so difficult for the substitute teacher. He didn't like it, but what could he do? I took a teddy bear to school the next day, for the substitute, and told her it was from our family so she would know that she wasn't alone in her battle. Jeff was still considered a target by his classmates, so speaking up in class might have made things worse. If we would have told the principal, could anything have been done? I'm not sure. She didn't seem to be the teachers' ally this year.

Things got so bad at one point, that the substitute threatened to cancel the gingerbread house project. Soon after this point, one of the girls (who had been one of the biggest instigators) brought a card into school. Her mother, another parent-volunteer, required all the students in the class to sign it. It was an apology card for the substitute.

Jeff's teacher returned after being gone about six weeks. By this time, the class had better behavior. A substitute, or any teacher, shouldn't have to battle the class to teach the students who want to learn.

## N) SAFETY & SECURITY: *Child Watch*

The current plan for dealing with an absent child was to call the school first thing in the morning to let them know your child would be absent that day. This is inconvenient if you have just spent the whole night sitting up with an ailing child. The school only had one secretary. If she was busy, your call didn't get through. We also didn't have any answering machine or voice mail for the school. This was a problem and we tried to come up with a solution.

The first solution we came up with involved running a second phone line and buying an answering machine. The cost of a second phone line was prohibitive. My husband suggested arranging for a voice mail service. Maybe, we could get a better rate if we promised a potential donor advertisement. He checked around for potential donors and found one who would donate the service for the first year, if he got credit for it in our school's newsletter. The offer was more than fair. The principal said that her daughter's school had to pay $9 per month for their service. Because this involved the school directly, we had to have the principal's authorization.

At our October meeting, we were hopeful that the Child Watch system would be implemented soon. There were other areas this program would help besides keeping track of sick children. We would know sooner if a child were missing. There had been a case in Alaska where the non-custodial dad picked his daughter up on the way to school. Because her friends knew Dad wasn't supposed to be in the state, they told their teacher. The girl's mother was alerted, and the child was picked up at the airport. If no one had known anything until school was over, the plane would have been long gone. Now, it's more difficult to get a child out of the state, but this was the situation then. We also had to be concerned that animal attacks would cause a child to be missing.

We came to the meeting with a list of parent volunteers to check the voice mail, and compare the calls to the absent list. If there was a discrepancy, the parents would be called. As my parents taught me, it was a solid plan, but we would run into a major obstacle: The principal. She vetoed the whole idea, citing the fact that we only had one secretary and we couldn't possibly give her more work. We came up with the idea of five volunteers doing the job. Each volunteer would monitor the calls on the day of the week they normally volunteered. This was still considered to be some sort of invasion of privacy. She would only give her OK if we had one parent cleared to do it. That wasn't possible, so the Child Watch Program went down in flames.

*Disaster Preparedness*

Living in the state that has the highest annual incidence of earthquakes, we needed to have a good disaster plan. Basically, the current disaster plan said:
1) If you are heading to school, and there's a bad earthquake, head home.
2) If you are heading home, and there's an earthquake, continue home.
3) If you're in school, and there's an earthquake, hide under your desk.

Our Disaster Preparedness Chair came up with a great plan for teams of parents and teachers to become mobilized in an emergency. Supposedly, there would be training through the school for parents and teachers to work as teams. There was also a plan for an emergency information card for each child. These cards would have the child's information and two signatures on the front, of someone who was authorized to retrieve the child in an emergency. There was a place on the reverse side of the card for a countersignature. The person who picked the child up would have to sign for the child.

The Disaster Preparedness Chair even had a pledge for a donation of Ark Kits from a local business. They offered to donate enough kits to cover all the children in our school. These kits contained water pouches, granola-like nutrition squares, and a space blanket. Each box was about the size of a cigar box.

Because storage of these supplies might be a problem, the Disaster Preparedness Chair had solicited a local hardware store for materials to build a military specification, earthquake resistant, storage shed. She also recruited military personnel and parents to build the structure.

The principal shot this idea down, too. She refused delivery of the Ark Kits and the building materials. She said there was no place to store these items. The amount of donations we had been offered was amazing, and she was ungrateful enough to turn everything down.

I was speaking with one of the teachers about our frustration with trying to get an emergency plan in place. The teacher told me that she was glad that she didn't have to worry about Disaster Preparedness. I was shocked. Then, I found out more about the emergency plan that was currently in place. In the case of our school being structurally compromised, the students were to be moved to the neighboring school, which was a mile away. Our school wasn't as well built, but was on sturdier ground than the other school.

Betty suggested if we had to move the children anywhere, they should probably be taken to the church across the street, or the new department store that had just been built 8 blocks away. The former was closer. The latter was built with earthquake resistance in mind. Few of the parents truly understood who would be taking care of our children in an emergency. If we were naïve enough to assume that the teachers would be doing that, we would have been wrong. The teachers were only required to stay at the school for half an hour after a "disaster". This wasn't spelled out in anything the parents received.

While our school didn't accept the plan our Disaster Preparedness Chair presented, the principal did pass it on to the School District. Our Disaster Preparedness Chair was at a meeting where her plan was presented without any credit to her. She asked a question at the meeting about the plan that none of the presenters could answer. Of course, she knew the answer, because she had come up with the plan, but the presenters should have known it, too.

Even when the School District accepted the plan, our school still didn't use it. What a waste!

*Safe Home*

The Safe Home Program was like a program I grew up with in Minnesota. To participate in the Safe Home Program, your household had to pass a criminal background check. This applied to anyone who was over 18 years old in your house. If you passed the background check, you received a placard that showed you were a Safe Home. You would display this placard in the window, only when someone was home. If a child was in trouble, they could look for the sign and have safe haven. The program sounds good, doesn't it?

Our school discouraged this program, too. Supposedly, the Safe Home coordinator found out that it takes 6 months for the police to do the background checks and they had to be done annually. Six months would mean that two-thirds of our school year would be "lost". I wondered how other areas managed to participate in the Safe Home Program, if it was so difficult. Jeff would turn 18 before I found the loophole. There is a way around the 6-month waiting period. The required background check takes about 20 minutes and costs something. In our case, it was $20 per person. We needed the background check done because we were under consideration for hosting an exchange student.

*Security Violations*

In October, we started noticing some security problems with the PTA belongings. The first was open mail in our school mailbox. The treasurer asked me one day if I had opened the bank statement. Both the September and October statements had been opened prior to the treasurer collecting them. None of us on the board had any reason to look at the bank statement, and everyone said they hadn't touched it.

The school secretary put everyone's mail into the little cubbies, which were near her desk, so the treasurer asked her if she had seen anyone disturb our mail. The secretary said she hadn't. Since it was impossible to keep the culprit from opening our mail, the treasurer opened a post office box to receive important mail. This way, we could ensure that the mail hadn't been tampered with.

The other odd thing that happened was we got charged for 5000 copies on the PTA account. The code for the copier hadn't changed since we had been at the school. By this time, the PTA had only sent out about 1000 copies, and they were made on the president's personal copier. We asked for the copier code to be changed for security purposes. The principal refused to allow it. I wonder if our PTA was being required to pay for copies that had been made by someone who was running for public office. We'll never know.

*Hot Coffee*

I didn't care much for the new Kindergarten teacher. She taught Betty's son the previous year. The woman was addicted to coffee. That may not be a good enough reason to dislike her, but it added to my discomfort. The Kindergarten room was right next to a room that contained a small kitchen and the PTA desk. There was a window in the door that was between the rooms.

I would watch the Kindergarten teacher burst through the door to get her coffee fix. We almost needed a traffic signal for that door. Then she would walk back into the classroom and stand behind her students, looking over their shoulders with her coffee cup suspended directly above their heads. She wasn't intentionally threatening the children with the scalding coffee, but the potential for severe injury was still there. What if a child didn't realize the teacher was standing behind her, and pushed her chair back or jumped up?

I warned a few of the parents I knew, whose children were in the class. I don't know if they paid any attention to me, but at least I said something. As far as I know, the teacher never spilled her coffee on anyone, but she should have been a little more responsible.

### Surveillance Mirrors

Sally noticed that there were several places in the school that a person could hide. Having been brought up in the military, she was informally trained in security. When she looked a little closer, she decided that the school could probably benefit from surveillance (convex) mirrors. I thought her idea was good, because placing mirrors on some of the corners would make it a lot easier when we had to move television carts around. When I moved a television cart, the bottom of the shelf that the television was on was at about my chin level. This made it difficult to maneuver the cart without running into someone, while going around a corner. The mirrors could solve that problem.

It was the same old story, though. The principal didn't like the idea, so it couldn't be implemented.

### O) POLITICS: Invasion of the Parents

The teachers were discussing a potential strike. Some of my friends knew I was on the PTA Board, and a regular volunteer, so they asked if I could talk with some of the teachers to find out what they were fighting for. Maybe, as parents, we could find some way to support our teachers.

Melissa's teacher was the spokesperson for our teachers, so I asked her. Basically, the teachers wanted everything. Some teachers wanted to save the benefits, others wanted more money, and some wanted both. It was difficult to find a position to support. Soon after I spoke with her, the teacher's lounge was declared completely "off limits" to parents.

There were rumors of a teachers' strike, midday on a Wednesday. That could put the students in some danger, if the teachers all walked out. The PTA had to come up with a plan of action in the event this happened. We didn't have to tell the teachers what we were planning. The teachers on our Board didn't seem to be listening, but the principal was.

The PTA plan involved calling in parents to volunteer as "babysitters" until arrangements could be made for all of the students to leave the school safely. We didn't want children walking home to empty houses. As soon as the last student left, the parents would leave and the school would be closed.

Of the children's teachers, Jeff's teacher, planned to stay as long as the school was open, Melissa's teacher planned to go out on the picket line, and Matthew's teacher was undecided. I found out something about three other teachers I thought I knew. The teachers were being told if they went on strike, the parents would take over their jobs. I was amazed. How could these teachers honestly believe that the parents could replace them? I wasn't a teacher and I knew more about the situation. For the same reasons the parents couldn't volunteer to cut the school's grass in California, we couldn't volunteer as teachers. We weren't part of the union and there were liability issues. Besides, how many parents wanted the teachers' jobs, paid or not?

The teachers never stopped to think that the principal was manipulating them by threatening their jobs with the people who were trying to support them. After all, the principal was on the management (opposing) team. Hostility intensified inside the school.

The teachers decided to strike first thing in the morning, so the PTA didn't have to hunt up volunteers. The animosity between teachers and parents continued long after the strike. My teachers were happy that I was volunteering for them, but they were hostile towards other parents. Teachers I wasn't personally involved with were hostile towards me. The situation alienated a lot of the volunteers and they left. I don't know if the teachers ever really realized what had happened. If they were complaining about how difficult their jobs were when they had volunteer help, how was it without the help?

*Give or Take a Million*

During this year, the PTA President attended a meeting where the Superintendent was asked how much it cost to run the School District. The Superintendent gave an amount, and said, "Give or take a million." It would be interesting to note that the PTA income for our School District was probably about a million dollars at that time. We wondered if this was just coincidence or if it was part of the School District's financial calculations.

P) POLICIES & PROCEDURES: *Banned from the Bathrooms*

Around the time of the teachers' strike, notes showed up on the lavatory doors around the schools. Adults were not allowed to use the children's facilities. There were two faculty rest rooms for adult use, but when I tried to use one of them, I was greeted with hostility upon my exit. The attitude of the teachers was, "Didn't you know that teachers have limited time to take bathroom breaks?" Supposedly, I could have used it any other time. Without a schedule for teacher bathroom breaks, I couldn't synchronize my schedule accordingly.

I continued to walk past the children's lavatories, hearing unattended water running. Before the ban, I would go into the girls' lavatory and turn off the water. After the ban, I just kept walking. I tried to get all my volunteer work done in half a day, so I wouldn't need to use the school's facilities. If I had to be there all day, I drove home at lunchtime to use the bathroom.

R) REDUCE, REUSE & RECYCLE: *Several Teachers Have Complained...*

I tried to promote the paper-recycling program in our school, but I was unable to speak to the students about it. I made signs for the recycling receptacles that a kindergärtner could read. It showed everything that could go in there and everything that shouldn't. At the beginning of the year, I spoke to the teachers at a staff meeting about the signs. The teachers didn't look very interested in my project, but I thought it might have been due to the fact that it was 7:30 AM.

I tried to have announcements made, for teachers to place their recycling baskets outside their classroom on Wednesday mornings, so I could collect them without disrupting class. I still had to hunt for them, or allow them to become "fire hazards".

The week before the teachers went out on strike, I was told by one of the PTA Board members that "several teachers had complained about my (volunteer) activities, and I was requested to do my volunteering after school hours." I knew exactly who used the phrase "several teachers have complained." If the teachers couldn't be expected to work beyond their contracted hours, why could the principal expect me to have to pay for child care and work alone in an empty school? The program wasn't worth it.

The day of the strike, I crossed the picket line and spent two hours in the school with my children. We collected up all of the recycling containers, emptied them, and stacked them in a corner of the workroom. After the strike, I was in the workroom, and several teachers asked me where the recycling containers had gone. When I said I had removed them, they all gave me a curious look and said that they thought the program had been going so well. I told them that I just didn't have the time to run it after school.

*Aluminum Can Round Up 2*

I don't know who ran the Aluminum Can Round Up this year. It wasn't run through me. It was November and the snow was covering the ground. The round up was pretty much over and the janitor had put the bags out on the school's loading dock. The cans couldn't stay there, so the principal asked me (as Green Star Coordinator) what I was going to do about them. I was told if the cans weren't removed that day, they would be put into the dumpster. The program I wasn't running was becoming a nuisance to the principal and the janitor.

At the time, I had a van. According to the rules of the round up, if we delivered the cans to the recycling center, we got money for the cans. If the recycling center picked them up, we didn't. I started loading my van up with as many bags of uncrushed cans as I could. Going to the recycling center took 40 minutes round trip. I figured it would take at least four trips to remove all the cans. After my second trip, I returned to the school to find all the rest of the bags gone. There were only a few aluminum cans scattered in the snow.

I asked the janitor where all the cans went. He told me that the principal had called the recycling center, and they had sent a truck. I just didn't understand the logic of the situation. If she knew I was removing the bags, why did she call the recycling center? If she was going to call the recycling center, why did she ask me to do something about the situation? I don't understand why the principal allowed the school to participate in a program that was considered to be so inconvenient. Maybe guidelines should have been set up, so the cans could be weighed for each class each day, then they could be removed to the recycling center in a more timely manner. The principal's attitude towards this project showed how little she respected the time and efforts of the parent volunteers.

## S) SICKNESS & HEALTH: *A Touch of Baldness*

It was time for school pictures. Jeff's hair had a tendency to stand up in the back, so I gave him a squirt of hairspray and sent him off to school. I hadn't looked at his hair really closely, so I didn't notice anything strange.

When Jeff got home from school, he told me that a classmate said he was losing hair. Sure enough, there was a bald spot about the size of a quarter near the crown of his head. I suspected the hair spray, but more of his scalp would have been affected than this small circle.

A trip to the dermatologist determined that it wasn't parasitic. The doctor decided that it looked stress related. Some of the hair in the area seemed to be growing back, so this had probably gone on for a while. The doctor asked Jeff if he pulled at, or twisted his hair. He denied doing either activity. We left the doctor's office with a note for Jeff to be able to wear a baseball cap during school for the next couple weeks. We also cut his hair a little shorter. Being very fair in coloring, I couldn't give him a crew cut without making him look really strange.

His teacher didn't want to allow him to wear his cap. I thought this was strange, coming from a teacher who had pulled me aside the first day of school to tell me that I needed to buy new clothes for Jeff, because his pants were too short, and "appearance was everything in the sixth grade." She hadn't been able to see, right away, that the cap was meant to preserve his self-esteem. The doctor's note wasn't enough. She had to see the bald spot before she gave approval for the hat.

By the end of the two weeks, Jeff's hair had grown enough that it wasn't as noticeable, and he was able to stop wearing the cap.

### Contagious Acne

I had walked the kids to school and was about to start my volunteering activities when I was called to the office. Jeff was sent to the office on an errand for his teacher. The secretary noticed that Jeff had a rash on his face. Since it was close to his mouth, it must be impetigo, which is extremely contagious. My parental observation had determined earlier that morning that it was acne. Of course, I'm not a professional secretary.

The secretary told me that Jeff was to leave the school and wouldn't be admitted back until either his rash healed, or he had a doctor's note. I had very little choice but to get the doctor's note. Jeff was supposed to be taking a test that afternoon. The exercise was a waste of $65 and much of the school day. The doctor looked at the rash under a magnifying glass and gave us the verdict. It was acne. Specifically, they were blackheads. Impetigo has white heads. I returned Jeff to school with the note. We decided that the pattern was consistent with where his flute rested, so we made sure to disinfect the whole mouthpiece every time he used his flute. The secretary gave no apology for the inconvenience. One of my friends said I should have requested their requirement for a doctor's note, in writing. That way, I could have had evidence for a lawsuit, and the secretary should have had to pay for the visit to the doctor.

*Who's Administering Your Child's Medicines?*

I have had occasion to see medicines administered in the school. Since our school shared its nurse with at least one other school, the nurse wasn't always the one dispensing the medicines. Usually, it was a noon duty.

The whole process looked relatively efficient, but I wonder if they ever made any mistakes. If your child needed to take a medicine during school hours, the parent needed to provide a bottle with the proper prescription label on it, for school use. The medicines were placed in a box that had large index cards in it. The cards had student names on them, probably the name of the medicine, and there must have been a calendar on it, because I saw one of the noon duties check something off after administering some medicine. I don't know if they tracked students down who hadn't come in for their medicine that day, or not.

Over the counter medicines can't be administered in school without a prescription label. Some days, I would walk over to the school to give my children Dimetapp at lunchtime. If I timed it right, I could catch all three between lunch and recess. I thought it was quite interesting to walk on the playground and have a whole group of kids gather around me while I gave my children their medicine. I was never challenged. Who knows what I could have been dispensing to the other students? I don't think the noon duties knew who I was in my big coat, yet they never tried to disperse the group that gathered around me, or asked what my business was.

U) CELEBRATIONS: *Satan's Playground*

Every year, the school had a carnival around Halloween. It was considered the big money making fund raiser Part of the agreement with the fund raising company included supplies for the carnival. Everyone would usually come to the carnival wearing a costume. Who could object to it?

This year, the Program Chair was going to be out of town at carnival time, so the Volunteer Liaison took over the organizing duties for the carnival. This year, the carnival was scheduled on Halloween. The date was chosen to give children a safe alternative to walking around on the dark streets. Personally, I have no clue as to who started the rumor mill, but there was heavy sentiment against the carnival, and it was directed at the Volunteer Liaison.

People were angry with her for scheduling it on Halloween. What was she trying to do, promote Satan and give him a playground for the evening? They were saying that she was connected to the occult. Since there hadn't been this much public outcry against a carnival before, we could only assume that the attacks were personal. I didn't know very many people who were as spiritually positive as this woman, yet people seemed to want to stone her. Why were so many people against her?

In spite of a respiratory ailment, she managed to get the carnival together. It brought in a lot of money. Amazingly, there were several small children in attendance, without any parents. The only hitch in the whole process seemed to be a problem with one of the games. It could be conducted in the dark. It involved a Frisbee and a hula-hoop. Both of these items were capable of glowing in the dark. The object was to toss the Frisbee through the hula-hoop, which was suspended from the ceiling. Turning off the lights increased the difficulty level. Unfortunately, it also gave potential players time to steal things from the classroom. Someone was caught stealing something and the lights were left on after that.

It's true that Satan had a strong presence in our school, but the Volunteer Liaison wasn't the one who opened the door and invited him in. The people responsible for his presence were the ones who were pointing fingers.

V) SUPPLIES: *The Principal's Discretionary Fund*

This was the first year I heard about a concept called, "the principal's discretionary fund." This was supposedly an allowance every principal received, to help with minor problems in the school. I don't know how much each principal was allowed. As a parent, I never heard of it being used for anything in our school. As a PTA member, I only knew that we were the first entity that was petitioned for money.

A parent volunteer from another school told me that she had overheard the principal talking about plans for remodeling her office, with the discretionary funds. While discretionary means the opposite of delegated (or designated), this still seemed sort of inappropriate to the parent volunteer. There were several other areas where the money could have been utilized better to further the education of the students.

If principals get discretionary money, there should still be some paper trail to show how it's being spent. If it's being spent on educating the children, we could get a better picture of what the schools actually need.

Z) LAST IMPRESSIONS: *Flushing Coats and Changing Schools*

I walked over to the school to pick up my kids. When I walked into the school the secretary pulled me aside and told me that she had been trying to call me. As the kids were getting ready to leave school, one of Jeff's classmates had taken his winter coat and flushed it in one of the toilets. The janitor had managed to rescue it, but it was now a sodden mess. Without a coat, Jeff could freeze on the walk home. My husband had the car that day and he was across town. I took my heavy coat off and put it around Jeff. I was glad I was wearing a sweater. We got home as fast as we could, with me carrying the wet coat in a large garbage bag. I don't know who flushed the coat, but this was definitely an indication that I needed to move my kids.

The next day, my husband had a day off, so we looked at some of the schools that were around. I didn't think to try the neighboring school right away, because I had been turned away the previous year. Instead, we tried one of the charter schools. Unfortunately, they were full and we couldn't get into the lottery until May.

My husband suggested the neighboring school. I was doubtful, but gave it a try anyhow. They had openings for our kids. The only problem was where did Jeff want to go? They had both traditional and optional classroom settings. He could have fit either class, but he needed to make the choice. We told the principal that we would let her know after lunchtime and ran over to our school to pick Jeff up for lunch.

We discussed his options during lunch, and he chose the Optional Program. Back at school, Matthew and Melissa were unaware of what was happening. By the time school was dismissed, I came back to the school with several large trash bags, so we could empty their desks. I had resigned from the PTA about a month earlier for health reasons, so I didn't have any more obligations at this school.

I led my crying children out of the school with a heavy heart. I would miss my friends, too, but this school wasn't safe anymore.

# Chapter 9
## The Neighboring School Spring 1995

A) FIRST IMPRESSIONS: *Being Zone Exempt*

Matthew had a male teacher who was into science. Matthew was fascinated by the Madagascan cockroaches the teacher had. I wasn't really happy about the floor plan of the school. The classroom Matthew was in had two classrooms behind it. That meant there was a good bit of traffic going through his classroom.

Melissa also had a male teacher, and her classroom was similarly situated in the pod. Each pod in the school had ten classrooms. Four that bordered the hallway, and six that one could access through the hallway classrooms or from the outside of the building.

Jeff's teacher was a woman. In the Optional Program, teachers were referred to by their first names. This made me slightly uncomfortable. Linda's boys had called me by my first name, but her rule was to use a title before the name. I was Miss Shelly to them. There was no title of respect in front of these teachers' names. Parents were required to volunteer at least half a day per month if your student was in one of the optional classes.

Their playground was quite interesting, also. They had a large hill that was suitable for sledding and several huge rocks placed around the playground. They didn't have an ice rink like our former school, though.

C) PARENT TEACHER ENTITY: *Phases 4 & 5 Search for the Guilty and Punishment of the Innocent*

I tried to join the PTA at the new school. I became a member, but I knew that I wouldn't ever really fit in. Soon after I arrived at the school, I heard the PTA President repeating some gossip. She was talking about the "Corrupt PTA" at my former school. She was telling some of her friends that our Board was being ordered to hand over the books to the original PTA President. If they didn't, the police would be called and my former board-mates would be arrested. I knew that they had already retained a lawyer's services and were probably putting together their defense.

I asked the PTA President if there was a question about her books, would she be willing to hand them over to a third party without getting some sort of documentation about the original condition of the books? This woman just looked at me as if I was crazy. She opined that they were criminals and should be arrested. I truly wanted to enlighten the woman about her information source right there. I doubt that she would have taken my word that her information was coming from a woman who had written questionable checks on the PTA books for two years.

E) DIFFERENCES & DISABILITIES: *Vindication*

Sally had been sniped at by the teachers the whole time her son had been in elementary school. Teachers said her son was too loud and disrespectful. Teenagers often have difficulty modulating their voices. When I was his age, I had gone from talking too quietly to talking too loud, because teachers told me to speak louder. The disrespect aspect, I didn't understand. Any time I had been around this boy, he seemed very respectful, but he was extremely truthful. There were no gray areas when it came to rules for him. If the rules said things were one way, he insisted that people around him follow the rules. This even extended to correcting adults around him when he perceived them to be wrong. I just figured Sally needed to teach her son some tact. Another difficult lesson to teach any teenager.

By the time Sally's son finished elementary school, she was worn out by the teachers. There was something different about her son, but she couldn't figure out how to make him fit in more with his peers. She worried that he might be blatantly honest to the wrong classmate and end up being stabbed, or worse, if he went to Junior High School. Some of the teachers had claimed she was over-protective of her son, but this was the only child she had. She didn't coddle him and had tried to help him be as self-sufficient as possible for a kid his age.

Sally decided she would home school her son. It would be five years before Sally would find out what made her son so different from the other kids in his school. She was abused by the teachers for being a bad parent. Yet, they hadn't offered any helpful suggestions. In fact, even the "experts" didn't have a name, or diagnosis, for her son's problem until he was 11. It didn't reach Alaskan doctors until Sally's son was 17. He had Asperger's Syndrome. It's a form of autism. The people who have Asperger's tend to have very high brain functions, yet they can't pick up social cues easily. This makes it difficult for a child to function properly in school. Only about 1 in 500-5000 people have this condition. One in 20 people have varying degrees of dyslexia, and educators often don't recognize this more common disability. Still, Sally (who had no formal medical or educational training) was expected to know how to deal with a son who had Asperger's autism. I think she did a damn good job, considering her lack of professional guidance.

If education were the school system's main function, it would seem that they would almost know how to troubleshoot students by now and be able to figure out if the students have disabilities early. I know every student is an individual, but there must be some patterns that show up for learning differences.

*The Perfectionist*

I volunteered in all of the kids' classrooms, but Jeff's teacher required all of her parents to volunteer for a certain amount of time every month. This was part of the optional program's charter. Parents were required to be involved. Everything we did had to be just so. If we missed a step or made our marks differently, the teacher seemed unreasonably upset.

Each of the students had assigned chores in the classroom. One of the chores involved a lot of writing. Jeff was assigned this task, but didn't complete it in the time allowed. The teacher noticed that he wasn't completing his homework either, but his handwriting was meticulous. She assumed he was a perfectionist and that was what was taking so much time. Being a perfectionist may have been one of his problems, so the teacher fixated on it. She told me that I needed to get him away from the perfectionist attitude. He needed to "get over it".

I looked at her and realized she was a perfectionist. How did she expect a twelve-year old boy to overcome a personality trait that she hadn't been able to overcome yet. I picked up a book about "gifted" children and tried to read about dealing with a child who was a perfectionist. Unfortunately, he also looked like an underachiever. I was overwhelmed by information and went into a type of paralysis. It would take me years to figure out what I had been looking at. The answer was so close, but I felt like I was slogging through knee-deep mud.

## G) TRANSPORTATION & FIELD TRIPS: *Camp Challenge*

The fifth and sixth grade optional classes had a tradition of going away for camp, one weekend in May. The students planned what food and other supplies they would bring. Planning the menu involved deciding what kind of meals could be prepared for the whole camp and figuring out how much they would need to feed everyone. Of course, they had to be aware of food allergies. Other supplies they would need depended on the activities and what was already available at the camp.

Students would live in cabins and tents, and there would be small group activities that would be led by parents and teachers. Small group activities included: Carving, Cooking, Drawing, Fishing, Photography, Fly-tying, and Writing. The students also learned about Ecosystem Issues, Aquatic Studies, Survival, Orienteering, and "Leaving No Trace".

Parents and students packed everything up on Wednesday morning and Camp ran until just after lunch on Friday. Parents took turns as chaperons. This year, my husband spent a night in a tent with Jeff's group, and part of the next day doing activities.

I assembled the booklet the students used for the Camp. It contained a map of where the camp was, and a map of the camp itself. There were also schedules for each day. If there was any doubt as to which activity the student was scheduled for that day, or where they were supposed to sleep at night, this was also clearly noted. I left some blank pages in each booklet for the students to use as journal paper. The booklet was bound and the cover was laminated. It was a nice manageable 8.5" x 5.5". I received a lot of compliments on it.

The kids had fun at Camp Challenge. Melissa's class would go to camp two years later, and I would spend the day working with her group.

## K) CURRICULUM: *No Short Cuts*

I was sitting in Jeff's class correcting papers, when they were discussing breaking down numbers into prime factors. The teacher was asking the students about dividing numbers by other numbers up to 10. I raised my hand when she got to nines, and said I knew a simple way to figure out if a number is divisible by nine. It was different than her way. She refused to listen to my method, but I'll tell you, for future reference. If you take a lengthy, multi-digits number and want to know if 9 fits into it, you add up the value of all the digits. If that sum is divisible by 9, then the whole number is divisible by 9. If this works, then you also know the number is divisible by 3.

The teacher told me that she wouldn't allow any shortcuts or alternative methods. When I was a student, nines seemed to be the bane of my existence. I didn't know, to check to see if your answer is right, you add up the digits to equal a multiple of 9. If your answer only adds up to 8 or 10, it needs to be rechecked. Not everyone understands things in the same way. Sometimes, they need an alternate method.

## M) DISCRIMINATION, HARASSMENT & ABUSE: *Mom, Please Don't Volunteer at the School, Anymore*

The Volunteer Liaison, at the neighborhood school was still volunteering. It was still the same. Her teachers appreciated the volunteering, but other teachers were hostile. She felt that she needed to be in the school, to watch over the children. There was so much evil around these days.

The PTA was still being labeled corrupt. The president and treasurer had a lawyer, on retainer, if necessary. Their umbrella covered the Volunteer Liaison, too. The Programs Chair had shown that his allegiances were elsewhere. He's the one who had stirred the situation up first, by not wanting to be a co-chair. The president and treasurer also paid for an independent audit, out of their own pockets.

The Volunteer Liaison's children told her one day that they wanted her to stop volunteering at the school. They didn't like what the other adults were saying about their mom. Within the hearing range of many children at the school, school employees and parent volunteers spewed so much slanderous filth about the PTA Board.

The school employees are supposed to be professionals. There was supposed to be a School District policy of "zero tolerance" for prejudicial statements. The biggest lesson that was taught that year was hatred, and the school wondered why there were so many discipline problems.

## O) POLITICS: *A Cohesive School*

When we started at the new school, I noticed the lack of friction between the teachers and the parent volunteers. I asked some of the parents how they managed to survive the fallout from the strike. How did they manage to regain a good relationship with their teachers so fast? The parent volunteers couldn't understand my question. There hadn't been any friction to overcome. Being the only representative from the other school, they probably just thought that I had personal problems.

I tried to figure out why they didn't have the problem. There are a couple reasons that they could have avoided the friction. The first option involves the principal's personality. She might have decided that education was more important than politics. Keeping the stress level down at her school, at a very stressful time, might have been her goal.

The other reason there could have been a lack of friction had to do with the way their school operated. The new school had the Optional Education program. About half of the school ran on this program, and parents were considered to be an integral component for the operation and success of the program. If the principal had put a wedge between the parents and the teachers like our principal had, she could have jeopardized the program.

It took months for the damage to be repaired in our old school, while the new school hadn't missed a beat, getting back to the business of education. I think that the school administrator should look at the big picture when a strike is threatened. How will their participation in the contract negotiation process impact the education process in the long run? There is a difference between how a CEO can run a company that manufactures goods for profit, and how a principal runs a school where they are molding children's minds. Over a year of productivity was lost in the neighborhood school because the (professional) adults were distracted from doing their job.

*Anatomy of the Teacher Contract Negotiations*

In May, the Anchorage Daily News had an article about the teachers' contract negotiations. It took up parts of six pages and I thought it was fascinating. No logical person could have solved the problem. The negotiations had started in the spring of the previous school year. During the summer, the School District sent out papers to the teachers, informing them that their medical/dental program would be negatively impacted, arbitrarily. This was an act of aggression.

The teachers were divided on what they wanted. Some wanted more money, some were more concerned about benefits, and some wanted everything. With so much division within the ranks, an arbitrator was called in from out of state. The arbitrator was given all the information about the wishes of the various groups and how much money was available to make this happen. He left the state for a few months to figure this out.

During the time the arbitrator was doing his calculations, the School District got more money and everyone knew about it, except the arbitrator. When he arrived back in the state and presented his solution, the teachers became very angry. They thought he was on the administration's side. They didn't realize that he hadn't been given all the facts.

The teachers went on strike and three days later a contract was agreed upon. I understand the contract still didn't make any of the teachers happy. One of the things they lost was medical and dental benefits. Up to this point, the School District was paying the teachers' insurance premiums. Now the teachers would have to pay something. Orthodontic coverage was also a thing of the past. Their co-payments went up. Their premiums and benefits were still better than most of the families whose children they taught, and whose taxes paid for their benefits. Welcome to the real world.

Of course, I'm leaving out several details, if I'm able to sum up the situation in so few words. There was so much politics and intrigue, behind the scenes, that wouldn't interest many people outside the affected population, so I left it out. The situation was very unfortunate and several months were wasted trying to solve the problem. Hopefully, someone learned something useful for future contract negotiations, but I'm afraid that might just be wishful thinking on my part.

## S) SICKNESS & HEALTH: *Medical "Emergencies"*

I had been talking on the phone to Susie, one evening. Our conversation lasted about fifteen minutes, but it was memorable because she had three interruptions on her end by the school nurse. The first time the nurse called, she commented on Susie's son's speech impediment and suggested that Susie put him in braces. At the time, Susie didn't have the $5000 necessary to buy braces outright. As a Native Alaskan, she could get them for a reduced price and she was already on the waiting list. Unfortunately, nothing can speed up bureaucracy.

The second time the nurse called, she had a complaint about Susie's son's hearing. Susie had been aware of this problem for several years. Her son had been misdiagnosed for two days while running a high fever as a baby. By the time the doctor finally realized the boy had an ear infection, his eardrum had ruptured. Therefore, his hearing was impaired.

The third call was for the most ridiculous reason. It was springtime, and the nurse was complaining that Susie's son supposedly had a constant runny nose. Susie informed the nurse that he was allergic to pollen and that she gave him allergy medicine in the morning, but she was unable to bring him more at lunchtime. Since the medicine wasn't prescription, she couldn't send it to school with him, so she would send a box of tissues with him in the future. That way he could blow his nose.

We wondered if the nurse was checking all of the students so thoroughly, or if Susie was just getting special treatment because they thought her son was being abused or neglected. No charges ever materialized, but it did seem like a waste of time for problems that weren't life threatening.

### The Jaundiced Eye

Mary's daughter had run down the path near their house, one afternoon. Like many other nine-year olds, she didn't heed her mother's warning to slow down and she tripped over an exposed tree root. The next day, Mary's daughter arrived at school with a large bruise on her shin and a limp, so Mary was summoned to the school.

Both mother and child gave the same accounting of the accident, but the principal and the nurse gave Mary dubious looks. They proceeded to ask her why she didn't prevent the child's injuries. Mary's daughter had been about 10 feet away from her when she fell. There wasn't any humanly possible way to have broken the girl's fall from that distance.

Mary offered to produce witnesses, if there was any doubt about her daughter's safety. The matter was dropped, but Mary was wary any time her children injured themselves in the future. Who knew when the school would decide that you were a bad parent? They were required to alert the authorities of any suspicions of neglect or abuse. I thought it was interesting that the school almost routinely picked on parents whose children were noticeably cared for. What was the actual motive behind the witch-hunt?

### Mystery Malady

Around the time my mother died, Jeff became ill. I received the call from the school around 10 AM. Jeff had vomited and he seemed to have a fever. I needed to come to the school to pick him up. I kept him home that day.

The next morning, he wasn't running a fever and felt like going to school. He hadn't been nauseous since I had brought him home from school, so I let him go. At 10 AM, the nurse called me. He had been sick again.

I kept him home for the next day for observation. Despite seeming to feel fine upon waking, he vomited again at 10 AM. I took him to the doctor. I asked what could be causing the problem. Did he have the flu or did he have something like an ulcer? The doctor did a blood test. It wasn't an ulcer. There was a flu virus in his blood. I kept him home for two more days without incidence. We have no idea why his body decided it only wanted to rebel at 10 AM. Maybe it was because I hadn't fed him anything solid for the remainder of the day, after he had been sick.

Z) LAST IMPRESSIONS: *Phase 6-Praise and Honors for the Non-Participants*

The PTA at the neighborhood school was replaced. The Program Chair became the new president. His first vice president was the woman who had been the president with the questionable expenditures. She had access to the checkbook again.

A shock wave went from our school and affected the PTA Organization all the way up to the national level.

OUR president had come into the PTA with a hidden agenda. None of the rest of us knew anything about it, not even his wife. He had come into the presidency to clean house. We thought we would be changing the PTA for the better, with our ideas for programs, but we had come up against so much resistance. At that point, the president decided he would allow the school to hang itself with its own rope and put his own agenda into play. There wasn't anything illegal about the president's agenda.

No legal action was ever taken against the remaining Board members. They had done everything by the book and had paid dearly for the "privilege" of serving on the PTA Board. The treasurer advised that husband and wife not have chairs together on the Board, in the future. Instead of having an activity that they could be involved in together, it nearly shredded their marriage. Health problems of Board members included: Cancer for the Disaster Preparedness Chair; respiratory problems for the Volunteer Liaison, the treasurer, and myself; and high blood pressure for the treasurer. During this year, I lost my mother, and the president lost his. He wouldn't be allowed to attend his mother's funeral because it was out of state, and he refused to leave his wife alone to deal with the vultures that were circling the PTA.

*Our Dreams Among the Ashes*

In just one year, we had gone through all six phases of a project. We had been doomed from the start, and didn't know it. All of the programs that we wanted to implement ended up being implemented by the new PTA Board, in a skeletal form. I would live with guilt, because I felt that I had betrayed my friends when I left the PTA. I felt especially bad about getting the treasurer involved with this mess. Would she have tried for the opening if I hadn't suggested it? We watched in horror as our good intentions went down in flames, but we had no chance of succeeding without the support of the principal and the teachers.

# Chapter 10
## Junior High School 1995-1996

### A) FIRST IMPRESSIONS: *Children in Two Schools*

Jeff was in Junior High School now. We had arrived home from our summer vacation just in time to answer the phone. The Junior High was calling to tell us that it was the last day that Jeff could register. My husband took Jeff to the school, and they made it just in time.

Since the school was a few miles away, Jeff had to take the bus and get up a little bit earlier. His school had six classes per day, so his day was full with Math, Science, Social Studies, English, Gym, and Band. They had a principal and a vice-principal. The principal was a woman who smiled a lot and said the usual things a principal says. The school was broken down into teams of about 150 students who shared the same core class teachers. Jeff was on the "gifted" team.

Melissa was in the fifth grade. She had a female teacher who had taught a 1$^{st}$/2$^{nd}$-grade combination class the year before, and this year she was teaching a 5/6-combination class.

Matthew had two female teachers by the end of the second week of school.

### B) BUILDINGS & GROUNDS: *160% Capacity*

Being a seventh grader, Jeff had to share a locker with another student, because the school was overcrowded. Supposedly, the school was built to house around 800 students. In reality, with the addition of eight portable classrooms, the halls could still be filled with 1200 students between classes, without the mention of adult staff members and parent volunteers. By mathematical calculations, the school was near 160% capacity. The capacity of the school is determined by the fire codes. Walking through those halls between class periods was like trying to swim upstream.

### C) PARENT-TEACHER ENTITY: *Introduction to PTSA*

This year, the school had a Parent Teacher Student Association. After being burned by one PTA experience and judged unacceptable by the last group I tried to join, I wasn't much interested in participating in the new PTSA.

#### *Disaster Preparedness in the Neighborhood School*

Melissa was still attending the neighborhood school half a day per week, for the "gifted" classes. Requests for emergency supplies were being sent out for the rest of the school. Requests included foods like crackers, peanut butter, and tuna. They also included a request for an emergency pouch for each child. This included a set of mittens and a clean pair of underwear. All of these pieces were to be placed in the large, rolling trashcan that was sitting in each room. Each room also had a pile of wool blankets. Ironically, they were usually placed on window ledges. I'm sure if we had an earthquake, they would make great glass catchers.

The gifted classroom had no blankets, there was no request for supplies, and I doubted most of the parents of students from the other school knew the disaster plan. If they did, it would have chilled their blood. The neighboring school had a much better plan for evacuating the school. If the school was compromised, the school could send the children to the nearby grocery store, the synagogue, or to the neighborhood school. The store was the best bet. The school was the last resort. The neighborhood school still planned to evacuate to the neighboring school without any backup plan.

I went to the neighborhood PTA meeting to ask what provisions the school made for the gifted students who attended the school for three hours per week. My reception at the meeting was very revealing. The first vice president came into the meeting and demanded to know why I was there. I told her that I was there to discuss Disaster Preparedness. The librarian, Matthew's first grade teacher, the principal, and the PTA secretary came in. They all gave me dirty looks. The president arrived. Throughout this setup, I had been reading, to give a relaxed image. The blood was rushing in my ears. I was definitely stressed and this was serious business.

The president noticed me, but wanted to exercise his power by making me wait. He wanted to run the meeting his way (poor, foolish man). He was no match for the women on the Board. Soon, the women were demanding that he recognize me, so I would leave. They were saying that my presence at the table was making them gag. I was only too happy to accommodate their wish.

When I was recognized, I asked about the disaster plan. The president confidently told me that the students would be evacuated to the neighboring school. I asked what they would do if the other school were compromised. The response had something to do with the fact they had a two-way radio. It didn't answer my question. Matthew's first grade teacher piped up at this point, and said, "Removing the emergency supplies from the building is my first priority." The other adults at the table nodded their heads in agreement. I was astounded. I thought her students should have been her first priority. I could imagine Matthew's first grade teacher struggling to drag a rolling trash can out of a building filled with debris, while first graders lay injured and bleeding in her classroom. I told the assembled board that they really needed to consider the fact that they were responsible for these children and they needed to make appropriate arrangements. Then, I left. I had said my piece.

Melissa said some wool blankets did show up in her classroom, but no paperwork was ever sent home, outlining emergency procedures.

## E) DIFFERENCES & DISABILITIES: *The Resource Side of the Spectrum*

This year, I met a woman named Dolly. Jeff had gone to elementary school with Dolly's daughter. Dolly was a divorced mom who had worked hard to earn a decent living for her family. Her work schedule kept her from volunteering in school, so that's why I hadn't met her sooner.

While Jeff was on the end of the education spectrum labeled "gifted", Dolly's daughter was on the other end, and labeled "resource". Dolly's daughter had a comprehension/retention problem. While I was begging teachers to help me figure out why Jeff couldn't write, Dolly was pleading with her daughter's teachers to teach her. One teacher's response had been, "What do you want me to teach her?" Like Jeff, the girl had an Individualized Educational Profile, so the teachers should have been able to make a plan that was suitable for the girl's needs.

Both children were pulled out of their regular classes for special education. While they were out of the classroom, the rest of the class was getting information and being given homework that Jeff and Dolly's daughter would be responsible for, also. The rest of the class had class time to complete some of the assignment. It was additional work for the special education students. Looking back, we wonder if the special education teachers ever worked with the regular teachers to develop decent education strategies for the students they had in common.

In Junior High, I was being told that I needed to monitor Jeff's homework. Dolly's daughter went to the other Junior High, and when Dolly asked about homework assignments, so she could monitor her daughter's progress, the teacher told her that her daughter should be old enough to manage her homework alone. Her daughter's teacher went so far as to make an announcement to the class, the next day, that they should all be old enough to do their homework without their parents' aid. Dolly's daughter slipped further back.

### Drop Out Risk

I was speaking with the Gifted teacher one afternoon, while we were waiting for the students to arrive. The teacher told me that we have to be watchful for gifted students, because they are at a higher risk of dropping out of school than your average student is. Resource students may drop out due to frustration, but gifted students will drop out due to boredom. In order to help our students reach their potential, we have to keep them interested and challenged.

## F) PROGRAMS: *Optional Education*

Melissa started the fifth grade on the Optional list. She thought she might like to try the format that Jeff had tried the previous year. Unfortunately, there was a waiting list for the Optional Program. Two weeks into the school year, there was an opening. By that time, she had developed a rapport with her current teacher. She asked the teacher for advice. The teacher told her that the decision was up to Melissa, but she suggested that Melissa might want to observe the Optional class for an hour one day. That way, she could make a more informed decision. Melissa observed the class and decided that there wasn't enough structure for her liking. She seemed to feel that the teacher had little control over the class. I didn't see the teacher she saw, so I don't know if her observation was biased. She really liked the current teacher and felt she shouldn't leave a good situation. I think she made the best choice for her.

## G) TRANSPORTATION & FIELD TRIPS: *The Suspicious Tail*

One morning, after dealing with business at the school, I went out into the parking lot to get into my car. Melissa and some of her classmates had just boarded the school bus for their gifted class. I could have pulled out of my parking space in a hurry and left the area ahead of the bus, but the parking lot was extremely icy. I decided that option wasn't safe, so I let the bus pass me. I had to follow the bus for about four blocks before I could turn towards my house, or I could drive a mile out of my way. I followed the bus.

Halfway into the drive, the bus stopped. It seemed as if it had stopped in the darkest part of the block possible. I didn't know if they were having any trouble. Usually, if students are misbehaving, the bus driver will pull the bus over and stop. He hadn't pulled over. The bus was so close to an intersection, that I didn't think I could get around it with enough clearance to miss oncoming traffic, so I sat still.

I turned on the dome light in my car, and pulled out a book to read. I looked up from my book and noticed several students were looking out the back window and waving at me. Since I knew most of these kids, I waved back. The bus finally resumed its route after about five minutes. It headed towards the school and I headed home.

When Melissa got home from school, I asked her what the problem had been with the bus. She told me that the bus driver thought I was following him in a suspicious manner, so he had stopped the bus and called his dispatcher for advice. While he was on the radio, the kids had recognized me. Melissa had verified it, and they had tried to tell the bus driver that I was just heading home. For some reason, he refused to listen to them for a long time.

If I had malicious intent, the bus driver's actions would have made it easier to carry out a threat. Could he have put the bus in motion fast enough and long enough, if I would have had an efficient weapon? The street was icy and he couldn't have been able to get much speed before he would have needed to stop at the intersection. Unless I had some sort of James Bond type car, the driver's best bet would have been to keep the bus moving. That would have given me little opportunity to stop my car, get out, and brandish a weapon. He should have driven the bus directly to the well-lit school and parked as close to a door as possible, if he thought there was imminent danger. Maybe the kids could have gathered information on my vehicle during the ride.

### Invincible Kids

I had been on several field trips with the kids. There was always a formula for how many adults were required to accompany a class. The ratio for elementary school was one adult to five or six children.

For this particular field trip, we were going to be walking. In the course of the walk, we would have to walk along a blind curve to go down hill. On the other side of the street, residents had lost mailboxes because cars came down the curve too fast. This way, at least, we would be walking facing traffic. The fact that we wouldn't be visible until after we rounded the curve bothered me, but it didn't seem to concern the students.

I was walking with fourth and fifth grade students. As we started to go around this curve, rather than staying close to the curb, the students spread out all over the street. I thought they seemed like a mindless herd of cattle. When I advised them to walk single file around the curve, they looked at me as if I was totally insignificant, and spread out further. I prayed that a car wouldn't come speeding around the curve.

These students either didn't understand or didn't care, that we (the adults) were responsible for their welfare until the field trip ended. If they were to get injured on the excursion, it could look like the adult in charge was negligent. While we were walking, a car did come around the curve. Luckily, it came up slowly enough that students were able to move out of the way. I was never so relieved for a field trip to end, as I was that day.

H) HOMEWORK: *Study Skills and Housework*

Jeff was still having trouble with his homework, so his teachers called me in for a conference. The conference couldn't have been planned for a worse time. I woke up that morning with strep and dragged myself into the school. Jeff had shown some interest in a computer class that was being held after school. This was meant to be a reward for finishing his homework, but the homework wasn't getting done.

The teachers sat on one side of the table and told me that I needed to do something about Jeff's homework. They asked if I was requiring him to do housework. I told them that I had cut back on the housework, in an effort to give him enough time to complete his homework. They suggested that I needed to give him more housework to discipline him for the homework. There was some sort of educational correlation between homework and housework. Supposedly, both activities required discipline.

I told the teachers that we had been informed my husband would be losing his job soon. This might be impacting Jeff. The teachers suggested we get counseling for the situation. I felt getting counseling while we were being held hostage wasn't going to be very effective. My husband's employer had moved the release date back a couple times. He was considered to be essential personnel until the downsizing, so he found it hard to get a new job sooner.

Another thing the teachers asked me was, "Do you have a computer?" Cautiously, I answered that we did. I was advised to have Jeff do his homework on the computer. Since many of his textbooks couldn't come home and homework was started at the school, I wondered how he was supposed to do the homework on his home computer? There was no offer from the teachers to allow him to use the computers at the school. We didn't have enough money to buy him a laptop computer. Besides, the School District advised against carrying valuables in school. One of our friends' sons had taken an old laptop to school, and someone kicked him in the back, severely damaging the computer he was carrying in his backpack.

The conference ended with the teachers recommending me to enroll Jeff into the after school study skills class. They also advised me to monitor homework (that may or may not come home). The teachers promised they would send home a weekly list of his homework while I was to encourage computer use, even though he wouldn't be allowed to use one in school. These were teachers who were certified to teach gifted children, yet they didn't recognize Jeff's problem. It was educational, yet I wouldn't get any support. The weekly homework list fizzled out after the first week. So much for the teachers being consistent.

Jeff took the study skills class, but it didn't improve anything. The teachers would require it again in the 8th grade. It wasn't a matter of learning the work. It was a matter of transmitting it back in a timely manner. What was the difference between homework and tests? I would learn much later, the only tests Jeff failed were essay tests.

### J) VOLUNTEERING: *Returning to the Scene of the Crime*

I had been away from our neighborhood school for several months when Betty asked me how to use some of the machines in the school. She had often come to the school, to volunteer, only to be told that her services weren't needed because she didn't know how to use the necessary machines. After determining when she was scheduled to volunteer again, I annotated my calendar to help her, since no one else seemed to be inclined to show her what she needed to know.

I walked into the school with Betty and we felt the temperature drop about 20 degrees. I watched the eyes of the adults get big. They were afraid and I seemed to be the focus of their fear. The children, on the other hand, were quite happy to see me.

We did some laminating for Betty's teacher. We were discussing the best way to feed the papers into the machine to make the least amount of waste. While we were running the project, one of the teachers lectured us on wasting the lamination. We were to make sure that we fed the machine properly. I thought this lecture was ironic, since she was one of the teachers who refused to bring her lamination in when we had tried to do a consolidated lamination. She always had to do hers separately.

The other machine Betty didn't know how to use was the binding machine. We grabbed some scrap paper, and went in search of the binding machine. We were told it was in the library. There was a class in the library, so I peeked into the librarian's office to see if the binding machine was there. It wasn't, so I started to leave the area. The librarian abandoned her class to follow me. She asked what we were doing, in a hostile tone, then directed us to a room behind the library. We located the machine, and I showed Betty how to use it.

By the time we finished our projects, I was happy to be leaving the building. I was starting to get a headache. After we left the building, Betty asked why the adults seemed to be so afraid of me. I think it's because they had an idea about what I knew about them. I had blended in with the woodwork for three years and heard a lot of things. Proving any of it would have been difficult. How much more garbage was out there that they thought I knew, but didn't?

If they had been conducting their business in a principled manner, they would have had no reason to fear me.

### M) DISCRIMINATION, HARASSMENT & ABUSE: *The Teacher Tamer*

Linda's younger son was in Kindergarten. I tried very hard not to say anything to prejudice her against the teacher. The new teacher in the Kindergarten was the teacher who had taught Betty's son in the first grade. Was it just Betty's son she didn't like, or did it go deeper?

Everything seemed to be going OK for a while, at the beginning of the year. One morning, Linda had to take her husband out to the airport, at about the same time school started. I was asked to come over to make sure the boys got to school on time. The younger boy's clothes were set out on a chair, but he refused to get dressed. I dressed him, but as soon as I turned my back, he was down to his underwear and hiding as far under his bed as possible. I made sure his brother was ready, then we pried him out from under the bed, and got him dressed with just enough time to get out the door. If I didn't know better, I would have thought the child was abused.

What I didn't know would have shed some light on the situation. The boy was required to pull cards all day in class. Linda said a couple times she had been called twice in one day, because he had to pull a blue card. How much trouble can a kindergärtner get into in three hours?

One day, after we dropped the kids off at school, Linda and I went out to breakfast. We came back to the school to pick up her son, at lunchtime. He didn't come out with his classmates. The teacher approached Linda, frantically. Her son was out of control and something needed to be done. Linda rushed into the school and was shocked by the scene in the classroom. Her son was in the corner holding up a chair like a lion tamer. He was fending off the principal. When the teacher approached, he waved the chair at her also. This would be his last day at this school.

Linda moved her son to another school, where they realized he had a hearing problem. This school was willing to work with the boy. Linda had suspected something was wrong, but she hadn't been sure. The previous school had been extremely slow in trying to test him at all.

The change was amazing. He was back to being his polite and happy self. He loved his new kindergarten teacher and progressed at a decent pace, until they moved to Texas, that summer.

N) SAFETY AND SECURITY: *Emergency Number Please*

The schools ask for emergency numbers at the beginning of the year, and carefully file them away for emergencies. The only problem is, when there is an emergency, will the numbers be used?

When Jeff entered the Junior High School I filled out the paperwork, as I had done for several years. Since my work was mobile, I put my pager number down as my work phone, with the notation that this was a pager.

Time passed, and we had an emergency that could have put Jeff's life in danger. I suffer from migraines and have heard of children having them. One of Jeff's classmates in the second grade had a waiver to wear a hat with a bill, in class, because the fluorescent lights caused the ailment. When Jeff's headache hit, he didn't know what was happening. He only knew his head hurt, he was having trouble seeing, and he wanted to vomit. He managed to make it to the nurse's office, where he was allowed to lay down for half an hour. After that, he was told to catch the school bus home. With some guidance from his friends, he managed to get on the right bus.

The driver noticed that Jeff was extremely uncomfortable during the ride home. He was worried that Jeff wouldn't make it the block and a half from the bus stop to our house, so he drove the bus up to our driveway and waited until Jeff got into the house.

I was surprised to hear a bus pull up in front of our house. I opened the door, and Jeff nearly fell into the house. I tried to get him comfortable enough to tell me his symptoms. I realized he had a migraine and drove him back across town to the doctor's office.

The irony of the whole situation is that our doctor's office was less than a mile away from the school. If the school had called me to pick up my nauseous son, it would have saved Jeff from suffering through five extra miles of driving.

The bus driver could have lost his job for getting Jeff home safely. If it would have gotten down to that, I would have fought for the bus driver.

*Emergency Number 2*

The second time we needed the emergency number, again, it wasn't used. Jeff decided to stay after school for a dance. The decibel level was so high that he was having trouble with the vibrations and the noise. Jeff ended up in the office, which was across the hall from the cafeteria where the dance was being held. He couldn't get away from the vibrations. He waited an hour for us to arrive, because we had no idea he was in trouble. He had tried to call the pager, but he couldn't call it from the school, so he left a message on our answering machine. He hoped that maybe I hadn't left to get his dad from work already. Unfortunately, I had and was in transit.. He either didn't think of calling his dad's work, or couldn't remember the number. Either way, it didn't matter. The time would have been the same.

I went to the school to pick him up from what I thought would be a happy event, and found my son in near migraine condition. The secretary in the office said that Jeff had looked miserable and she wished she could have done something for him. I asked why I hadn't been called, and Jeff told me that the phone wouldn't allow him to call pagers. I asked the secretary about the problem. I was informed that all the phones the students have access to are blocked for pager and cell phone numbers, in an effort to hinder drug deals.

When I asked how Jeff was supposed to reach my emergency number, since it was a pager if the phones he had access to wouldn't allow him to call me, she asked me, "Do you have a cell phone?" I asked her what good having a cell phone would do, if he couldn't make that call either. She informed me that there was one phone that the call could be made from, and that was way back in the corner of the office, behind the counter. I asked her if Jeff could use if the phone she indicated if another emergency arose. She looked at me as if I was from another planet. I told her that I didn't care if he made the call or if an "authorized adult" made the call, I wanted to know that they would make an effort to reach me for a future emergency. She assured me that they would, but I was dubious.

*Emergency Number 3*

In the elementary school, Mary was an emergency contact for a friend who worked. The friend's child acted up one day, and Mary was called to remove the child from the school. When she came to collect the child, the secretary lectured her about disciplining the child. Mary reminded the secretary that she was only the emergency contact, and if the school had a problem about discipline, they needed to discuss it with the child's parents, not her. After all, she was only there to remove the child.

About two weeks later, Mary was visiting her invalid mother, who was her emergency number. If Mary wasn't at the school, or at home, she was usually at her mother's house. Mary's daughter had a serious allergic reaction to something and was in the nurse's office. Mary had no clue that her child was in distress, because the school didn't call her emergency number.

Mary left her mother's house and headed home. When she got home, she checked the answering machine, and heard the message from the school. The call had been made well before she left her mother's house. When Mary arrived at the school, she was upset. She pointed out the fact that she had been called immediately to deal with her friend's child, which hadn't been life threatening, yet her emergency number hadn't been used in a potentially life threatening emergency. This was unacceptable. To avoid further problems with the emergency number, she invested in a cell phone and gave that number to the school, as her only number.

*Emergency Number 4*

Linda was a military wife, and had filled out the emergency card, just like Mary and I did. Her problem was slightly different. About six months before the school year ended, Linda's husband was being sent into combat. He would be gone for the remainder of the school year, therefore, his work number would be of no use as an emergency number. Linda, being a conscientious person, went to the school office and tried to make arrangements for another number to be put in the place of her husband's work phone, and listed as a second emergency number. After all, what good would it do to call his office if he were thousands of miles away.

She explained the situation to the secretary, and asked that my name and number be put in place of her husband's name and his work phone. The secretary dutifully removed the number and asked for Linda's husband's new work phone number. Linda patiently explained that her husband would be out of the country and she didn't know what the number would be. The only way that her husband would have to be contacted about an emergency would have been if Linda was dead, or otherwise incapacitated. At that point, the military would contact him. Otherwise, he would be too far away to bother with  He obviously couldn't do anything about a child with the flu, if he was 18 hours away. The secretary looked at her blankly.

Somehow, Linda finally convinced the secretary to make the requested change. With the relatively high percentage of military families in the area, one wouldn't have thought that the request was so unusual.

O) POLITICS: *Advocating the Year Round School*

I was very interested in the concept of Year Round Education. Sometimes, people thought that was all I could talk about. I had tried to figure out why it wouldn't work in Alaska, besides the stubborn attitude of the people involved. I couldn't see much difference between Alaska and California. Alaska was following the same path California had, yet Alaska was supposed to be different.

There were all sorts of discussions about the need for more schools, yet I knew existing schools were in disrepair. Without a large population base, like California, it would be more difficult to fund problems if we had new construction and seriously aging buildings at the same time. Year Round Education could be a temporary bandage to help stem the hemorrhaging of school district money. If we could cluster at least four schools into the year round program, we could work on one school for a year, while the other three schools accepted the overflow students. By the end of four years, we could have a group of schools in good repair, and we could move on to another group. The solution sounded logical.

I put together a package for the School Board members to look at. The first six pages were a balanced argument for trying a year round program. I backed it up with some facts and figures I had collected from schools in the Lower 48 states. I sent it to the School Board with hopes that they would consider it.

My next move was to try to get a proposition put on the municipal ballot so voters could vote on the suggestion. Maybe areas that seemed more receptive to the idea in the voting booth might be good candidates for trying the concept.

There were two ways I could get the proposition on the ballot. The first way involved collecting thousands of signatures. I figured that would take too much time. The other way was to present my case in front of the Municipal Assembly, so I requested an audience with the Assembly.

I thought my presentation was well planned, but I spoke the wrong language. I pointed out the cost of a new school. I believe it was $12 Million, at the time. Illustrations I provided explained the track system, and commented on savings for things that went into the school, such as playground equipment, desks, and textbooks. The Assembly lacked comprehension, and decided to "pass the buck" in a relatively logical manner. I was asked if I had seen the School Board about this. My meeting with the School Board was scheduled for the following week. The leader of the Assembly told me to come back after I had spoken to the School Board.

I received a friendly letter inviting me to speak to the School Board, signed by one of the members. The tone of her note led me to believe she had actually read my packet. I went to the meeting with a hopeful attitude.

At the meeting, I signed in. I would have three minutes to cover my topic. Since I had sent some information already, I assumed that I could build on the information already provided. I couldn't have made all my valid points in three minutes.

It was my turn to speak. They tape all these meetings so people can watch them on TV. I haven't had the courage to try to see my three-minute performance. I was a bundle of nerves and it probably showed on my face. I spoke about why I thought we needed year round education and spoke about specific problems I had seen. Things like the Junior High School being so overcrowded and textbook shortages.

After my presentation, the Board members only made three comments. One Board member stated that the Junior High wasn't overcrowded. Another Board member said she was unaware of any textbook shortages. Of course, that meant only that she was unaware, not that there wasn't a textbook shortage. I was also told there could be no funding for my idea. I wasn't really asking for money. Operation costs went up for the first year or so after a conversion to Year Round, but after that, they drop sharply. The price would have been a lot less than building a new school.

I returned to the Assembly, and they asked me what the School Board said. I told them they said, "No". The Assembly agreed with the School Board, and sent me on my way. I had failed. Welcome to Anchorage, California.

## P) POLICIES & PROCEDURES: *Competition is Bad*

The school newsletter mentioned that there was going to be an early morning meeting to discuss Technology, Reading, and Conflict Resolution. Parental involvement was requested. I thought the meeting sounded interesting and I felt I could make a contribution in the area of Reading. I left the house early and went to the meeting.

When I got to the meeting, I seemed to be the only parent in attendance. I looked for the Reading group, but they seemed to have completed their objective a couple days before. I knew very little about Technology that would be helpful to anyone, so I looked into the Conflict Resolution group. This group was looking for ways to minimize friction between students.

I don't know if I was supposed to be there, but I offered a couple (I thought) good suggestions. The first suggestion considered looking at various groups as teams. You start out with your class as a team. From there, your grade is a team. If you have a buddy class, together you're a team. Finally, the whole school's a team. If you see a team member being harassed on the playground, ask the victim to join your group's activity. If the victim has friends, it makes him a less desirable target. The teacher's response was shocking. I was told they couldn't consider it because, "Teamwork had gang-like connotations." The teachers actually had shocked looks on their faces. (The McGruff campaign would promote a similar concept (to mine) in 2005.)

I had tried to illustrate the concept of teamwork further, by referring to their canned food drive. As it currently stood, the class that brought in the most cans of food received a prize. I said, rather than giving a can count for each class, they could stack the food in the gym and take a picture of what the whole school donated, and the students could watch the pile grow. It would definitely be a visual example of how much power they had as a group to change their corner of the world.

Again, the response I got was confusing. The teachers were angry, and they told me, "Competition is bad, and can't be allowed in the school." I didn't see how my suggestion could be criticized that way. The school was already promoting competition. I was promoting cooperation, but then you get back into the gang mentality. Forget about the fact that the school sells clothing in the school's colors to promote school spirit. What's left besides cooperation and competition?

The school chose to stay with their Resolving Conflicts Creatively Program (RCCP), and working to teach more student mediators how to deal with problems between students. I knew I was out of my league, dealing with these teachers. Like the fool I am, I had taken the bait again. SUCKER! I knew, the next time they asked for parent involvement, they didn't really want any input. I obviously had nothing of value to contribute.

## R) REDUCE, REUSE, & RECYCLE: *Recycling at the Neighboring School*

I started participating in the recycling program at the new school. They already had a program in place, but it was feeble. Like the old school, this school didn't have a whole lot of student involvement with the recycling efforts. There were no standardized collection receptacles, so I would often have to hunt around the room for the recycling container. I provided some boxes for collecting the paper. This school was actually a little better at putting only recyclable paper into the boxes.

One of the high schools was running a paper collection project as a community service, and making a small profit. They had a dumpster with a padlock on it, for collecting recyclable paper. I paid for a key that year, to participate in the program.

I noticed a couple other problems with wasting paper in the school. In one container, I found a big piece of construction paper with a small circle cut out of it (in the middle!). I remembered being a student at that age. The teacher usually had pre-cut squares and rectangles. This action would give us just enough paper to cut the shapes that were required for our projects. The teachers needed to speak with students about cutting from the edge.

The previous year, Melissa's teacher had asked me to cut up small squares of construction paper for a mosaic project. It had evolved into a confetti project, instead. When the teacher made a similar request for the current year, I modified it a little. I made long strips, which the students could cut, as needed, to make the little squares. There shouldn't be any confetti on the floor after the project. If there had been a paper shredder around, we could have run the sheets of paper through it, and made strips in less than half the time.

I tried to rescue construction paper that was still usable. I requested teachers put the scraps in a box that was near the die cutter. Some of the pieces were actually big enough to make letters, while others were relatively smaller, and could be used to cut out shapes used in the tessellation projects. When I had a good supply of scraps and some time, I would cut out the shapes for the tessellation projects. I put these pieces into large zipper bags for future use. One day, someone posted a note with a shabby scrap attached to it. The note said, "This couldn't possibly be used any further". I got two more shapes out of it, and re-attached it with a note of my own. The note said, "NOW it's unusable."

I thought it was wonderful at this school that their teachers managed to coordinate their lamination. The teachers put their projects in a box with their name attached. The librarian, or a designated parent volunteer, would laminate once a week. The finished product would be delivered to the teacher. The laminator at the old school had been freestanding on a cart. There had been plenty of room for the lamination to drop down to the floor. At the new school, the laminators were on a counter, perpendicular to the wall. One had to feed the materials in from the side, and carefully watch the output, so it wouldn't back up into the machine again. If I had designed the area, I would have put a large slot in the back of the counter. The lamination could be fed from the front, and directed through the slot, to collect in the cabinet below.

Melissa's teacher was generally interested in paper conservation. They had their usual Daily Geography, Math, and Language exercises, every morning. There were two questions for each subject, each day. We tried making transparencies for the overhead projector, but too many kids complained about their eyes hurting, from trying to read the transparency and write the questions in the dark. Some teachers took their daily questions and copied them on a worksheet that they hacked up into 1" x 8.5" strips for each day. Each child received a little slip of paper, and the slips turned into so much litter by the end of the day. Another option was to put all the questions on one sheet of paper, but there wasn't any room to write the answers on the paper.

The fifth and sixth graders had the same Language and Geography lessons, but different Math lessons. I managed to make a two sided worksheet, usually 8 ½" x 14". Each grade had the first page the same, and the second page was age appropriate. They were to use a piece of notebook paper to show their work and answer the questions. At the end of the week, the students could correct their papers. If the original worksheet was in decent condition, it could actually be recycled for the next year.

While recycling the papers, I saw several teachers had copied several pages of stories that had questions at the end. Because students answered the questions on the last page, the whole packet was discarded. I felt that teachers should have required the students to write their answers on a separate piece of paper, and the packets could be collected for future use.

## S) SICKNESS & HEALTH: *Mystery Malady 2*

Matthew was having some difficulty in class. He liked to be funny, so the teacher thought he was just trying to be funny when he started belching in class. The belches were quite loud and definitely disruptive. The teacher was sure that Matthew was just trying to get attention, so he was sent home at the end of the day, with a reprimand.

The next day at school, besides having problems belching, he was having flatulence problems. The teacher gave him permission a couple times to leave the room and use the bathroom. When the problem persisted, the teacher thought it was just another way to get attention. She spoke to me after school. Had Matthew eaten anything strange lately? The ailment was a mystery, and it seemed less troublesome at home.

The third day, I hoped we had him straightened out. I had given him clear liquids, in an effort to flush his system. The symptoms worsened to such a degree that I was called to the school. The nurse told me that the situation was intolerable. I needed to take him to a doctor. We made an appointment for that afternoon. Matthew was diagnosed with an ulcer. He was given medicine and sent home. We waited a whole day before we sent him back to school. No one could believe that a child so young could get an ulcer.

It would be years before I would really learn about the H. pylori bacteria. When I did hear about it, H. pylori would be considered a hazard to living in the Bush. It's the bacteria that can cause an ulcer, and it doesn't usually like garlic or broccoli. An ulcer caused by bacteria can hit any age.

A couple years later, Mary's son would have a mystery malady, where it looked like he was vomiting vanilla pudding. The nurse called her and was reprimanding her for feeding her son pudding for breakfast. What kind of parent was she?

Mary took her son to the doctor and he was diagnosed with a bleeding ulcer. Mary's son was 10, so people couldn't believe that he could have really had an ulcer. Her son wasn't being mistreated at home, but school was another story. Daily intolerance and piles of homework with short deadlines was stressing her son out. Mary reminded the school that she had previously complained about these problems, yet nothing had been done. Would something be done now that it was noticeably having a negative impact on her son's health? Being in a constant state of anxiety can impair anyone's immune system, leaving it open for attack.

### You Can't Teach a Child Who's Dead

Mary's daughter developed a sinus infection, and was put on antibiotics. As soon as she seemed well enough to return to school, Mary sent her back. Within a few days, the girl wasn't able to function well enough to attend school, so Mary requested homework. This isn't unusual for a child who misses some school.

As time progressed, so did the infection. The doctor ordered stronger antibiotics. The classroom Mary's daughter had was the same room that Jeff had in the fourth grade. He had missed half a month of school before we got him straightened out. Every time they thought Mary's daughter was fit enough to send back to school, she would have a relapse within a couple days. The doctor worried that the infection would spread to her brain and they were having trouble finding a strong enough antibiotic to kill the infection, that Mary's daughter could function with.

At this point, Mary requested homework assignments and lesson plans from her daughter's teacher for a long-term basis. The teacher complained that it was extremely difficult to accommodate her request, and she urged Mary to return her daughter to school soon. After all, she couldn't educate a child who wasn't in school. Mary suggested that the teacher needed to find a way to accommodate the request, otherwise, she would be within her rights to petition the school district for a tutor. It wouldn't shine a very good light on the teacher.

This teacher had recently lost an ancient and beloved pet. The effect of the loss on the teacher was as profound as if she had lost a child. Mary had been sympathetic about the teacher's situation at that time, but the teacher was less sympathetic towards Mary's situation. Mary was consulting with out of state specialists and worrying about losing her daughter. At this point, I would have told the teacher that she couldn't teach a child who was dead, either. But then, I'm somewhat more impulsive than Mary is.

I think Mary handled the situation with incredible finesse. She asked the teacher, "How far in advance are your lessons prepared?" There was plenty of lead-time. The teacher provided the materials that Mary requested. Her daughter physically missed four months of school, and completed the year with A's in all of her core classes. The teacher told Mary that she wondered if she still belonged in a classroom, if a parent (who lacked the extensive educational training) was able to teach a child as well as she could. The teacher retired a year later.

The teacher hadn't considered that this is how the State runs its correspondence school. If a parent is able to follow a comprehensive lesson plan, and the student is self-motivated, the educational process has a good chance of being successful. If the parent runs into a problem, the teacher is available for consultation. This teacher had a great lesson plan to follow, which left the parent with few unanswered questions, That's why Mary was so successful.

*An Incident on the Ice*

I was at Linda's house one afternoon, when her older son came home. He came in with a relatively shocking story. At lunchtime, the students were allowed to skate on the skating rink. They put on their skates in the building and walked across the playground with blade guards protecting the blades on their ice skates. At the edge of the ice rink, they removed their skate guards and stepped out onto the ice.

While they were skating, one of his classmates fell on the ice. She asked for help getting up. When some of her classmates went over to help her up, the noon duty yelled at them, telling them that she needed to get up by herself. After a couple attempts, the girl was unable to do it herself. She was having trouble supporting weight on one of her feet. There was no way she could make it into the nurse's office on her own. The noon duty was unwilling to help remove the girl from the ice, or allow her friends to accompany her to the building. They needed a pass to get into the school, and the noon duty wasn't going to give them one.

Three of her classmates helped her into the building, and to the nurse's office. The nurse told the girl's mother that she had a sprained ankle, when her mother picked her up at the end of the day.
Making a child walk on a sprained ankle is bad enough, but this girl's problem was worse. Upon full medical examination, the girl's ankle was found to be broken. She was in a cast for the next six weeks. It's a good thing that her injury wasn't a matter of life and death.

T) TECHNOLOGY: *The Computer Lab*

The computer lab at the neighboring school was nothing compared to the fabulous Technology Learning Center, which was "state-of-the-art", at our last elementary school. The new school had twice as many students and the lab was half the size, with half the computers. Our previous school had a gifted grant writer, who enabled us to qualify for numerous grants. I doubt that people at our former school really appreciated how lucky we had been..

The students at the new school still got their work done in the time allowed. It just required more cooperation.

## U) CELEBRATIONS: *25ᵗʰ Birthday for the School*

This spring, the neighborhood school celebrated its 25ᵗʰ birthday with a big party. An announcement was sent out with a request for guests to bring gifts of school supplies. When I heard about the party, my first thought had to do with the concept that the building had been built to last 30 years. In five years, it would be past its prime. Would they renovate it, or replace it? The party was nice enough, and the gym was packed. There was a table for gifts that was covered. I went there to see a couple of the teachers. I mildly wondered what happened with all the gifts that were collected, since the original PTA President was in charge of the party.

## Y) MOBILITY: *The Concept, in General*

By the time Jeff moved into the seventh grade, he was on his seventh school. Melissa was currently on her fourth school, and Matthew was on his third. According to E. D. Hirsch, in his book, "The Schools We Need and Why We Don't Have Them", mobility (changing schools) can be as devastating to a child's education as coming from a single parent household or being poor.

Two of Jeff's school changes were "natural". The Kindergarten school had fed into the elementary school. Moving from an elementary school to the Junior High school was also a natural move. In California, if we had lived in a different area of the School District, we would have been looking at a forced move between schools with the rezoning, when they built the new school. That move was voluntary, on our part. We obviously had to move our children when my husband changed jobs. Getting the zone-exemption for the neighboring school may not have been the best move educationally for my children, but I felt that my children were at risk from the adults they had to deal with daily at the school we were zoned for. I've heard other parents complain that, while they didn't change houses, their children had to change schools repeatedly because of rezoning. Living in areas with a high military population, I know these families are highly mobile, and have to cope with the constant upheaval on an irregular basis. Mobility in our society is becoming a fact of life.

My children entered school being curious and intelligent. I don't know how much their education was handicapped by mobility. My husband and I have always promoted learning. If my children aren't successful, how much of their failure was due to mobility? How much of it was caused by the adults around them who failed to do their jobs properly?

### Mobile Matthew

When Matthew started the third grade, there were three third grade teachers. He started out in one class, but by the end of the second week, he had been moved to another class. Between applicants to the Optional Program being accepted, and people moving out of the school zone, one classroom had suffered a significant population loss. Matthew was moved to even out the discrepancy.

Even though I really liked his first teacher, the three teachers worked as a team, so he still had one subject with her. The original classroom was one of the classrooms you had to cut through to get to the other classrooms. We hoped moving him might help him concentrate a little better.

# Chapter 11
## Middle School Model 1996-97

### A) FIRST IMPRESSIONS: *Breathing Again*

Jeff started the eighth grade. This year, the school was converted into a middle school. There would be an extra period in the schedule, for a second elective. The school district was quite excited about this momentous advance in education. I politely looked at the literature, but wasn't impressed.

Melissa started the sixth grade. I liked her teacher. I think the rest of the students did, too.

Matthew started the fourth grade. He had Melissa's fourth grade teacher. I thought a male teacher would have a positive effect on him. We were finally stabilized after the Reduction In Forces (RIF) action. My husband had found a new job in town, and I was starting to unpack our boxes again.

### D) FUND RAISERS: *The In-Store Book Fair*

Fliers were sent home with all the students. There would be a book fair at the new bookstore in town on a certain Saturday, for two hours. People who wanted to support our school should go to a special checkout in the store, during those hours. The profits from that checkout would go towards our school.

On the day of the book fair, I went to the store and bought some books at the proper checkout. This type of book fair seemed popular this year. Betty went into the bookstore on a Saturday when another school was running their book fair. There was no line at the designated checkout, so she paid for her books there and pointed out the lack of a line to a couple other customers, who also bought their books there.

After the book fair, I asked the librarian how it had done. She said it was similar sales to some of the best years they had in their school since she had been there. It seemed like it was more convenient. The school didn't have to designate space for the books and disrupt classes, so the students could make their wish lists.

A couple years later, I noticed the book fair at the school, again. Supposedly, the book fair was meant to bring people from the neighborhood into the school. I don't know if this meant they wanted more community involvement, or if it was supposed to be a draw for the parents of the students. If, finding out how your child was doing in school wasn't enough to draw a parent into the school, how would selling books at conference time improve the situation? If it was meant for community involvement, there was a chance of security problems.

### *Missing Money*

I volunteered to help check the fund raiser orders for accuracy before they were sent in. This was on a Saturday morning. We made sure that all the addition was correct, and all the money was in each envelope. There were about three orders in my stack that had missing money. The addition had been accurate, but either there was a check missing, or there was cash missing. Without some indication as to how each customer paid, there was no way to tell what was missing. Cash can be lost or taken so easily.

The easiest orders to verify were the ones where each customer paid by check. With some of the orders paid in cash, it was difficult to tell which customer didn't pay the full amount. I had to call parents of the students who turned in the incomplete orders.. I could tell the parents what I saw on my paper, and how much money had been turned in, but explaining it over the phone was quite confusing and time-consuming.

To avoid this embarrassing situation in the future, parents should double check the math for the orders, and convert any cash into a check or money order before sending it to school. It's harder to make a check disappear mysteriously.

E) DIFFERENCES & DISABILITIES: *Special Education Funding*

Supposedly, Special Education accounts for 18% of the school's population. Three percent of the population is supposedly "gifted", while the other 15% are supposed to be "learning disabled". This may or may not add up.

If 2-7% of the school population is Attention Deficit, that could mean "gifted" or "resource". One in 500 can be Asperger's autism. According to Sally Shaywitz's book, "Overcoming Dyslexia", approximately 20% of our population is dyslexic. Dyslexics can also be categorized as "gifted" and "resource". Of course, many of these students fly under the radar and go undiagnosed. The students with the most prominent problems can't recite a nursery rhyme or tell you which words rhyme on a verbal test.

English as a Second Language can also be considered a special education need. There is one other group who isn't specifically counted. That is Fetal Alcohol Syndrome students and children of parents who have taken drugs. I don't have any numbers on what the percentage of these students is in the population.

During one of the budget cuts, the School District decided to cut funding to the "gifted" students. That meant that the teachers who dealt with "gifted" kids had to share the money that was originally allowed for the "resource" students. With all these figures, special education seemed more like the rule than the exception. It seems like more than 18% of the students have learning differences. Maybe we would be better off learning how to teach to the differences, rather than segregating students in special classes.

F) PROGRAMS: *The Middle School Model*

Jeff started school this year, and was able to add French to his electives. According to the paper that we were able to pick up at Back to School Night, Middle School had several advantages over Junior High School. They considered the middle school to be different than a junior high, because it wasn't a baby high school. "Junior high school" had an infantile connotation. I loved the fact that "Evaluation of student achievement was to be personalized in nature and strictly individualized" rather than a letter grade compared to others. Jeff's report cards still had grades on them and his achievements (i.e., fantastic test taking ability) weren't individually evaluated.

There was supposedly a multi-material approach, so students could learn at different rates. Textbooks were passé. Flexible schedules and team teaching were also emphasized. Students could complete a course in less than the structured semester if they worked at their own speed. That sort of made me wonder how these students were expected to occupy the remainder of the semester.

There was supposed to be a higher level of interaction between students and teachers, rather than teachers lecturing classes. Community involvement and use of volunteers were supposed to be greater than in the junior high school model. In other words, it was supposed to be a kinder, gentler educational environment.

*Library Aide*

The job of being a library aide was usually reserved for sixth graders, but Matthew's teacher offered to help him get the job during lunchtimes once a week. Matthew was having trouble with the noon duties. Another student was causing some problems, and Matthew always seemed to be the target. Matthew's teacher could see the problem. He had watched through the window at lunchtime. Since there was no way to talk any sense into the noon duties, he devised his own plan for occupying Matthew. The first part involved having Matthew sit in the classroom and do some creative writing, after lunch. The teacher liked Matthew's stories and imagination, but sometimes this option wasn't feasible.

The teacher suggested Matthew be considered as a library aide, and his skill was found to be acceptable. He was able to check books in and organize them on the cart. He did this job quite well. He didn't miss the running around during recess much, and averaged about twice a week outside. At the end of the school year, the librarian gave Matthew and the other library aides a nice gift bag. Matthew was so proud, and asked if he could be a library aide the next year. The librarian told him he would be welcome to help next year.

### The Spelling Bee

Matthew was in the Spelling Bee this year. He passed the school level of the competition, and went on to the district level. Our neighborhood school had discontinued the Spelling Bee because it was hard for children to lose. I didn't understand that concept. There were all sorts of competitions during the school year that usually revolved around fund raising  Didn't students feel bad about that?

Matthew got to the district level of the Spelling Bee, and it was held in the university auditorium. Everything seemed to be going well. Matthew liked to read, so he had a broad vocabulary. I believe there were a couple things the people who read the words were allowed to do to help a child who might be having trouble. Besides saying the word, a child could also ask for the definition, and maybe how the word was used in a sentence. When Jeff had been in a Spelling Bee, in the third grade, one child was eliminated by the word "pen". He thought the word was "pin". It had seemed silly to ask the definition of such a simple word, but the definition would have made the difference with an unclear pronunciation.

No amount of help was able to help Matthew in his case. His word was "writhe", and he kept asking to have it repeated. They gave him the definition, but that didn't shine any more light. He just wasn't familiar with the word. His guess ended up being "rive".

He tried again the following year, but was beaten by his nearest opponent from this year. Competition had worked to make her try a little harder.

### Parents in Our Schools Days

In November, they had three days where parents were invited to come to the school and interact during the school day. The objectives were: to meet some of your child's friends, participate in classroom activities, and get to know the school's support staff.

Parents were reminded of the rules against smoking, drinking, or carrying a weapon on the school property. Parents were instructed to make arrangements ahead of time for a lunch, if they were going to buy one that day. Checking in at the office and getting one of the visitor badges was also emphasized. The People Mover also provided a free bus pass so parents could ride a bus to the school if they needed transportation.

I thought this concept was ridiculous. I was in the school on a regular basis, and students still acted uncivilized when I walked into the room. Were the parents going to get a realistic picture of how the class truly functioned? All I could think of was how much disruption there would be. This is nothing against parents or teachers. If students aren't used to parents always being in the class, they tend to act differently.

After the fact, I asked a few of my friends, who were teachers, how the Parents in Our Schools Days went. They all said that it was very difficult to control the class with all the visitors. Very little learning was accomplished. I think parents should be more involved on a regular basis. Then, their presence wouldn't be such a novelty.

### H) HOMEWORK: *Not For Love Nor Money*

Jeff was still having trouble turning homework in. I asked his English teacher if I could borrow a textbook over the weekend, to see what was going on in class. The teacher told me that there was a textbook shortage, so she couldn't allow anyone to remove a textbook from the classroom. Not even a parent could borrow one for a weekend. Coming to class, myself, to find out what the homework for each day was, wasn't an option. The teachers had offered to let me know what homework was required for each week, but without a book, I couldn't monitor it. The promise of a list of weekly homework assignments only lasted about one week anyhow.

I spoke with a couple of my friends about the problem. One of them suggested that I might approach the principal and ask her which textbook was being used by the class, and if she could tell me where to buy it. This seemed like a great idea. The price of a textbook was much smaller than having Jeff tutored for his credits.

I went into the principal's office, and presented my problem. She smiled at me and cheerfully announced that students were being weaned from textbooks, so no amount of money could help the situation. There was no possible way that I could buy copies of all the materials that were being used in that class. There was no offer of a list of materials, in case I felt I could afford the cost. There was just the smug smile, and I felt as if she had actually patted me on the head and sent me on my way. The school suggested a way for me to remedy Jeff's situation (monitoring his homework), but they would be damned if they were actually going to cooperate with me to reach our mutual objective.

I did receive a textbook a couple weeks later. When I asked Jeff what his assignment was, he told me that they were done using the textbook. I asked why he had brought the book home and he told me it was because his teacher told him I had asked to see one. It didn't matter that the reason I wanted to see a textbook was to follow his homework.

Three years later, one of Jeff's friends would be in the same position with the homework. The principal would advise the parents to go out and buy her a textbook. It was the same school, same principal, same teacher. Why had they changed?

*Summer Assignment (Gifted Only)*

Linda's boys were getting ready for summer vacation in Texas. Her older son came home with a homework assignment for his gifted class. Over the twelve week summer vacation, the gifted students in his age group were supposed to read a book called, "The Weirdo", and write a book report on it. Linda's first problem with the assignment was the fact that only gifted students were getting summer homework. It seemed like they were being penalized for understanding lessons quickly. Most gifted students would probably be exercising their minds during the summer vacation, whether or not there was a school district mandate.

The second problem Linda had with the assignment was the scarcity of the book in the library system. There were only five copies of the title in their local library system. With 300 students who were given the assignment, and the usual time allowed for checking out a book being two weeks, about 30 students would be able to complete the assignment without having to buy the book.

This brings us to the third problem. Like me, Linda might buy a book that her son needed to complete an assignment, if there was a shortage. After looking at this book, she refused to buy it. Within the first chapter there were several graphic killings. The book was inappropriate for a fifth grader, in her opinion. Did she really want this book in her house? Was there really any redeeming message buried in the book, to make it worth reading that first chapter?

Linda spoke to the school board that summer. She pointed out that there needed to be enough books available for the students to read if it was a school assignment. She objected to the material, and to the fact that the gifted students were being singled out for this assignment. The school district decided not to have a mandatory book the next year. The following year, everyone was assigned a summertime reading assignment.

I)  DRUGS & WEAPONS: *Bethel School Shooting*

On February 19, 1997, 16 year old Evan Ramsey walked into Bethel High School (in the Alaskan Bush) and opened fire.  He killed the principal and one classmate.  Two others were wounded.  Other students knew he was bringing a gun, and had watched to see what would happen.  Evan is in prison and will be eligible for parole when he's 86 years old.

In "The Bully, the Bullied, and the Bystander", Barbara Coloroso covers this incident in a concise two paragraphs.  Basically, Evan was bullied, and the principal told him to ignore the harassment.  Seeing no other options to relieve his torment, he took the gun to school.  The bully isn't the one who will bring the gun to school.  The student who is bullied is, yet little notice is given to these students who are screaming for help.

K)  CURRICULUM: *Questionable Reading Material*

When I saw the book on Jeff's dresser, I was initially shocked.  The book had been difficult for me to read as a 30 year-old woman.  What was it doing in my 13 year-old son's room?  The book in question was Maya Anjelou's "I Know Why the Caged Bird Sings", and it was required reading for Jeff's Gifted English class.  As I said, I had read the book, and it had disturbed me as an adult.  The concept of rape is harsh, and the girl in the story was extremely young.

By the time I saw the book, Jeff was almost done with it.  I didn't ask him how he felt about the book.  If he had any problems with it, it was too late to do anything about it.  At his age, in English class, I remember choosing between books like "Durango Street" (gangs), "Death Be Not Proud" (cancer), "Old Yeller" (rabies), and "Treasure Island" (pirates).  I thought "I Know Why the Caged Bird Sings" might not have been appropriate for 8th graders.  By 10th grade, it might have been more suitable.

In a school system where you have to sign a permission slip if your teacher chooses to show a film that is rated PG or higher, I was surprised by this choice for reading material.  I have read other work by Maya Anjelou.  I preferred "All God's Children Need Traveling Shoes", but that might have been considered too political for middle school.

*Speed Writing*

Melissa's teacher had an exercise called, "Speed Writing".  She gave the students 10-15 minutes in the morning to write anything that came to their minds.  This wasn't going to be graded or corrected.  It was an exercise to allow the free flow of ideas.  Later, if there was a writing assignment, the students could look at their speed writing folder, to see if there was anything they could use to build a story.  The disorganized ideas could be tamed into a legitimate writing assignment.  Melissa sort of liked the exercise.  I don't know if Jeff would have done well with it.

*Mom Goes to School*

I had tried everything I could think of to figure out why Jeff wasn't succeeding.  I had sent him to the Study Skills classes twice.  He understood everything, but nothing was improving.  Without the textbooks, I couldn't see what he was supposed to be doing. So I had to find a different way to see how things fit.  I decided to get a first-hand look at the core classes.  I contacted all of his core teachers and informed them that I would be attending their classes the next day.

I got my supplies together and went to school with Jeff.  His first class was French.  This class wasn't a major concern as far as promoting him to the next grade.  After French, we went to Science class.  The teacher found a chair and wedged me between two cabinets, at the front of the room.  The lesson was about titration, and the teacher spent the whole time demonstrating three experiments.  I could feel the collective ennui of the class.  It was hard for me not to fall asleep with this riveting demonstration.  I figured, she could have involved at least nine of the students in the experiment.

Social Studies class was next. I had an actual seat because there was someone absent. This teacher explained to me that there was an area where students could pick up copies of homework papers, if they missed a day. Each day's homework was in a hanging file folder, labeled with the date the assignment was given. This file was in front of the classroom. I wondered if Jeff picked up homework for days he missed. This class shouldn't have been a problem, but it wasn't one of Jeff's favorite subjects.

We ate lunch on the bleachers, in the gym. After lunch, we had math class. Jeff was in Algebra. The teacher had students taking turns providing answers for the homework from the night before. It was Jeff's turn. He sat by the overhead projector and started reading off the answers. Some of the answers were "yes' or "no", and one of his class mates asked, "Is the answer for number six "no"?" Jeff answered, "Yes". The class tittered a little bit. He proceeded to write answers that were more complicated, on the transparency. I didn't understand the class, but he seemed to be functioning well in class.

Homework was the biggest problem. Since it constituted 30% of his grade, it contributed to a failing grade. I wasn't any closer to solving the problem.

*Taking Notes*

Melissa's "gifted" pullout lined up with her social studies class. Often, the teacher would have a video on the day she had her class. There was no way that Melissa had any opportunity to study for the test that the teacher usually gave the next day, unless she managed to get some notes on the video. Melissa took the best notes in class, and was very responsible. Unfortunately, she had to rely on someone else to take the notes for her. The teacher told her it was her responsibility to find someone to take notes for her.

One classmate took notes that were both hard to follow, and nearly non-existent. Another classmate took great notes, but there wasn't any time between the time Melissa got back to class, and the bell rang, to get to look at the notes. The other student took the school bus home and had after school activities that didn't allow for any time to get together.

If we had any idea which video was shown, we had a slim chance of finding it in a video store or the library. We also tried to look up the subject in the encyclopedia, and the Internet. Some subjects were vast, and hard to figure out what information was important.

The situation would have been a lot easier if Melissa had the opportunity to view the video, or even part of it. The teacher could have changed the day (or time) they saw the video, because there wasn't any surprise about the "gifted" class schedule. It happened only once a week, for half the day. The teacher could have allowed Melissa to view the video after school, or during lunchtime. Melissa was the only student in this class who was pulled out for "gifted" classes. Would the teacher have dealt with the situation differently if there had been five students missing the class?

L) CRIMES & PUNISHMENTS: *Your Son Must Be in a Gang!*

I had made friends with another mother who was volunteering in the library. It was a slow day, and we were talking. She asked if I had any children in high school. I said that my oldest was only in the eighth grade.

This woman's son was a football player, and he was on the honor roll. His only interest in gangs was being part of the football team, if that could be called a gang. He was a big guy, and it wasn't easy for him to share a bus seat with another person without spilling out into the aisle. School buses just weren't built to accommodate six-foot tall young men.

A couple days before, her son had been on the school bus, heading home. He was going to study at a teammate's house. While he was on the bus, a smaller student kept kicking his foot and trying to provoke him. He refused to take the bait. When they got to his friend's stop, he and his friend got off the bus. The smaller kid and two of his friends got off at the same stop. There was some pushing as the students got off the bus, and the driver could tell that there was a problem, so he reported what looked like a gang conflict.

The next day, the two football players were called into the principal's office and told that they were going to be suspended for fighting. This woman's son demanded to be allowed to call his mother. When the mother talked to the principal, the principal said that he had dealt with problems like this at his previous school, and the situation appeared to be a classic gang scenario. Bigger boys picking on littler boys. The woman refused to allow her son to be suspended.

I never saw her after that. I wonder if she might have moved her son to another school because of the incident. It seemed like a clear-cut case of prejudice, to me. In future years, I would have to deal with this principal. After those experiences, I would be inclined to believe this mom, because the principal barely dealt with actual facts.

*A Crime Against the State*

The day before Halloween, I was expecting another Avon representative to pick something up from my house. I had never met her. I was running dishwater, when the doorbell rang. I opened the door and my life went into a blender. The woman at the door wasn't the Avon representative I had been expecting. She was a social worker. She showed her credentials and had a complaint against me. Someone had reported that my children were in danger, because of me.

I let her in the house, because not letting her in might have triggered seizure of my children from school. Whoever had reported me used a German spelling for my name. The ages of my children were also inaccurate. Supposedly, my children had no father, or man around the house.

The charges against me included my house being filthy, my son (Jeff) had a breathing problem, and my writing (in my pajamas). On this particular day, my husband had just left town for the week, on business. We had had a very early morning, so Melissa was resting on the couch. She always looks pale. I had just come in from volunteering all morning at the school, and was trying to finish the dishes so I could go to conferences that afternoon. Matthew was playing out of sight, and the social worker never asked to see him, even though she could hear him. My living room contained a few boxes that I was still unpacking, and a stack of boxes that I had broken down and was going to take to the recycling center the next day. I also had my Avon orders set out to deliver that night.

The social worker inspected the upstairs of my house in a superior manner. She commented on the fact Melissa was resting. She shouldn't have been tired at that point in the day. According to the complaint, by an anonymous person, I was writing subversive materials, and what was worse, I was doing it in my pajamas! This book was something I was working on at the time. I also wrote letters to the editor. The social worker told me that the condition of my house, and my other questionable activities were grounds enough to have my children removed, but she didn't take the kids away that day. She just threatened. Then, she left.

The entrance of this woman into our lives made my life much more difficult. Matthew wet his bed for the next week, generating two loads of laundry a day. I had been making some progress getting Matthew to write, now, neither boy wanted to write. If writing was considered to be a crime against the state, they didn't want to have anything to do with it. This book was put on a shelf for almost three years because this upset me so much.

I went to Social Services and requested to see a supervisor. I asked what the guidelines were for how clean my house had to be if my youngest was 10 years old. The paper said he was 8. The supervisor told me that the parameters were subjective. The determination of the cleanliness of my house depended on what the social worker thought was clean.

A week after the visit, we got a note in the mail saying that there were no grounds to remove the children at this time. Supposedly, they had spoken with the schools and found out my kids were doing well. I thought this was quite interesting since the original complaint said that my children's schools were not known, and the teachers were asking what was going on because the kids had all changed. No one had talked to the teachers, and both boys weren't doing fine in school. They were failing. We almost needed counseling for being abused by the social worker, but that wasn't going to happen.

This same social worker was written about in the paper, soon afterwards. Several complaints had taken her to a house. She had commented that the mother shouldn't have marijuana sitting around the house, but she didn't do anything to remove the child who was in danger, until the 17th visit. By that time, the child had been violently raped by her mother's boyfriend, and needed emergency medical care.

I think people should be held accountable if they falsely report someone for child neglect and abuse. We just had a disorganized house. I hadn't realized that there was a time limit for unpacking a house after an aborted move. Most of the personal information in our complaint was false. The social worker carried out my "enemy's" cheap revenge, while another child was truly suffering. It took a long time for my kids to recover, and it affected their schoolwork.

## N) SAFETY & SECURITY: *The Mountain View Stake Out*

Betty's son had come home from school early. It was lunchtime, and he was bleeding when he walked into his grandmother's house. Betty's mom called Betty at work, and asked if she knew where her son was. Betty said she thought he would be in school at this time. Betty's mom told her that her son was at her house. He had been beaten up on the playground, and had waited in the office to see the nurse. No one would let him see the nurse without a pass from a noon duty. In order to obtain the pass, he had to get past his assailant. Since no one would see him without the sacred pass, he decided to walk the six blocks home.

Betty called the school. Her son had a substitute teacher, who had just realized she was missing a student. Betty asked about the treatment her son had received, and the school told her that it was standard policy. A student wasn't supposed to be in the school during lunch recess without a pass from a noon duty.

Betty was unable to get her son to tell her who his assailant was. She asked the school if they could sort of watch him a little bit, to find out who it was. Her son shouldn't have to be sent home bleeding. Someone had to see what was going on. The school said it was impossible to find out who was picking on her son. After all, they were dealing with hundreds of children.

I decided to make a visit to the school. I found out what time lunch recess was, and arrived at the school soon after it started. I was parked in the parking lot near the playground. There was some playground equipment near the school, and the school curved around it protectively. There was also a long open space, which bordered the parking lot. This area had some swings and a small sledding hill.

I didn't have to go too far to find my target. In fact, Betty's son came within three or four feet of my car and didn't even recognize me. For twenty minutes, I watched these children. I was wearing a red coat, my car was running, and I was either just standing next to my car, or sitting in it. I tried to look predatory, by intently watching the children play. During that whole twenty minutes, not one adult challenged my presence. In fact, I didn't see any adults on the playground during the whole time I was there.

How easy would it have been to abduct a child from this school? I'm not a predator, so my logic could be flawed. I think I could have easily pulled a child into the car, gone to a car wash, turned my coat inside out, and maybe gotten away without a problem. That is if I was a determined predator. In Alaska, there are lots of open spaces to dispose of bodies.

Betty's mom also went to the school one day. Her grandson didn't pay any attention to her either. Like me, there were no adults anywhere near the area for the twenty minutes that she tried to look menacing.

O) POLITICS: *Dialog With the Commissioner of Education*

After my defeat at the hands of the Assembly and the School Board, I considered other options. I reasoned that if the school districts in Sacramento were dictated by the state when it came to funding, maybe Anchorage was dictated by the state also. Not knowing whom I wanted to write to, exactly, I wrote a letter to the Governor. It was forwarded to the Commissioner of Education. I've never met this woman, but her correspondence was gracious.

She thought my ideas had some merit. However, among other obstacles I would encounter, the law was against me. Particularly, Alaska Statute 14.17.160 student counting periods. This is the law that caused teachers to become anal retentive about attendance in February. Even if both October and February were counted, there might need to be a third counting period (that wasn't currently allowed for), to get an accurate count in a year round setting. The extra counting period might be an added expense for the budget.

She told me she was looking into solutions for budget problems facing the education community in Alaska. She advised me to try to change the law, and encouraged me to approach the School Board again. I knew that approaching the School Board again was inadvisable. They already had their minds made up. I also knew that I didn't speak the right language to communicate with people who had such narrow viewpoints.

I wrote two more letters about questions I had concerning education. Ms Holloway was nice enough to respond to my letters. I decided I had gone as far as I could with my available resources. More correspondence, at this point, would only be a waste of her valuable time.

*1993 YRE Study*

I was told that there had been a comprehensive study done in Anchorage, soon after I arrived. I should get a copy to look at. I went to the School District Office to ask for a copy of this study. One thing I was surprised about was its size. It was over 200 pages long. I expected to pay for my copy of it, but no one could find a price for it, so I got it free.

In the report, it states that the Academic Concerns Subcommittee felt there was no single issue that would be an insurmountable problem for implementing year-round education. It just seemed that there were so many little objections. They suggested site-based choices for the schools. That meant that a school could decide if they wanted to become year-round. There was allowance for three schools to choose this option in the 1993-94 school year, but no one chose to take it.

I noticed a major similarity between the response of parents in California, and the parents in Alaska, when it came to Year Round Education. Despite the number of variables of the two groups, their complaints were all the same. The one difference between Alaska and California was the climate. So many people had claimed that the Alaskan summers were so short, and the winters were so hostile, the children needed to have the summers off. I puzzled over this remark for quite a while and still can't figure out the logic behind it. I would've thought they would need some relief from the hostile winters.

The Family Concerns Subcommittee wasn't able to resolve problems with seasonal work and subsistence lifestyles. In this case, "subsistence lifestyles" means being able to go fishing. In Alaska, there is a window every season for hunting something. I would think the subsistence people would be looking at YRE, because of this aspect. Seasonal work includes people in the construction business. While their children are out of school, they can't go on vacation because they have to work. Without YRE, these people have to decide between having no vacations, or pulling their children out of school (incurring unexcused absences) and taking vacation time during the school year.

I was also surprised by some of the problems for dealing with food services, transportation, and building maintenance. Providing lunches for a year-round schedule seemed to be some sort of hardship for food services. I would have thought that could have generated more revenue. Were they saying "no" to more money?

Transportation argued that they needed the whole summer to do maintenance on the buses. In other businesses, there is a periodic maintenance schedule. Couldn't they buy a few extra buses to allow for some of the buses to be taken out of circulation for periodic maintenance? After all, how many buses could they work on at one time? What happened when buses were pulled out of circulation, when they broke down or were in an accident? Did the system fall apart when that happened?

Building maintenance might have been more of a problem. It's hard to deal with any major projects if the school is constantly full of students. How do office buildings deal with maintenance?

One of the most ironic problems had to do with teachers and the curriculum issues. Teachers were concerned that there wouldn't be enough time to work with other teachers so all the students would have the same curriculum. In a few years, we would be audited as a School District, and be found lacking because of varying curriculums. Teachers were also concerned that there would be problems scheduling conferences, team teaching potential would be reduced, there would be more combined classes, and students would miss assemblies.

On the plus side, YRE could help disadvantaged students and ESL students. It could also lower stress, which can lead to burnout and illness. Burnout can lead to loss of good teachers. The regular breaks also allow students to relieve stress.

Many people who were surveyed suggested that the overcrowding issue would become a non-issue as the Alaskan economy dropped off and the population declined. At this point, there were about 50 schools in the Anchorage School District.

Basically, the report consisted of a lot of "Not in my back yard", union opposition, and "the situation is impossible". It made me sad, because the situation could only become more difficult if they refused to learn California's lesson in time.

## P) POLICIES & PROCEDURES: *Improper Language*

I had been working with the recycling program for the school. After collecting up all the recyclable paper, I usually checked it for foreign objects in the workroom. This process took about half an hour. One of the teachers' aides wore cologne so heavy, it nearly caused me to pass out. All she had to do was pass by me, and my sinuses blocked up. I had seen her pass by groups of children, and their attitude seemed to change for the worse. They became extremely irritable. This woman only smelled like, "Death".

I would take my allergy medicine before I went to school, but her cologne overrode the allergy medicine. I couldn't leave the workroom fast enough after she passed through. There was no air circulation in this room, so the fragrance just hung in the air. I tried to get my work done as quickly as possible, to get away from the offending smell, but I never could move fast enough.

One day, as she breezed through the workroom, my head blocked up and I snapped. I asked her if she really liked smelling like a "street walker". The woman ignored me and walked off, but another parent didn't ignore me. My comment was reported to the principal.

The principal called me and left a message on my answering machine, that she wanted to talk to me when I came in to volunteer the next day. I called the principal and asked why she wanted to see me. After all, I wasn't going to be in the school the next day. By this time, I was home schooling Jeff, and couldn't give much time to volunteering at the school.

The principal said that my unfortunate description of how the woman smelled was unacceptable. The other parent, near the workroom had complained, because I made the comment within the hearing of her three year-old child. The principal said I should have pulled the offending woman aside and spoken to her privately. Since this was the woman I suspected of turning me into Social Services, we weren't on friendly terms. Besides, if I had gotten much closer to her, to speak privately, I might have vomited on her. Come to think of it, that might have been a more effective way of dealing with the situation.

I apologized to the principal for offending the other parent and informed her that I wouldn't be volunteering in the school anymore. I couldn't come to the school if my complaint about her fragrance was the only complaint, and nothing could be done about it. I couldn't afford the recovery time that I had to deal with from each exposure. My only other option was to be drugged into near insensibility.

The principal sent me a note the next day, begging me to reconsider volunteering at the school. I didn't go back for the remainder of the year, because I had my hands full.

# Chapter 12
## Home Schooling 1997

### Q) ALTERNATIVE EDUCATION & GETTING CREDIT: *Not Making the Grade*

On February 28, I received the mid-quarter report from Jeff's school. A form letter from the Counselor was enclosed with the report. Jeff was either failing or nearly failing all of his core classes. The letter pointed out that Jeff would need to pass three out of his four core classes for three out of four semesters to move into high school. In this letter, the Counselor also made an offer of help if it was an educational problem. I only had to let her know what the problem was.

I didn't know if it was an educational problem because I had never been able to monitor any of Jeff's homework, since all his materials had to stay at school. There was obviously a problem, and the school wasn't interested in helping me find a solution. Looking into the smiling faces of the counselor and the principal, I was sure they were amused by my predicament. This problem couldn't go on any longer. I had to try to save my son before he got into High School. But what chance did I have, if the trained professionals couldn't even figure it out?

### P) POLICIES & PROCEDURES: *Storming the School*

I immediately went to the school, and told the secretary that I was there to pick up Jeff. She asked if I had a blue excuse slip for him. I informed her that I wasn't removing him for an appointment, but for good. It took the office half an hour to locate him. It's a good thing it wasn't an emergency.

When Jeff arrived in the office, he was confused. I told him that I was removing him from the school, so he had to empty his locker. While he emptied his locker, I went to the registrar's office to remove him from the rolls. She asked me what day I was planning on removing him. I told her the removal was effective immediately. She started to tell me that I needed to give a full day's notice because books had to be turned in, and paperwork had to be done. The problem couldn't wait a day. (I didn't want the school to have a chance to make an end run around me.) I told her that any books Jeff had at the school would be turned in before we left the building and I expected a receipt. Any books we had at home would either be turned in before the end of the school day, or the next morning. If there was any other business, the school could either call me or write to me. Since the school seemed to think that Jeff's learning difficulties weren't their problem, it was up to me to do my best to help him.

Jeff acted as if my actions were completely unexpected. The timing was the only real surprise. There were only three options, and two were distasteful. The third was out of reach. The first option was getting him tutoring through Sylvan. Unfortunately, to get him the credit he needed, it was about $4200 per subject, and he needed four subjects. This option also required more time than we had before the next school year would start. The second option was having him repeat the eighth grade at this school or we could drive him to another school. Repeating could only damage his self-esteem. The last option was a long shot. We were already midway through third quarter. Would the correspondence school be willing to work with me? I had to try, but Jeff had to be out of a school to be transferred.

I contacted the State's correspondence school. I begged them to send me curriculum for the second semester of the eighth grade. Late enrollment was difficult, but I emphasized that the school he had been attending had indicated to me, in no uncertain terms, that this was my problem to solve. They sent me the paperwork to have his transcript transferred to their files.

### K) CURRICULUM: *The Waiting Game*

It took a month for Jeff's curriculum to arrive. While we waited, I checked out educational videotapes from the library to keep him actively thinking about school subjects. I quizzed him on pages of, "It Pays to Increase Your Word Power", from Reader's Digest. We also invested in some High School Math computer programs to help his Math skills. In order to keep him on track for High School, I had to do something. Pulling him out and letting him vegetate wasn't an option.

When the curriculum came, English and Science weren't too different from what he had been doing when he was in school. The Social Studies curriculum was drastically different. It was US History, and they had been covering more world-oriented Social Studies in the eighth grade. His Math was also quite different. In this class, he had taken a step back. Instead of the algebra we asked for, he was given eighth grade math. I'm not sure if this modification in his curriculum was because of his transcript, which had him near failing in all his classes. Even though he had tested well in algebra for the time he was in the class, his level of competency may not have been immediately apparent.

I would learn later that by moving Jeff out of the school, I might have broken the law. Since Jeff was still labeled "gifted" and had an Individual Education Plan, moving him to the correspondence school could have violated his rights. The correspondence school had no resources for dealing with IEPs.

## S) SICKNESS & HEALTH: *PMS Mom and Hormone Boy*

We started into the schoolwork, and it wasn't a pretty sight. Trying to pull a 14-year old out of school and teaching him in relative isolation wasn't the easiest thing to do. As summer approached, we had our windows open more often. Jeff was complaining about how he wasn't getting any summer vacation and he wasn't able to see his friends. The battle of wills was getting louder. I knew the neighbors could hear everything. The frustration reached epic proportions when he threatened suicide. For a teenager, this might have been a sympathy tactic, but my family had a definite history of depression. I had to take the threat seriously. I still felt I had to fight for my son, even though he was fighting against me. By this age, a boy will usually rebel against his mother, but I was in charge of this particular situation. I had to show him I meant business. I made an appointment with the psychologist.

When we arrived at the appointment, I was shocked by the apparent youth of the counselor. She looked like she was barely out of High School. I decided to dismiss her appearance and gave her a chance to display any of her wisdom for the problem at hand. Jeff and I were both obviously distraught, so I explained the situation to her as factually as possible. I explained the problems and the methods I had used to try to resolve them. I also stated that I was frustrated by the situation and was looking for an objective viewpoint, to see if I was missing anything. The counselor asked to speak to Jeff alone, so I left the room.

Almost half an hour later, I was called back into the room. The counselor explained Jeff's viewpoint to me. Jeff mentioned the RIF process we had just gone through. He felt that he wasn't in control of his own life and that things were changing too fast for him. The change of educational venue had come as a total surprise to him.

The counselor recommended that I was to let Jeff have more control over his life, and I was supposed to control more of the chaos in my own life. Since the RIF situation was over and the Social Services problem was remedied, my life was already less chaotic. The only chaos I had in my life was trying to be a teacher on top of my normal life. Most teachers don't have to work and teach.

I listened to the counselor's recommendations and I wondered if there was an echo in the room. She told me that I was supposed to start doing everything (that I had told her) I was already doing, when we came in! Hadn't she been listening to me?

I paid the fee for the counseling session, but I felt as if my money had just been stolen. I refused to make another appointment. I couldn't afford the bill, as it was. Our insurance didn't cover the counseling, and I didn't really want to have to work longer and harder, so I could pay someone to tell me that I had to do what I was already doing.

The arguments continued at decibel levels that I thought would bring Social Services to our door again. Thank goodness, our neighbors didn't call the authorities.

H) HOMEWORK: *Fumbling Around in the Dark*

The English curriculum was the most difficult for Jeff. While I could get him to do worksheets and tests, I couldn't get him to write any papers. I had never seen two of the concepts they discussed in the lessons. One was diagramming sentences. If we had ever done that in school, it had been done a different way. I don't think I had ever labeled every part of any sentence before. The other concept that I wasn't familiar with was the story web. Outlines had been a real obstacle for me in the fifth and sixth grades. I had truly dreaded them. Like the outline, this tool was supposed to help a student plan a paper. The concept totally eluded me, even though I read everything I could about it.

Jeff had problems with doing a rough draft, a revision, and a final copy. He thought it should be able to be done right on the first try. My perfectionist son. While I have had compliments on my letters to the editor of the local paper, and my letters home to friends and family, creative writing was something I couldn't teach my son. I couldn't present the concept in terms he could understand. I knew how he felt. In High School, Math had been an uncharted, dark tunnel for me. Since becoming an adult, there has been a little more light in that tunnel. Jeff needed to see even a little bit of light, and soon.

We finished units in each subject and turned them in. I was surprised by the results. People could argue that I helped my son pass these classes, but they would have been wrong. I excelled in English and Social Studies. Jeff was making As and Bs in Math and Science, my worst subjects. Trying to grasp some of the concepts in the eighth grade Math book were giving me a headache. Some of the lessons had to be explained to me, by Jeff! If we couldn't make sense of a lesson, we could spend hours comparing the answers for sample problems to what we actually came up with. Once he grasped the concept, I let him run with it.

Science was something we could do together. They sent all the necessary supplies, and the experiments were outlined in great detail. I supplemented the social studies lessons with videotapes from the PBS series, "America". I know Social Studies was a tolerated subject.

I communicated with the English teacher about Jeff's writing. It didn't have to be handwritten, if I could get him to produce anything. He just had to show rough draft, revision, and finished product. I believe he finally wrote two papers. I tricked him into one, and it may have been therapeutic. His longer paper was about how much he hated home schooling. He got a decent grade on it, and the teacher was able to judge his writing skill level.

When all was said and done, Jeff graduated from the eighth grade the day before he entered the ninth grade. His grades were: A for Math; B for Science; C for Social Studies; and a D+ for English. At the time Jeff hated me, but if I hadn't done it, how much time would this smart kid have been held back in the eighth grade, for an obvious problem?

## Chapter 13
## High School 1997-98

A) FIRST IMPRESSIONS: *One Foot in High School*

Jeff had just graduated from the eighth grade the day before he entered High School. We had endured a long battle, but it was over, even if the war still raged.

Melissa was now in the seventh grade. It's amazing how many people didn't realize that she was my daughter, unless I was standing right next to her. Hopefully, that wouldn't happen too often. After all, she's my good student, who does everything right.

Matthew was in the fifth grade. His fourth grade teacher suggested a teacher who would challenge Matthew. I trusted his judgment. After all, he had done such a terrific job understanding Matthew.

E) DIFFERENCES & DISABILITIES: *Gifted Education Revisited*

I went to the middle school for Melissa's Open House. Melissa was on the "Gifted" team in school. One of the parents brought up a very valid point. I hadn't paid attention to which time Melissa had which class, but it became extremely obvious when the gifted students had their class, after this mom asked her question.

The teacher had each class' assignments on the board. Most of the classes had a specified page and either odd or even problems only. Only one class required the entire page. This was the assignment for the gifted class. The mom asked, "Why did the gifted students have to do so much more work than the regular students?" If these students learned things faster, it didn't mean that they should be expected to do twice the work. Extra work should have been given for remedial students, not to the gifted students.

I don't remember if the situation was remedied that year, but the logic made sense to me. The excessive homework meant that our kids worked twice as hard to get the same grade as their non-gifted classmates. The teachers would have protested if they had to do twice the work, for the same amount of money.

*Lisa's Daughter and English as a Second Language (ESL)*

Spanish was Lisa's first language, but her children were raised in a non-Spanish speaking community. They knew Spanish, but they spoke with their friends completely in English.

Lisa's daughter was attending an English class where the teacher was getting a divorce. She spoke to the students about it. Lisa's daughter was very outspoken. She wasn't interested in the teacher's personal problems. They were there to learn about English. Could the teacher please stick to the subject? The teacher called Lisa, and told her that her daughter had been disrespectful to her. This was intolerable, so she wanted the girl moved out of her class

Lisa allowed her daughter to be moved to a different English class. There was only one class that had any openings. It was an "English as a Second Language" class. It didn't seem to matter to the school that Lisa's daughter spoke English quite well already. At conference time, the teacher told Lisa that he didn't understand why her daughter had been put into his class. She obviously didn't fit the profile, and should have been put into a more challenging class. Unfortunately, the school wouldn't move the girl to another class, so she finished out the year being bored, in the ESL class.

F) PROGRAMS: *Caring About Drug Free Youth (CADFY)*

Melissa took this performance-oriented elective, and really enjoyed it. This performance group went to various elementary schools to speak out against getting involved with drugs. One performance I saw covered the concept that marijuana is a "gateway" drug. By starting on marijuana, you'll usually go to harder drugs. I sort of wondered if the ADD medicines were considered to be "gateway" drugs also. Hmm.

In the spring, there was a drug awareness conference in town, and the CADFY students were invited to attend. Melissa told me some things that had shocked the teachers at the conference. If a student is only painting her thumbnail white, the student is most likely using "White-Out" or another corrector fluid on their thumb. It is an inhalant, but it doesn't last very long, so it has to be reapplied often.

In Alaskan winters, it isn't unusual to see teenagers standing on the corner, waiting for the bus with their hands over their ears. Many teens choose not to wear hats. If a student has loose sleeves on their sweaters or sweatshirts, these students may not be warming their ears. They may have solvents on their sleeves, and are sniffing them. The positioning of the hands over the ears puts the edge of the sleeve in easy sniffing reach.

The last thing that I remember Melissa telling me about, she believes she had actually seen herself. Students are allowed to drink sodas in school. An empty soda can with a small amount of solvent at the bottom, is an efficient inhalant method. A student can appear to be drinking the soda, until you look closely. Does the student get the soda can near their mouth, but seems to be distracted from ever actually drinking it? Looking back, Melissa remembered at least one classmate who never seemed to be able to get that can all the way to her lips during lunch.

One of the annual CADFY projects involved the students in the CADFY classes coming to school one day, dressed in black. At regular intervals, a CADFY student would leave the classroom and come back with white paint on their face, carrying a white carnation, and wearing a sticker. These students represented kids that die every day due to substance abuse. The interval is determined by the death statistics for a day. These students aren't allowed to speak, once they are "dead", so there are some scheduling considerations as to when a student "dies". The sticker proclaims how the student died. Melissa's sticker said that she had "burned to death while huffing".

Mid-year, I bought Melissa one of those Chicken Soup books for teenagers. In it there was a reference to a suicide prevention program called "The Yellow Ribbon Program". A family had started this because their son committed suicide, and they hoped that none of his friends would feel as isolated as he had felt. Whatever had caused the problem, he hadn't felt that he could talk to his parents. Would he have told a friend? This couple passed out cards to their son's friends. A teenager signed the card as a pledge that they wouldn't try to take their own life without trying to reach out to someone who might be able to get them help. People who fall into this helpful category are: teachers, counselors, parents, and friends.

Melissa ordered some cards for her school, but they had to be sent to the school. The day the cards arrived, we got a call from the school. A package had arrived at the school for Melissa, and the principal demanded to know what was in it. We hurried back to the school, because we couldn't think of anything, on demand. The box was about the size that you get checks in. Melissa opened the package, than tried to explain the cards to the principal. Could they hand the cards out at their CADFY performances? The principal said she would have to check the matter out with the counselor.

The counselor said that she didn't have any time to deal with this program, so the principal officially forbade the class to circulate the cards. Melissa distributed them unofficially. Considering the counselor is supposed to be a mandatory reporter on disruptive trends (depression, abuse, and neglect), it didn't seem like these innocuous cards would be contrary to her mission.

H) HOMEWORK: *Cubbies and Manila Envelopes*

Matthew's teacher had a shelving unit with little slots or cubbyholes in it to place work for the students. This was generally used to sort corrected homework and fliers that had to be sent home once a week. After the papers were sorted, they were placed in a manila envelope that had the child's name on it.

Parents were to remove the papers, and sign the envelope. It was to be returned to the teacher before the next week's work was due home. This was a slight variation on the system in California.

After seeing how homework was handed out normally, I wished the teacher had required the homework be placed in the cubbies. That way, everyone would have the homework they needed, and the teacher would know who forgot to pick theirs up. As the system was, homework papers were handed out just before the bell rang. All the kids scrambled to get out of the classroom, and the floor would be littered with homework papers that had been left behind.

## I) DRUGS & WEAPONS: *The Drug Test*

One of Melissa's friends came to school. She needed glasses and usually wore contacts. In her hurry to get to school this morning, she could only find one contact, couldn't find her glasses, and forgot to take her ADD medicine. In school, she was shaky and was having vision problems. The counselor saw her and decided that the girl probably had a drug problem.

The girl's mother was called, and the counselor informed her that someone needed to pick the girl up from school. She wouldn't be admitted back without a drug test. The counselor also suggested that the girl be monitored after school, to make sure she wasn't indulging in any drugs.

Of course, the girl did have a drug problem. Because she forgot her prescribed ADD medicine that morning, she was having symptoms of withdrawal from "speed". No other drugs were found in her system, and her mother was at wit's end trying to figure out how her daughter could be monitored after school. Everyone she knew worked the same hours she did. I offered to have her daughter come home with Melissa after school. They could do their homework together.

This arrangement went on for about six weeks. After that, the mother was sure that her daughter wasn't taking any drugs, and as far as the school knew, her daughter was still being monitored.

## K) CURRICULUM: *Everyday Math Will Be Taught Exclusively*

Mary's son was in the fourth grade when she first heard about "Everyday Math". The teachers had been learning about it for a while, but after Christmas vacation, it would be implemented exclusively. From what Mary had heard of the program, each year was supposed to build on what the student had learned the year before. It didn't seem like they should just plug the program into the school on all grade levels, mid-year. They should have introduced it as if they were closing a zipper. Starting at the bottom, and working their way up.

By springtime, it was evident that the students were having problems with the program, so some experts were sent to the school to try to figure out why the students were having difficulty. The experts spent two weeks making no more progress than the teachers had. The students barely understood the materials either way. It seemed the program might be flawed.

So much money was invested in this program, by the School District, that it had to succeed. Teachers were banned from supplementing the program with outside materials, unless they wanted to lose their jobs. Mary's son's teacher was going to retire at the end of the year. She was willing to risk the consequences, to help her students succeed.

Teachers were expected to use the program exclusively, and to increase their class' scores at testing time. Could they meet both requirements? I don't think so. I understand slipping scores required teachers to use supplemental materials. No school wants to have a population that's failing. Failure is unacceptable, and I think the principal can be held responsible for this. My hypothesis is, there was a tacit agreement between teachers and principals, to supplement Math materials. This covert activity would be quite widespread in a few years.

*The Teacher from Hell*

Two years earlier, Linda's son had this Kindergarten teacher, and absolutely loved her. My friend Lauren had her first son entering Kindergarten this year. I told her she was lucky to have this teacher for her son, because she was absolutely wonderful. I was so wrong.

Lauren's son started school and was abused and degraded by this teacher. She was always yelling at him and isolating him from the other students. It seemed that the teacher's husband was seriously ill. For some reason, she was taking her frustration out on this five-year old boy.

Children aren't disposable. They can't be treated like garbage, just because a teacher is having a bad day. If a teacher has such a serious problem, they shouldn't be working with the children.

Lauren pulled her son out of the school, and started home schooling him. She also started home schooling his little brother and a couple of the neighbor's children. When they get to High School, they can choose whether they want to attend the regular school or not. For now, they're happy where they are, and their grades are great.

## N) SAFETY & SECURITY: *Unauthorized Entry*

Matthew came home with an interesting story one afternoon. After lunch that day, an older man, who was somewhat disoriented, had entered the school through a door that led from the playground. He went into the Kindergarten room, which was right next to Matthew's class. It took a while to get someone to remove the intruder from the classroom. I don't know if the school had any policy revisions to deal with an intruder who just walks into the building.

There is a way that the doors can be locked from the outside, but opened from the inside. If they had been set this way, the incident might have been prevented. If anyone complains that students having recess won't have easy access to the building, the noon duties could be carrying a key for the door.

## *Losing Her Lunch*

The School District tells you not to bring anything valuable to the school, in case it gets stolen. Melissa had to share her locker, because she was a seventh grader. Her locker partner gave all her friends the combination. Sometimes, Melissa would go to her locker to pick up her lunch, only to find it gone. She would come home starving, because she found it hard to eat breakfast.

In the Middle School, you weren't allowed to eat snacks in class, so she couldn't nibble on a breakfast bar when she finally got hungry. She also wasn't allowed to carry her lunch into class. This couldn't be helping her grades.

Despite multiple efforts to change her locker, she was unable to. Finally, she took matters into her own hands and started sharing a locker with an amenable eighth grader. She was finally able to secure her lunch.

## O) POLITICS: *Substitute Shortage*

After the early retirement of several teachers, the substitute pool was severely depleted. Many of the empty teaching positions were now being filled by former substitutes. Supposedly, there were about 3,000 teachers teaching in our system. On an average day, it can be expected that 10% of the teachers will need to have a substitute. Some of these teachers are ill and others are taking classes.

Melissa came home one day and told me about the substitute they had in one of her classes. He was a very disagreeable man. He told the class outright that he hated children and had retired from teaching. The students asked why he was a substitute if he hated children. He responded, "Because there's a teacher shortage."

Substitutes can decide which jobs they want to accept. They get a straight fee for the day, but no benefits. I wonder how often this teacher chose to sub. Was being hostile his way to keep the students from trying to "sink the sub"?

In Jeff's Biology class, his teacher had an emergency and wouldn't be in school for a couple days. Jeff's class was the first class of the day, and a substitute hadn't been located yet. The teacher in the room next door realized there was no teacher in Jeff's classroom, so he turned on a video for the students to watch. Jeff's class was a pretty well disciplined group. It had taken nearly half the class time for the neighboring teacher to realize there wasn't a teacher in the classroom. Other classes might have been more noticeable about being unsupervised.

## P) POLICIES & PROCEDURES: *Pink Hair*

One of Melissa's classmates decided to dye her hair hot pink. One of the school's rules declared that no student should have hair of an unnatural color. The girl and her parents both knew about this rule before she colored her hair.

When the girl came to school, she turned quite a few heads with her neon hair. The principal called the girl's parents and informed them that their daughter would be suspended until she dyed her hair to a more natural color. In order to achieve that objective, the girl would have needed to bleach her hair again, and apply more dye. Over-processing her hair could potentially cause her to lose her hair. I think, coming to school bald might cause a little more disruption.

Her parents refused to make her change her hair color. They felt that the hair color was a fashion statement, and wasn't a threat to anyone. The less notice given to the hair color by the adults, the sooner the problem would go away. I think the parents understood that their daughter was just trying to be shocking. After all, students this age start trying to push the envelope. When I was that age, I remember my classmates trying out various messages on their T-shirts. How far could they go before the administration voiced an objection?

I think the parents chose their battle well. I think their intervention would have been more effective towards problems with the education or safety of their daughter. If the school had spent the energy on educational problems, rather than addressing shock value issues, who knows how successful they could have been?

In the end, the girl was allowed to have her pink hair, and the novelty wore off. Then she started wearing her hair with two or three dozen pigtails sticking straight out, all over her head. After all, there were no rules against it.

## *Recess Problems*

Matthew was still having trouble at recess. Because it was winter, the playground was icy. The sledding hill was off limits. Matthew complained that the noon duties kept putting him "on the wall". Basically, it is a punishment where a student has to stand still near one of the walls at the school. I wondered what he was doing wrong.

I went out to the playground to watch, at lunchtime. I saw Matthew run though an area, and the noon duty immediately put him on the wall. The noon duty watched eight other children run through the same area, without disciplining them. I wondered about this.

After lunch, I spoke with the assistant principal. I said that I thought Matthew was being unfairly targeted. I named the noon duty that had singled Matthew out. The assistant principal told me that there was no one with that name as a noon duty, so I described her and said that she was Melissa's classmate X's mother. Maybe the girl's mom had a different last name. I still got a blank look.

I asked the assistant principal if there were any guidelines that could help Matthew to know which areas were off limits. The assistant principal told me that I should have attended the noon duty meeting the previous evening if I wanted my questions answered. I hadn't had a clue about the noon duty meeting. It wasn't something that was advertised to the general school population. This woman would be of no help to me. Things were melting down in Matthew's class, and we would be leaving soon. After that, I didn't think I would have to deal with this clueless woman again.

## Q) ALTERNATIVE EDUCATION & GETTING CREDTIT: *The Algebra Test*

Jeff got a rocky start for high school. Because of the problem we had getting his Math curriculum in the home schooling program, Jeff was put back into Algebra. He had only the first two weeks to change his schedule, and the administration wouldn't move him because he didn't have a second semester grade to show for Algebra. Since he hadn't completed the course, they wouldn't promote him.

Jeff was lucky though, he had a teacher who decided to give the class a test to see what everyone knew. The test the teacher gave was the final exam. Jeff passed the test with over 90%. That meant he was eligible for the Geometry class. There was very little the teacher needed to teach him, so spending a whole year in the class would have been a waste of time. He was moved into the Geometry class just under the wire, but he missed the review time. He still had a few gaps he needed to fill in, but he managed to make the repairs before the year ended.

His Geometry teacher required 10 proofs for each assignment. She felt that if you could come up with 10 proofs, you understood the material. Jeff was good at Math, so coming up with 10 proofs was going to be easy. Writing them down might have been a little harder. Melissa wouldn't be so lucky when she got into Geometry.

### Eliminate Electives

I heard one of the School Board members on the radio recently. They were discussing graduation standards. This woman suggested we concentrate on the basics, and eliminate the electives. At the current time, students need 22.5 credits to graduate. 7.5 of them needed to be electives. Electives include variety in Social Studies and English classes, and foreign languages, as well as the arts and music classes. If we eliminated the electives, students would only need 15 credits to graduate. A student could finish high school in three years, rather than four. If they were college-bound, they would have to take the recommended two years of a foreign language that many colleges ask for, through private means.

Art and music help with critical thinking, but these programs are already severely cut back. Sports programs are still heavily promoted, however. I was happy to hear that this woman wouldn't be around much longer. She was moving out of state. Hopefully, no one would pay too much attention to her opinion.

### I Can't Teach Your Child

When Matthew's fourth grade teacher had suggested placing Matthew in a certain teacher's class for the fifth grade, I had trusted his judgment. Everything seemed to be going fine, until third quarter.

It seemed like Matthew's teacher started loudly complaining to me, any day that I showed up in the classroom, that she couldn't teach my son. I thought this was extreme, since his classmates were also in the room. A couple weeks into third quarter, Matthew's desk was placed facing the wall. The teacher could be teaching his classmates, who were facing the teacher, but he would have to twist in his chair to see the lesson, since she was behind him. A couple times, I noticed homework being handed out at the end of the day. None was put on Matthew's desk, because it was so far away from the others. I had wondered why he hadn't been bringing any homework home.

I noticed the video camera and recorder (left from a previous project) were still sitting in the classroom. I suggested that I could bring a tape in, the camera could be pointed at Matthew's desk on a day he would be in class all day, and the button could be pushed on the recorder. My presence in class wasn't going to help me figure out how he was misbehaving, but passive surveillance could. If a piece of cloth were placed over the recorder's display, no one would realize it was taping. After all, the camera and recorder had been sitting in the classroom for weeks. A minor adjustment in direction of the camera wouldn't be noticed.

The teacher said she couldn't tape Matthew without the principal's permission. Since it was nearly impossible to get an audience with the principal, unless you misbehaved, I chose to move Matthew out of the school.

I don't know what the teacher's problem was. I do know that she was getting complaints from her own son's teacher about behavioral problems. Did Matthew really have behavioral problems, or was the teacher transferring her frustration onto me? I tried to home school Matthew unsuccessfully. He was weak in several areas of Math, and he absolutely hated Social Studies.

His teacher's usual method of punishment was placing students in the hallway. After I pulled him out, I found out how much time he had been spending in that hallway. Without a watch or other clock to look at, he didn't know how much class he missed. The teacher never told him how much time he had to be in the hallway. Other teachers would see him out there, but they had no idea he had been out there a long time. They only saw him when they were passing through the hallway. Because there was another classroom between his classroom and the hallway, the teacher would forget about him, and he couldn't cut through the other classroom without permission. He usually had his Social Studies book with him when he was sent out to the hallway, so he had read it cover to cover.

My friends asked why I didn't know my son was being abused this way. After all, I volunteered in the school. I told them, it was the same way that other parents don't know their children are being abused. The children aren't abused when their own parent is in the school. The teacher knew when I was going to be in the school, so she didn't put him out in the hallway when she knew I was there. I doubt that the long periods of isolation helped him keep up with his class work. There should have been another way to work with him.

It seems that putting a student outside a classroom was acceptable punishment in the School District. My friend Elaine's son was told to sit outside the classroom, once. His classroom was a portable, and it was winter. When the boy realized there would be no reprieve, self-preservation took over. He went into the main office to warm up, until class ended. Of course, he was punished for not having stayed outside and freezing. Elaine spoke to the school. No other student was placed outside during her son's class time. It's hard to say if the teacher was disciplined.


R) REDUCE, REUSE & RECYCLE: *Conserving Newsletters*

In the neighborhood school, they tried to reduce the amount of paperwork going home by sending one copy per house, through the child of your choosing. Your oldest might not be the most responsible, so you might want your papers sent home through a younger child. If this had been the way things worked in that school, they could have saved at least 72 pieces of paper with just the newsletter, in our household.

In this school, they actually used the concept of one paper per family. The cubbies or envelopes had an indicator, if a child was supposed to take home the family's papers. It was about time that someone cut down the amount of papers being sent home, but this year, I only had one child in the elementary school, so it didn't make much difference in our house.


S) SICKNESS & HEALTH: *Migraine Medicine*

When Jeff entered the high school, we took his medicines to the nurse's office. He would be allowed to carry his asthma inhaler on his person, as long as he had a special sticker on it. I was surprised when the nurse said he could also carry his migraine medicine, because it's a relatively controlled substance. It has a tranquilizer in it. I didn't want anyone trying to lift the medicine off him.

The other problem with him carrying his medicine on his person, was trying to take it. Besides being better to take it privately, in the nurse's office, I wondered if he would be able to see his pill and find the nurse's office. If his vision was going, he might need help getting to the nurse's office.

I felt more secure if the nurse administered his medicine and called me immediately. The nurse seemed to think I was overprotective, but accepted responsibility for the medicine. I wondered if she ever had a migraine.

## W) SEX: *He Said, She Said*

Melissa had been doing really well in school. She seemed to be relatively happy. One day, she came home from school looking very pale, and promptly vomited. She said, during the school day, people she didn't know kept asking her if she was Melissa McDonald. When she answered that she was, each person asked if she had "done (a certain boy) for a dollar." After the first couple times that strangers asked her who she was, she shut down. The idea of performing oral sex on the boy in question nauseated her.

Her Social Studies teacher noticed her unusual pallor and asked if she was ill. Melissa told her what the problem was and the teacher advised her to get help from one of the principals. Melissa put in a request to see a principal, but by the time report cards came out almost two weeks later, nothing had been done about her request.

The first week, kids had been asking her if the rumor was true. Sometimes, boys would walk down the hallway, waving a dollar and announcing, "Melissa, I have a dollar." The rumor had started when the boy in question had announced to his Science class that she had done him for a dollar. The teacher wasn't in the room at the time. One of Melissa's friends was in that class, and told her about it.

At conference time, the teacher asked if the problem had been addressed, because Melissa's grades were still down. When I told her, "No", she suggested I should contact the principals. After that, Melissa was repeatedly pulled out of her Math classes to defend herself. The harassment increased, and I decided to get into the act. Major mistake on my part.

I dressed in my best "Donna Reed" style outfit, complete with pearls, and stood outside the school with a sign that proclaimed that this Middle School supported sexual harassment. A principal came out and invited me into the school. After listening to my complaint, they said that they had seen several students from each side of the issue. Unfortunately, witnesses in favor of Melissa's story happened to be people she knew. The witnesses who defended the boy heard the boy make the statement, but chose to lie about the situation. Therefore, since no impartial witnesses could be found, it was a case of "He said, She said". The principals refused to ask any of the students in his Science class, who Melissa didn't know. I feel my involvement, at this point, actually made matters worse. It might have been dying down some already.

The boy's mother was very upset about the situation. Why was Melissa saying such bad things about her son? I asked her why her son was saying such bad things about Melissa? Matthew had heard the boy make the claim, but again, he's biased. Melissa had no classes with this boy, and hadn't even thought about him for most of the year. The mother said she was going to make her son write an apology note to Melissa.

The school delivered the note to Melissa. The contents basically said, "I'm sorry you feel you have to make up stories about me. I really like you, and I would never say anything like that." This incident almost cost Melissa her Math grade because of being pulled out of class so often to answer the charges. The Math teacher had no clue as to what was going on. The lesson Melissa learned from this situation was if you have a problem, don't tell anyone about it. Telling only makes things worse for you.

I would remember this situation when I heard a news story with similar proof a few years later.

119

## Chapter 14
## Return to the Neighborhood School 1998-99

A) FIRST IMPRESSIONS: *Beating My Head Against the Wall*

Jeff was still having trouble with his writing. After failing the summer school class, where the teacher had helpfully told him to "write more", we enrolled him in a Graduation Supplemental Services (GSS) class for his ninth grade English requirement. We hadn't even gotten to the hard stuff, yet: Composition. If we couldn't get him past the easy roadblocks, how would we be able to get him to write compositions? Melissa started the 8th grade with a good attitude, but it quickly faded in the first two weeks. The violin she had loved to play was quiet more often. The school had changed orchestra teachers, and it had been a change for the worse. She also had a Social Studies teacher with such a heavy accent that Melissa could barely understand her. It didn't make the subject she disliked any easier to deal with.

I was still attempting to home school Matthew, but it was becoming a battle of wills. I would have to cut my losses and put Matthew back into the neighborhood school. There was a different principal, and new teachers at the school. Maybe the attitude had changed. I could try to adjust my thinking and give the assistant principal, from the neighboring school, the benefit of doubt. I could act outwardly as if she might do better as a principal. I could still paste a smile on my face as I kept my eyes open. We would see how she would do.

There was no way that I couldn't be required to interact with the school personnel. I was Matthew's parent. I'm sure he wasn't happy to have a lightening rod for a parent.

C) PARENT-TEACHER ENTITY: *Just a Friendly Family Group*

Jeff was in Band class. With the desperate financial situation for music programs in recent years, parents of band members thought we could use a tool that the sports programs have been using successfully for years. The tool was a booster club.

The idea seemed sound enough at the first meeting. We needed to do something. Our High School was allowed $500 out of the budget to cover five bands. Our band wasn't as proficient as East High's band. They had actually won a prestigious award for a recorded album. Had there been more community support at the other school, or were their students just so much more talented than our students were?

The turnout for the first meeting was quite small but we had enough people to chair a board, with a few parents to spare. Our first mission was to develop some viable bylaws. We had an incomplete set of bylaws from another school that had been trying to launch a booster club for the past two years.

During the second meeting, I was the secretary. It was a straightforward job. We discussed the wording of the bylaws. At one point, someone mentioned that the language sounded quite legal. Some of it had to be, especially language pertaining to money matters. There was some discussion about removing some of this legalese. I spoke up and said that every paragraph that related to money needed to stay in the bylaws, to protect us. After what I had seen with the PTA, the bylaws were the only things that had protected my friends.

The president of the group said, "Why do we need so many rules? After all, we're just a friendly family organization." I responded, "That may be fine for now, but when we add money to the equation, everything changes." I couldn't believe the reaction I got from these parents. Most of them had children older than mine. With all this life experience, one would think that they wouldn't be so naïve. For instance, the president had several years of leadership experience in various school activities and organizations. Even if the rest of the parents were looking at me as if I had arrived from another planet, it would seem the president should have understood my point. The rest of the group was more concerned that the language of the bylaws be politically correct.

I took the minutes for the second meeting and turned in a pristine example of my work at the next meeting, with my resignation. The band booster club limped along for the rest of the year, and became nearly non-existent after that.

It took me a couple years to figure out why the group failed. The first problem was lack of viable bylaws. To be able to develop decent bylaws, we should have looked at a minimum of three examples of bylaws for established organizations that fit our status. Organizations like PTA and Little League might have been good places to ask.

Our second problem was the naïve attitude of the charter members. Even without this problem, our organization had more risk of being unsuccessful than a sports booster club did.

The band had most of its practices during the school time, and it's relatively private. They have fewer performances that the public actually sees. A flute player doesn't have the visibility and prestige of a favorite quarterback. The schools have pep assemblies for sports. Between the pep assemblies and the mandatory attendance at sporting events to earn their grade, the band is barely noticed or acknowledged. The sports are in the spotlight.

With the sports, the practices take place outside of school time. They are usually out in the open, where spectators can see. There are more public performances and people are expected to pay for these performances. At sporting events, there's extra money made when people buy food from the concessions stand. There's rarely a concession stand for a school's musical performance.

Until people realize that being part of a musical group is a positive "belonging" situation, booster clubs for the music departments will fail.

## E) DIFFERENCES & DISABILITIES: *Impossible Goals*

Dolly's daughter was still having comprehension and retention problems with her Math, in High School. Her counselor dealt exclusively with special education students. The girl failed her first year of Math, so she was placed in the same class a second time. Midway through her second year, the class had a long-term substitute teacher who realized that Dolly's daughter wasn't grasping the concepts. She should have been in a class that offered her a little more assistance.

When Dolly confronted the counselor about the situation, the counselor defended himself by saying he thought she just needed to stretch and reach for a higher goal. Stretching may be fine, but if she failed the first year, he should have realized he placed her in a class that was too advanced. Somebody should have seen the danger signs sooner.

In a curriculum where a student needs 22.5 of a possible 24 credits to graduate, Dolly's daughter had lost 2 valuable credits. What was the IEP process for if the school was just going to throw the students into whichever class was convenient, and not necessarily the one that met their needs?

### *Can You Test for Dysgraphia?*

I believe I had been reading a Time magazine article, while I was in a doctor's office, when I first saw the term "Dysgraphia". The description was quite enlightening. It felt as if a window had opened. I wrote down the symptoms. Some seemed like Jeff (*):

Generally illegible handwriting
Inconsistencies: Mixtures of upper/lower cases and/or print/cursive or irregular size, shape, or slant of letters.
Unfinished words or letters, skipped words *
Position of words not consistent with lines and margins
Irregular spacing between letters and words
Cramped or unusual grip on writing implement *

Strange wrist, body, or paper position *
Talking to self, while writing, or paying more attention to writing hand
Slow or labored copying or writing, even if writing is neat *
Content doesn't reflect student's other language skills *
Major erasing, and rewriting *
Heavy pressure on paper *

I went to the school and asked the counselor if they could test Jeff specifically, for Dysgraphia. The counselor said that they could, and Jeff was run through a battery of tests. The verdict came back. Jeff didn't have a learning disability, he was gifted. His writing problem was probably just laziness.

I was angry when I found out that Jeff had been subjected to the same testing he had done several times before, for his gifted certification. I could have told the counselor that particular testing wouldn't be of any help, unless they could interpret past results with a new light. Was Jeff really lazy? I tried to push him harder.

F) PROGRAMS: *An Unacceptable Exhibition*

Melissa was in Orchestra class, and they had their Winter Concert. The Orchestra shared the night with the Dance class and the Choir. Of the three performance groups, I thought the dancers were least prepared. I gathered that the Dance class was allowed to choreograph their own presentations. Since this was the first year to have the Dance class, I'm not sure what the curriculum was. To me, it seemed like there had been very little supervisory input in the choreography. The dancers, who had so much energy, seemed to put it all into moves that bordered on obscene, because of duration and lack of variation. I felt sorry for the students, who seemed to lack guidance. An adult should have intervened long before the performance. Who was responsible for the performance of the students? The same person who takes credit for any successes the school has.

I received a letter from the school about a day after the performance. It follows:

"Dear Parent,
I appreciate your attendance at our Winter Concert on Thursday night. The Choir and Orchestra performances were outstanding and reflected our School's fine musical tradition. Thank you for your continued support!
I want to personally extend my apology for the dance portion of the program. While this segment did give students the opportunity to perform, many of the elements of the performance were inappropriate. In the future, every attempt will be made to make sure every student performance at our School will meet the highest of standards."

The principal signed the letter. I wonder how the dance students felt when they found out about this letter. The principal was in charge of the school, so why was she shocked about the performance? She should have shown some interest sooner. I believe Dance class was dropped the next year.

*Bilingual and Indian Education*

There were two programs in the school that weren't there when I was a student. Indian Education, which dealt with students whose parents were Native Alaskan (and provided cultural education for the rest of the students), and Bilingual Education, which primarily dealt with students who spoke Spanish. I saw more of the Indian Education program than I did the Bilingual. The students learned about Native dancing and music one year.

In a school district that has over 80 languages, it seemed like it would be extremely difficult to do a bilingual program that didn't exclude anyone who needed it, and actually did justice to all the languages. Having been an exchange student and serving in the military, it seems to me that immersion is the most productive way to learn a language. This means jumping in with both feet.

I remember seeing a television interview with author, Betty Bao Lord. She's a Chinese author. In the interview, she mentioned that when she came to the United States there was only one other Chinese student in her class. The other girl spoke a different dialect, so they couldn't communicate. Her educational survival depended on learning English, and fast. So she did.

Matthew had a friend who was Russian. The boy had been in this country a little over a year. When you learn a second language, you might be a little slower processing it. Matthew's class had several substitute teachers, while his teacher was attending outside classes. A few times, the substitute would explain the assignment to the class, then expect them to get started quietly. The explanation would be quick and the Russian student had trouble grasping the information at the speed it was given. Matthew noticed the confusion, so he explained the assignments to the boy at a slower rate. The Russian student wasn't wearing a sign that said, "English Is My Second Language", so the substitutes thought the boys were just visiting. Matthew always got into trouble for talking and was never allowed to explain. Sometimes, the directions just had to be slowed down a little.

Is the bilingual program a crutch, or does it really serve a purpose? I don't know. It depends on how people whose children participate in this program, feel.

## G) TRANSPORTATION & FIELD TRIPS: *Who Carries That Much Insurance?*

Matthew's class was going on a field trip, and the trip they were going on would be using privately owned vehicles for the transportation. I went to the office to get the Insurance Confirmation Form, as I had for the past several years. This time, the secretary challenged me. She needed to see proof that my insurance was sufficient. Her comment was, "Who carries that much insurance on their car?" It was 8:30 in the morning, and my insurance policy was sitting on my desk at home. I ran home to get it, because I wasn't sure there was enough time to get the information from the insurance company, over the phone.

The insurance confirmation form says:

"The undersigned states that he/she wishes to provide pupil transport on an individual basis for school sponsored programs, i.e., field trips, etc., at Generic School for the (current) school year and that he/she is licensed to drive in the State of Alaska and will carry auto liability insurance in the minimum amount of $100,000/$300,000 bodily injury and $10,000 property damage throughout the school year."

Supposedly, the bodily injury requirement was considered to be more than the normal person would carry on their car. I wasn't a normal person. I was a parent volunteer, who would be transporting six students. If the office thought that no one had that much insurance on their cars, why did the schools solicit parents to drive for field trips? Did the secretary scrutinize every other parent who volunteered to drive this year, as much as she scrutinized me?

## H) HOMEWORK: *Only One Way*

Jeff was taking an English class, where he had to write reports. He wasn't turning anything in, so the teacher spoke with us about the problem. I told her that I had tried to get Jeff to write, but I wasn't sure what the problem was.

The teacher had heard him give oral presentations. His vocabulary was fantastic. When a classmate had asked how he knew so many words, he told them that he had the vocabulary of a high school senior from 20 years ago. He read like crazy. A book wasn't meant for show, he devoured them. The teacher just needed something tangible, to be able to grade, and she would accept about any medium Jeff would like. She said she would accept reports that had been typed on the computer or reports on audiotape. She was willing to go off the beaten path because her brother had a learning disability and nearly failed in High School, because there was no allowance. He's very successful now, since he can modify his work to fit his abilities. Jeff didn't have to prove his spelling, and he wasn't learning how to construct sentences in a foreign language, so writing by hand wasn't a necessary requirement.

Jeff refused to try either option. He had been told, for so long, by so many teachers, that there was only one way to do the assignments in their class. He also didn't want to be different. I tried to explain to him that he didn't have to be obvious about handing his material in, but he wouldn't budge. I think it didn't help that his mom was pushing for an option. Teens want to feel they are in charge of their own lives, and I was using a very heavy hand to push him forward. He limped through the rest of the semester, only turning in about a quarter of his homework. He barely passed the class.

*Group Projects*

The concept of group projects had bothered me for a long time, but if you can't offer a solution for a problem, it's hard to complain effectively. This year, Melissa had been put in a couple groups. They couldn't get together after school, and the other students wouldn't bring their work to school. All the kids had computers, but it seemed like ours had the only working printer.

Melissa had her part of the project done a while back, and the other kids said they would e-mail her their parts, so she could print it all up together. One of her teammates sent a very brief paragraph with no references. The other teammate sent only references like "Encyclopedia Britannica pages 84-85". Both of her teammates sent this information to her at 10 PM, the night before the project was due. Since her grade depended on it, she did repair work on the report until about 1 AM. Then, she had to wind down to get some sleep and be up again at 6AM. The group received a good grade at Melissa's expense.

Betty's son had to do a group report towards the end of the year. I liked his teacher's solution for the inequity of participation. The report would officially be divided up into sections. Each student was assigned a section. When the time came to read their report, each student would read their section. The group would get a grade for the whole report, and each student would get a grade for their portion. No one in the group could hide behind anyone else.

I). DRUGS & WEAPONS: *Contact High*

Melissa was in CADFY again this year. In this class, they pledged to stay drug-free. Melissa took that pledge seriously, but staying drug-free wasn't that easy. Especially, on the school bus.

Melissa got on the school bus after school, and there were only a few seats open near the back of the bus. After the bus leaves the school, students aren't allowed to move to another seat. Our stop was the last stop.

Melissa was sitting on the bus when another student produced a bong and promptly lit it. He passed it around to his friends, who all took a hit. Melissa doesn't like the smell of marijuana, because it makes her nauseous. It seemed like half the bus was getting high, but the bus driver didn't seem to notice. Or maybe, the driver was enjoying the marijuana, too.

It's hard to turn someone in if they can hear you make a complaint. Melissa wasn't about to become a martyr. Since she was the last person off the bus, she mentioned the bong to the bus driver. She also provided the offending student's name. When she came home, she called the school and made a complaint.

Of course, nothing was ever done about it. About an hour after exposure, Melissa munched out on all the chocolate we had around. Very unusual for my daughter who can only tolerate chocolate in small amounts.

K) CURRICULUM: *The Mass Exodus*

Melissa was in Orchestra class. The teacher she had loved so much the previous year had left. She had burned out on Middle School Orchestra, and was taking a breather dealing with elementary students. This is a perfectly normal and acceptable activity for a teacher, but this isn't what her students were told.

The new teacher spent the first two weeks of class telling the students how horrible they were, and how their last teacher left them because they had been so offensive. The music the new teacher assigned didn't challenge any of the students either. Many of the pieces were arrangements they had played in elementary school.

If any one would have cared to notice, students evacuated that class as fast as rats jumping from a sinking ship. One of Melissa's friends chose Home Economics over Orchestra. Like all the other students who participated in the mass exodus, he gave an excuse that the school accepted. In his case, he said he thought he would take the opportunity to learn how to cook.

I saw the former teacher at the winter performance. When she finished speaking to the current teacher, I asked her if the students had truly driven her away? She was shocked by my question, and vehemently denied any wrongdoing on the part of the students. She had just needed a change of scenery. Why had I thought she had been unhappy with the students? I told her the new teacher repeated the message daily, for the first two weeks of school. I wonder if she noticed that the students had performed without any life.

*The Japanese Petition*

Our high school was the only regular high school in the District that didn't offer Japanese. Jeff wanted to have Japanese offered, so he tried to show support for the language by having a petition. He got several signatures on the petition. Unfortunately, the petition was thrown out due to the fact that the majority of students who had signed it were graduating seniors. Jeff was determined to try again, the next year, and get "legal" signatures on the paper.

M) DISCRIMINATION, HARASSMENT & ABUSE: *Get a Restraining Order*

Jeff was five foot six and a hundred ten pounds at Christmastime. We knew Jeff was having trouble at school with a pack of bullies. Their favorite torture was chasing him in the halls at school. Jeff never slowed down to find out what they wanted. The halls were so choked with students sometimes, that the average person wouldn't realize he was being pursued. He knew who was calling him, so he just tried to stay as far away from them as possible.

One day, Jeff said one of the security people had noticed his problem. She told him she would get him a formal complaint form. After two weeks of waiting, Jeff finally asked the security person which form he needed to fill out. It took him two and a half hours to fill out the form.

The bullies continued to harass Jeff and his friends at lunchtime. Over a week after Jeff turned in his form, there was an incident. The bullies were blocking the doorway of the room where Jeff and his friends were eating lunch. His friend Taylor had to catch a bus to his next class. Unable to push his way through the obstruction without using his hands, Taylor raised his hands to push the obstruction out of his way and ended up bloodying one of the boys' noses. The penalty for fighting was a 13-day suspension. The hearing was scheduled to take place a few days later at the school district building.

I went to the school security office to get a copy of Jeff's complaint. The security principal wasn't there, but the security people looked for the paper. It was on a disorderly pile, on the principal's desk. No wonder the complaint hadn't been addressed yet. After I made the copy, I returned the original. I also made a copy for Jeff's English teacher. At least this was an example of his writing.

I gave a copy of the complaint to Taylor's father. I thought it might be helpful in the hearing. I also said we would be willing to testify. Even though we went to the hearing, we weren't allowed to speak and Taylor got 13 days suspension from school. Nothing was done to the students who started the conflict. Jeff and his friends were banned from having their lunch in the classroom.

A couple more weeks passed without any action being taken about Jeff's complaint. One day, Jeff was sitting on the school bus, getting ready to go home from school. Everyone is assigned to a school bus, and Jeff saw the ringleader of the bullies get on the bus. Jeff was near the back of the bus, so there wasn't much he could do about the situation. Almost as soon as the other boy sat down, the bus driver started moving the bus. Once the bus is in motion, it can't be stopped. There's too much chance of causing an accident at this point. The bus driver was a substitute, and there was no way that Jeff could let the man know that the other boy didn't belong on the bus.

Jeff got off the bus with Thomas, who lived on our street. One of the bullies lived on our street, so he and his buddies got off the bus, too. Jeff and Thomas made a run Thomas' house. As they were trying to get the door unlocked, a fully loaded backpack hit the door, just inches above their heads. The boys were being assaulted, and the school had delivered their assailants to the doorstep. The school is supposed to be responsible for our children from door-to-door. At least that's what they say. From the time our student leaves the house in the morning, until they get back from school, is supposed to be school jurisdiction.

I took the boys to the school to speak with security. I said that this problem had gone on a long time and the school needed to get involved. The security principal told us that it had been Jeff's responsibility to notify the bus driver of the stowaway. It wasn't the school's responsibility, because the incident did not happen on school property. He advised us to get a restraining order.

We went downtown to try to get a restraining order. This pursuit was futile also. When we got up to the counter to ask the woman for a form, she asked us what the relationship of the assailant was to our boys. When they answered, "Classmate", she dismissed us. We couldn't take legal action against these boys unless blood was drawn. Alaska State law apparently didn't allow for restraining orders unless there is a relationship.

A couple days later, I went to the school with Thomas' mother. We demanded to speak with the principal. The situation was becoming intolerable. The principal didn't want to listen, but we told him that we would petition a higher authority if he didn't do anything. He finally agreed to have a meeting with our boys, the other boys, their parents, and us. The meeting was scheduled for three days later.

On the day of the meeting, Taylor came in with his father. Thomas' mother and I also came in with our sons. Of the three boys on the other side, the ringleader came in with his parents, one boy showed up alone, and no one showed up from the last family. We had asked the security person to come to the meeting, because she was considered to be an impartial witness. She sat there for about five minutes, then the principal dismissed her without having her say one word. Nearly two months had passed since the security person had noticed the problem, and over a month had passed since Jeff had submitted the complaint.

There was a lot of discussion. The parents of the ringleader said they objected to the idea of their son being suspended. If he were suspended again, he would be withdrawn/failed from his classes, and wouldn't be able to graduate on time. I countered with the fact that their son's constant pursuit of Jeff was causing him to lose valuable weight. I considered my son's life and health a little bit more important than whether her son would graduate on time.

The boy's mother said that she had assumed that Jeff was one of her son's friends, since she had heard her son mention Jeff's name on the phone several times. I asked her if she didn't spy on her son and eavesdrop on his phone conversations. That was how I got much of my information about my children. I paid attention to their phone calls and knew who their friends were, because only friends usually called.

In the end, the principal's decree was: If he heard anything more about conflict between our boys, "Someone would be removed from the school in handcuffs," He didn't specify who, though.

The harassment stopped for the rest of the year and Jeff started gaining back the weight he had lost. The School's justice can sometimes be ponderously slow, and often the School's rules can't be enforced.

## P) POLICIES & PROCEDURES: *The Miracle of Music*

Betty said her son's teacher was fantastic. Often, when she passed by the classroom, music would be drifting out. The music wasn't just classical. If it was conducive to learning, it was fair game. The teacher wasn't the only one who chose the music. The students were able to make suggestions. The music ranged all the way from Beethoven to Britney Spears.

Betty had been helping in the classroom one day when the class started to get lively. It's hard to hold sixth graders down for long periods of time. As soon as they started getting noisy, the teacher turned on music. Like magic, the class was transformed into a much calmer and quieter group. This method worked well for times when everyone was working on projects or paperwork.

I had suggested bringing some music into Matthew's classroom the year before. His class had been quite active and I thought the music might save the teacher's sanity. I checked out a handful of varied music from the library, but none of it must have been acceptable to the teacher, because she never played it. I returned them to the library and paid the late fees on them.

## Q) ALTERNATIVE EDUCATION & GETTING CREDIT: *S.P.Y.D.E.R*

I heard a rumor about a year-round school in our District, but I was never able to find out who was in charge. The students who went to the school were members of SPYDER. That stands for Sports Programs for Youth Development & Recreation. The year-round program would work extremely well for students in competitive sports.

Melissa had a couple classmates who had been into gymnastics or dance programs, where there were competitions outside the State, throughout the year. Participation in the sport sometimes required missing school. Since most sports have their schedules set up well in advance, working a year-round curriculum around each sport's schedule shouldn't be too difficult. It would seem like a perfect solution for educational continuity.

# Chapter 15
## Placement Problems 1999-2000

A)  FIRST IMPRESSIONS:  *Enter the Stalker*

Jeff was starting his junior year in High School. We were hoping that he was on track to graduate on time. Melissa started her freshman year. She was on the swim team, and making friends. She was finally in the big school.

A week before school started, her happiness was shattered when a man followed her home. The man and his mother accused Melissa of stealing his son's bicycle two months earlier. They said that their informant claimed we were the only ones in the area who would have any reason to steal the bicycle. The bicycle had been stolen while Melissa had been working across town. I knew she had been working, because I provided her transportation. She wasn't guilty.

I called the police, and they investigated us about the theft. Nothing was done about the stalking situation. Supposedly, the boy who had sexually harassed Melissa two years earlier was the informant. After the police left, the man threatened to get the bicycle from Melissa, no matter what it took. He said he would be watching her. The informant's mother refused to believe that her son would do this to Melissa and she felt that I was unjustly accusing her son.

Melissa needed counseling and medicine. The school couldn't make any arrangements to work with me by getting her a tutor until we got her stabilized enough to get back into the routine at the school.

Matthew was starting the sixth grade. We didn't like the situation, but we had run out of options. If he was going to get any further, he had to complete elementary school. The school year wasn't looking fun.

E)  DISABILITIES & DIFFERENCES:  *We Can't Teach Your Daughter*

Melissa was 14 years old and she was acting much younger. I watched my confident daughter turn into someone who was fearful. She started walking close behind me, when we went anywhere. The day the stalker had shown himself, she had felt like someone was following her. It only took him two minutes after she walked through the door to knock on the door. He had to have been watching her.

I took her to the family doctor, who prescribed Paxil. No matter when we gave her the medicine, it was disturbing her sleep. Between being up all night, sleeping all day, and the horrible nightmares, the medicine only seemed to be aggravating the problem. She was physically in school for about two days before she threatened suicide. A "helpful" classmate kept trying to push her down the stairs. The lack of sleep was keeping her from being alert to this student's presence. The medicine was also making her extremely dizzy. I tapered her off the medicine in a week, but the sleep pattern was still disturbed.

I had asked the curriculum principal if there was any way that they could work with our situation. We had already started counseling. The counselor was worried about potentially home schooling Melissa, because she needed to have some activity where she saw people. Her only social activity was her swimming, but she couldn't be on the swim team unless she was attending her current school or a charter school within the District. I started checking the charter schools.

Unfortunately, every charter school I tried said the same thing. "We've already done our lottery for this year, but you can enter your daughter in our May lottery for next year." I needed a solution NOW. With all my options exhausted, I sent for materials from the State's correspondence school. The social and healing activity of being on the swim team was no longer available for Melissa. She was virtually isolated and her friends considered her home schooling as a show of superiority. She was shunned for most of the rest of the year.

## H) HOMEWORK: *Criminology Class*

Jeff took Criminology as one of his Social Studies electives. Each week, the students were supposed to look for newspaper articles that talked about crimes. Jeff said that the teacher wanted them to look for other papers besides the Anchorage Daily News. There were a couple places in town that carried out of area papers, but Jeff wouldn't remind me that he needed one until the day before his assignment was due. By then, I had run out of time to get out for one.

He was still writing slowly. The teacher had called me about his poor grade in her class. His output didn't reflect what she could see of him in class. I went to the school to discuss this matter with her, one day during lunchtime.

She told me that the way she wanted the assignments done was the only way, and Jeff should conform. I said that we had been trying to figure out what his problem with writing was for about 10 years. She advised us to have him take the Nelson-Denning test. This is a vocabulary test, which Jeff had taken three times already, and had aced it all three times. Taking it again wouldn't prove anything more. He barely passed criminology.

## K) CURRICULUM: *Japanese Petition Part 2*

Jeff tried to have a petition again for a Japanese class. He made sure that his signatures were legal, non-senior signatures. In a short time, he had collected over 60 signatures from students who were interested in taking Japanese. That was two whole classes. He would find out at the beginning of the next year that he was unsuccessful again.

Looking back, there could be several reasons for this failure. The first reason had to do with our school's goofy schedule. The teacher wouldn't be able to cover two schools, so they would have to be able to teach another subject besides Japanese, to get a full paycheck.

The next reason had to do with the school budget. Jeff had his petition signed after January. In January, they plan the budget for the next school year. His timing may have been off.

The last reason could have had to do with the administration not caring what the students wanted to learn.

## N) SAFETY & SECURITY: *Vaccinations and Social Security Numbers*

When I had taken Jeff and Melissa to the school to register, there were two requirements that I didn't like. The first one had to do with vaccinations. I had requested a notation be put in each of the kids' records that there would be no more vaccinations because of religious exemption. The other was requiring we give the student's social security number on the emergency form.

Melissa was unhappy when I calmly tried to decline these requirements. The school loudly tried to make an issue of these requirements. Teenagers are easily embarrassed by noisy disagreements. In this case, I felt it was my right not to submit to the requirements. Three different people told me that I had to give the social security number. Each person gave me a different reason. Personally, I didn't think that the school's security system was all that secure. After all, if I had wanted someone's social security number, I could have almost got it while we were in line. One could look down at the emergency cards as they shuffled through them to find our name.

The social security number is only meant for employment or money lending. The school really had no need for it. By having it in the school office or computers, outside interests could access the numbers and disrupt your child's credit rating, even before they had a chance to establish any credit history. I had dealt with the school system's ineptitude long enough to realize that I needed to actively protect my children's interests.

Betty's son went through the same School District policies, but didn't have nearly the trouble I had, registering her son. When the school asked for the social security number, and she said "no", they didn't pursue the matter.

If the school really needs to track the students, they should be given an alphanumeric student identification number, as soon as they enter school. It could have a two digit year, two letters for the state, numbers indicating the School District, and a number saying which student you were, entering the system that year. The number could follow you, no matter where you went in the US education system.

*Backpacks, Lockers, and Uniforms*

This year the School Board discussed eliminating lockers. I thought that was an interesting idea, since many students have to wait at bus stops in below zero weather. If they aren't allowed to wear their outdoor gear in class, and they have no place to store it, what are they supposed to do? Lockers are getting smaller in the High Schools, even if the kids are getting bigger. Luckily, they moved on to a different topic.

This time, the target was backpacks. Jeff carried half his weight in textbooks, back and forth from school. It would have been much easier if there was a set of textbooks for the classroom and every student had a set at home. This could have minimized the amount of "stuff" a student had to carry into the school, but the answer was too simple. Options under consideration were clear or net backpacks. Neither of these options was very durable.

The last security measure they wanted to deal with was uniforms. There was too much gang activity. If I remember correctly, many of the colors the schools use are used in gangs. This may eliminate most primary colors for school uniforms. By the way, how much emphasis is put on rivalry between school teams? Hmm, I think I sense gang activity happening. We need to stop it immediately.

My kids and I discussed the topic of uniforms. While uniforms would eliminate the individuality, and there would be no agony about deciding what to wear everyday, there might be a problem choosing colors. If the gangs take all the primary colors, maybe the school system would go for some of the colors that gangs don't usually choose, like lime green and hot pink. Better make that a plaid, then everyone will hate it equally. If we get some trendy gangs into the area, they may steal our uniform colors.

If we run out of colors, will we have to send students to school naked? Naked could be a problem. Besides the obvious temperature difficulties, you would have students promoting their individuality with tattoos and body piercings, and we're back to gangs again. We just thought we should take the subject of uniforms to the most extreme possibilities, for fun.

Kids will hate other kids for any reason. A uniform won't fix it. Teaching respect throughout the system might. Pushing the envelope is normal for teenagers, and the more rigid the limits, the more the teens push. Expecting a certain amount of accountability and a purpose for being a contributing member in the school community can make things much easier.

*Anniversary of Columbine*

Melissa was home, at this point, and was noticing the anniversary coverage on the news programs. It didn't matter whether it was local or national, it all made her nauseous. She couldn't understand why news people had to go back to all the victims' families and repeatedly ask how these people felt. Weren't these people in enough pain already, without having to prod them again? She also wondered if the renewed coverage of Columbine wasn't fueling more school violence. She wrote a letter to the editor about her concern. I don't know if anyone else got anything out of her letter, but people who knew us thought the letter was well written.

# Chapter 16
## Mobile Matthew 1999-2000

### A) FIRST IMPRESSION: *Problem Child?*

Matthew was now two grades behind his original class. It was his ninth year in elementary school. He had been held back through no fault of his own. The school he was in really didn't want him, yet they did nothing to help us get him out sooner. As you read this chapter, you'll feel our frustration as we tried to get Matthew proper placement. It had to be written chronologically. Otherwise, it would make you dizzy.

### SIXTH GRADE (First Semester)

### I) DRUGS & WEAPONS: *The Mad Bomber*

Three days into the school year, I received a call from the elementary school principal. She asked me if Matthew was noticeably interested in incendiary devices. When I asked her why, she replied that another student's parent informed her that Matthew had said he was going to build a bomb and blow up the school. This was the first I had heard of this idea, and I wanted to know more.

There was nothing around the house to indicate such an interest. Anything that could have been used around the house was relatively cumbersome, and I had seen no literature about assembling bombs, either. I'm not saying my son was perfect, and "wouldn't do something like this". Any teen can have a hidden interest. I just knew, from vast experience, that Matthew wasn't the most cautious person. We had "busted" him several times, because he left evidence around. Knowing his friends' parents helped make "busting" our son as easy as shooting fish in a barrel.

If Matthew was planning a bomb, he was doing it away from our house. There would have to be an accomplice. If that was the case, the principal had a bigger problem than just Matthew.

I asked the principal, who had informed her. She told me that I needed to ask Matthew that. If my son was hiding bombing supplies from me, what made her think he would tell me who had turned him in?

When Matthew came home, I asked him about his day. He told me that he had been called to the principal's office and asked a lot of questions. I was told, supposedly, Richard's mom had been the one to turn him in. She had said that she got the information about Matthew's plans from Richard. The only thing I knew about Richard was he was a video game enthusiast. We had his magazines all over our house, at one time. After having spent enough time around kids who speak "video game", you learn that words like "bombs" and a variety of weapons pop up in their vocabulary a lot, but only when they are discussing strategies for their favorite games.

Matthew rarely saw Richard. In fact, the last time he had spoken to Richard, they had been on the school playground a week before school started. Matthew couldn't even remember what they had talked about.

I was never able to reach Richard's mom, to find out what she had actually heard. Was she distracted and only partially listening to what her son was saying? Was he really telling her about Matthew's plan to blow up the school, or a strategy for a video game? Did she make sure she had her facts right before she contacted the principal? Did she think I was so unapproachable?

Despite the principal's threats to suspend Matthew, nothing could be done because there was no proof. What a way to start the school year!

### O) POLITICS: *Choose Your Fights Carefully*

Matthew was having a lot of difficulty with the elementary school staff, especially the people in the office. I wondered if their problem was with him or with me. As the school presented their position:

Matthew needed to be wearing a coat to school (since it was the middle of winter) or he wouldn't be allowed to go out for recess. My basic problem was trying to get him to wear a hat and gloves to school.

My job seemed insurmountable. Matthew didn't want to go to school because he was always being yelled at. The school was lecturing me for sending him to school without a coat and for getting him there late. It almost seemed like it wasn't worth the fight to get him to school, because no matter what I did right, they could find something trivial to complain about.

Matthew's lack of an obvious winter coat wasn't an issue, as far as I was concerned. He had been reading again. (How dare he read!) His current obsession was with the concept of multiple thin layers versus a few thick layers. He had figured out if he wore about eight layers of shirts and three pairs of pants, that he would still stay warm. His outer layer was usually a sweatshirt, and at least one of his inner layers was a thermal undershirt. I watched Matthew remove his layers when he came home from school, and replace them (in a different order) the next morning.

The school never realized that he was wearing multiple layers. Nor, did they consider the fact that I would be the one washing all these layers. Why would I want to promote this behavior? If they had known anything about sixth grade hygiene, sixth graders are the last to realize that they are reeking. I was sort of hoping that peer pressure would kick in at some point, and he would discard the idea of so many layers. I was more concerned about the prospect of frostbite on his ears and his fingers, so I was pushing for the hat and gloves.

Because of the lack of a regulation coat, Matthew wasn't allowed to go out for lunch recess so he could expend the excess energy that everyone seemed to complain about. The school was supposed to judge whether a student was suitably dressed to go outside for the twenty-minute outdoor activity. Students were expected to dress for –10-degree weather. If the temperature dropped below that, none of the students went out for recess.

One morning, I dropped Matthew off late for school and got the usual lecture about tardiness and lack of coat. In an effort to get Matthew some activity, I spoke with the substitute principal about a compromise. Since I was unable to make Matthew conform to the school's thinking, maybe they could let him out for recess when the temperature was above zero. The principal agreed to the compromise, because she understood my reasoning. You see, she had been Melissa's fifth grade teacher. Yelling at Matthew would only make him dig his heels in further. Feeding the "Negative Attention Monster" wouldn't accomplish anything.

It would have been helpful if the office personnel had tried to work with me. It was obvious to Matthew that they didn't respect me, and I was having great difficulty trying to respect them. When adults don't respect each other, how do they expect the children to respect anyone? Matthew was 13 years old. As adults, we should have been able to outsmart him, together.

*Maybe You Should Consider a Charter School*

Midway through the school year, the elementary school principal suggested that I might want to move Matthew to a charter school. She really didn't want him as her responsibility anymore. She could have saved herself a step, if she had put him in the sixth grade the previous year, as I had requested. In order to get into any other school, I had to pull him out of his current school. I knew a charter school wasn't an option, since I had already played this game with Melissa. Charter school rules hadn't changed.

I pulled Matthew out of the school, much to the surprise of his teacher. He couldn't believe that the principal had actually asked us to leave. I tried to see if I could put him in the other Middle School that was on our side of town. The principal shot me down when she informed me I could bring him back when he finished the sixth grade.

I went to the School District office and asked for the person in charge of Elementary Education. I requested the requirements for a student to pass the sixth grade. I wanted to find out what Matthew needed to be promoted. I was mildly surprised by the woman's response. She couldn't tell me. I had to contact the State correspondence school for that information.

Now, I had a child who no school wanted, and I wasn't going to try to home school him again. We were way beyond that point. Supposedly, the State offers free education for students under a certain age. My son was under that age, yet we couldn't find anyone to teach him. If I pulled him out of school completely, legal action could be taken against me by the State, for not having him in school. I contacted the Ombudsman's Office, and told them my problem. Within two days, I was informed that I had an appointment with the Middle School that Melissa had just left. What fun! I had to rearrange my work schedule, so I could take Matthew to the school, for their arbitrary appointment.

## SEVENTH GRADE (Third Quarter)

### K) CURRICULUM: *Benchmarks*

We were coming into the Middle School the week of the Benchmark testing for the 8th graders. I should have demanded that he be benchmarked with the 8th graders to help find proper placement, but I thought I would be overruled. Looking back, what's the worst thing they could have told me? I really didn't have anything to lose, and I missed my opportunity.

The people who were assembled discussed Matthew's records. His test scores showed him to be gifted in English. They couldn't understand why he was still in the 6th grade. The woman who was remarking on the test scores was the woman who couldn't tell me about elementary education. They placed him in a gifted 7th grade class for third quarter. I distrusted this school and the people in it, but maybe we could get him through this school sooner.

### S) SICKNESS & HEALTH: *Allergies & Sensitivities*

For Matthew to enter the middle school, we had to get a tuberculosis test. We went into the nurse's office, and she went over his records. She asked about allergies and current shots. I told her that we had a religious exemption on his records. She looked and found no notation, so I filled out the paperwork again for her to make the notation. She wanted to know which religion I was, and I told her that it wasn't really any of her business. She pressed harder, but I stood my ground.

We went over allergies. I mentioned that I thought Matthew was allergic to aspartame and formaldehyde. She asked what the symptoms were, and I said headache and stomachache. She said Matthew would have to watch for aspartame himself. For any other concerns, I was supposed to be my child's advocate. The school really couldn't watch out for every child. I knew Melissa had a severe reaction to being in a closed Science room and dealing with formaldehyde, the previous year. She had actually come home and vomited from the exposure. She also missed a day of school.

The school dealt with a chemical I knew my children were sensitive to, but I couldn't warn the school. Hmmm. I guess Matthew was always going to have to ask if there was formaldehyde in class that day. The reaction to formaldehyde wasn't considered to be an allergy, it was just considered a sensitivity. Only proteins can produce allergic antibodies. Formaldehyde wasn't a protein (but a poison). Therefore, it's a sensitivity. No matter the label, it needed to be in his records, if there was a problem.

I had been told that Matthew had needed a TB test. It was now called a PPD or Purified Protein Derivative test. I signed the paper, thinking the name had just changed not the form of the test. When the nurse pulled out a needle, I asked her what was in the needle. She seemed confused by my reaction. She said it was for the PPD test that I had just signed for. I tried to make myself clearer. What was the preservative in the needle? I needed to know whether it was formaldehyde. I had spent four days in a mental hospital because of my sensitivity to formaldehyde, which had triggered a stroke, before the doctor's figured out what was wrong with me. If my child was being given formaldehyde, I needed to know.

The nurse looked at me as if I was from another planet. I was being an advocate for my son, and she was reacting as if I was deranged. I refused to have Matthew take the test until I could find out what the preservative was. The nurse told me, in a challenging tone that he wouldn't be allowed in any of the District's schools without the shot. If Matthew were her child, would she have meekly submitted? Matthew got the test the next day. I was able to find out what the preservative was from my family doctor. It wasn't formaldehyde.

*Mad Cow Disease*

Mad Cow disease made me want to have my children vaccinated even less. I received a paper from Matthew's school about vaccinations again, just about the time they had stories on the news about Mad Cow Disease and a candy company. It seemed there was gelatin in this one type of taffy, and everyone was worried about it since the gelatin might have come from infected cows. I thought it was quite interesting that no one had brought up the fact that our vaccination supply might be compromised. After all, vaccines affected everyone, and they were chock full of varied animal cells (including cow cells).

I took the paper about religious exemption back to the school, since the nurse had obviously failed to file the form I had filled out in her office on the first day. I mentioned the story about Mad Cow Disease, and wondered if it was going to have any impact on our vaccination supplies. The nurse told me I couldn't be exempt from getting the shot for personal philosophy. The paper said the beliefs of my religion could exempt us from being forced to have the shots. It didn't require elaboration, or ask if I took the philosophy personally. I just thought the timing of their form was ironic.

L) CRIMES & PUNISHMENTS: *Noodle Flinging*

Matthew was in lunch one day, with his friends. Two of his friends were sitting across from him, eating ramen noodles. The boys decided to have some fun with their food. Each of the boys across the table decided to fling a noodle at Matthew. One boy's noodle hit him in the face; the other boy's noodle hit the shirt of the boy next to him. In the absence of available napkins, Matthew peeled the noodle off his cheek, and tried to detach the sticky projectile from his fingers. The boy next to Matthew had the noodle hanging out of his shirt pocket.

All four boys were removed from the lunchroom and assigned detention, for noodle flinging. The boys who actually flung the noodles tried to take responsibility for their actions. No one would listen to them as they told the authorities that Matthew and the other boy had only been targets. They hadn't thrown the noodles back. All four boys still got detention.

After the incident, I asked the counselor, "Why couldn't the punishment fit the crime more closely?" She told me parents objected to punishment that required manual labor. I felt a suitable punishment for noodle flinging (or food fights, in general) would be helping to clean up the lunchroom. I thought there might be substantially less debris, if this was the punishment. I have actually seen the lunchroom after a thousand "civilized" Middle School students have just finished eating. It looked like shoveling the floor would be more productive than sweeping it.

I think when parents enroll their student there should be a notation on the bottom of the registration paperwork. Punishment options could be: Detention; Suspension; Manual Labor; and Corporal Punishment. Parents can still be notified about the punishment, but the authorities can have a wider range of options to present to the parents, within the chosen punishment level.

EIGHTH GRADE (Fourth Quarter)

N) SAFETY & SECURITY: *Anniversary of Columbine*

Matthew started the eighth grade on the anniversary of Columbine. I remember it, because I was in the school trying to speak with his new Math teacher. The school, in its infinite wisdom, had scheduled Matthew to be in an Algebra class. I got to the school early in the morning to see what they were learning about, and found out that it was way above Matthew's head. I had never seen him bring any homework home that looked like this material. The teacher had initially been hostile about my unannounced appearance, but I hadn't really wanted a lengthy conference. Our situation was highly unusual, and I couldn't see digging a bigger hole, if it could be averted. This teacher also taught eighth grade Math, so we decided his schedule would need a little bit of shuffling. My "conference" took five minutes, at the most.

I was getting ready to leave the building just as morning announcements were being made. I stopped in my tracks. The principal was praising some students for reporting a student who had made some death threats on the school bus. The principal went on to say that the students who had reported this information hadn't been spreading a rumor or tattling, so they had handled the situation properly. There was no explanation as to how their method of "reporting" was considered to be different from spreading a rumor or tattling, but I was curious. Logically, I know that tattling gets someone into trouble out of spite, and "reporting" requires a good reason for providing information that will get someone into trouble. But I hadn't ever heard any school policy that pointed out the differences. Did students really know the difference?

X) SUMMER SCHOOL: *Fail-Safes and Marijuana Leaves*

Matthew had failed the eighth grade, so I enrolled him in summer school. Matthew hated summer school. I tried to appeal to his sense of logic. Wasn't 180 hours of school over the summer preferable to serving another 180 days in the Middle School that we both detested? Matthew didn't see it that way. He viewed my maneuver as stealing his summer vacation. He felt he had no choice in the matter, so he did the only thing he could, he quietly rebelled.

While teachers and administrators had expected me to straighten Matthew out, they had refused to work with me on re-enforcement. Matthew proved to me that my powers were limited. I might be able to pry him out of bed, wedge him into clothes, and deliver him to the door of the school, but I couldn't make him pay attention in class. He did very little work in class, and spent most of his time sleeping. Without any tangible class work, the teachers had great difficulty gauging his level of ability.

In Matthew's Social Studies class, they were studying the 60's, 70's and 80's. They did their research in the computer lab, and four groups of students used the same computers. One day, Matthew was looking up one of his bookmarks. On the way, another student's bookmark caught his attention, so he opened it. The first page displayed a large marijuana leaf.

Being able to open the page alone was supposed to have been extremely difficult with all the fail-safes that were supposed to be installed on all the District's computers. I don't know whether Matthew had the ability to circumvent security measures, but I do know that he did have the ability to change icons on the desktop. He had learned this lesson only a couple days before, so he decided to put his education into practice. He changed all the icons on his computer desktop to marijuana leaves. It only took a few minutes, and some of his classmates saw him do it. It took the school authorities a week to figure out who had done it. Even then, they couldn't figure out how he had done it.

When the administration figured out who had modified the icons, Matthew was summoned to the office, questioned, and searched for drugs. Since he spent most of his time in class asleep, he could be a potential drug user. The choice of marijuana leaves reinforced their suspicions. On my birthday, I received the call. Matthew was being expelled from summer school.

I went to the school to speak with the principal. They were still trying to figure out how he had made the change. Had they thought to ask Matthew? Apparently, the security program that was supposed to be on all the computers to keep students from accessing inappropriate web sites wasn't working on Matthew's computer. At first, the principal had thought that Matthew had done this to be malicious, but Matthew's demeanor wasn't defiant. Nothing else had been disturbed on the computer. It was basically a harmless prank, but the School District policy was clear: Any student who had anything to do with drugs would be expelled. There was "zero tolerance" of this activity.

## Chapter 17
## Graduation Fumble 2000-01

A) FIRST IMPRESSION: *Bumpy Rides*

Jeff was coming into his senior year. He was still having writing problems. I wasn't having a whole lot of luck with reason or trickery. Jeff couldn't verbalize his problem. I don't know if it was because he thought differently than I did or if he just didn't think I would understand. Would I have been able to explain the difficulty if I had his problem, at his age?

Melissa started her first year of High School in the usual fashion. She had the flu. I prayed that we wouldn't repeat last year. This would be her sophomore year, even though it was her first year. She was planning on finishing with high school in three years. We had only one credit from the correspondence school. Geometry had been beyond my ability to help, and Jeff and Melissa didn't speak the same language when it came to Math, so he couldn't help her. I had bought all sorts of books and tapes that were supposed to make the learning easier, but I think they overwhelmed Melissa.

Matthew was repeating the 8th grade. This time, they had him in the "Gifted" class. I hoped he would succeed this time, because I wanted him out of that school.

B) BUILDINGS & GROUNDS: *Building a New High School*

One morning, as I was returning home after driving my husband to work, I was listening to the morning talk radio program. The topic of discussion was the plans to rebuild one of the High Schools. The school may have been old and out of code, but I wasn't an expert. I had visited the school when Jeff had taken his SATs in the eighth grade. The school looked like it belonged in California rather than Alaska. There were covered walkways between some of the buildings.

The thing that disturbed me about the conversation on the radio revolved around the cost the Municipality was paying an architect for plans for the new school. According to the conversation, an Assembly member had said they were paying a company either $10,000 or $100,000 to come up with a plan. The amount of money didn't matter as much as the fact that they were paying someone ahead of time to come up with plans. Shouldn't an architect have an idea first, and present it to the Assembly (among other interested architects), for approval? At that point, the architect would be paid for his services. Wouldn't some of these companies have ready made floor plans on hand from previous projects? Besides our climate requirements, a school should be pretty much the same anywhere around the country. Shouldn't it?

*Closed Campus*

The School Board was discussing closing high school campuses for lunchtime. "Closing the campus," meant that high school students wouldn't be able to leave the school grounds for lunch.

Advantages to this reasoning were: less traffic problems coming and going during the lunch period and students not getting into mischief off school property. I don't know if the idea came up because of students arriving to their after lunch classes late, safety concerns, or if local fast food places had complained about student behavior. However it came up, it was cause for heated debate.

Our school had a forty minute lunch period. They had tried two lunches, but for some reason, that idea had been rejected. The logistical problems that I could see included long lines to get food and not enough seating for all the students. With only one lunch period, our lunchrooms could only accommodate about half of our 2000 student population. If students didn't bring lunches, the alternative was to wait in line for the food. Sometimes students got their food just in time to run to class. My kids had told me stories of classmates who had been told to dispose of the food they had waited so long for and paid so dearly for, because it wasn't allowed in the classroom. Food in our lunchroom wasn't cheap.

Jeff had suggested to his friends that they try to get everyone in the school together to give a live demonstration of what "closed campus" would mean. Unfortunately, the idea didn't catch on. Too bad. I would have paid good money to see such a demonstration.

## C) PARENT-TEACHER ENTITY: *The Advisory Council*

This year, I decided to check out the Advisory Council. I understand this entity was open to parents, teachers, and students. The various principals gave reports on activities within their jurisdiction. The activity principal spoke about the various sports and other student activities. The curriculum principal discussed curriculum matters. The security principal obviously discussed criminal activity on school grounds. There was a report from the Student Government and the School District had a representative. Topics of discussion included bullying and discrimination; Phase I of the new construction project, the upcoming Municipal election, and the administration principal's report.

The administration principal had an interesting presentation. She cited a publication called "Breaking Ranks: Changing an American Institution". The National Association of Secondary School Principals, in 1996, published it. Supposedly the ideal school would be small, autonomous, distinctive and focused, personal, committed to equity, provide multiple types of assessment, have parents as critical allies, and they would be schools that everyone would want to attend. As far as I could see, our school was moving farther from this ideal each year. High school students seemed to be treated more like kindergärtners than young adults who were supposed to be prepared for the outside world.

With a population of 2000 students, it was hard to have a small community. One of the proposals was to have multiple schools within the school. This way, security people and teachers could get to know students personally. One of the school within a school components could be a year-round program. I saw the School District representative nod at this suggestion, which was ironic, since it couldn't be very successful on a limited basis in the high school. One had to deal with the fact that there are a limited number of teachers in higher courses. Either the teacher could teach the entire course in the year-round format or, they could teach it in the traditional format. You couldn't expect a teacher to work the whole year. In other words, juniors and seniors could be eliminated from the year-round format, for lack of teachers.

The school had several goals. Among them was an expectation to increase the number of school-business partnerships, and increase student awareness and participation in the community. They also hoped to promote the use of technology. I thought this was funny, since the computers in the computer lab were so sanitized that you could barely do anything on them. Jeff's French teacher had taken them to the computer lab, only to find out she couldn't run her program because the computer lab teacher had disabled all the audio hardware.

The pamphlet the principal kept referring to indicated several times that the school needed to be conducive to teaching and learning, by acknowledging multiple talents and ways of learning, to help the students be more successful in the real world.

I left the meeting knowing I wouldn't return. I couldn't stand lip service. They couldn't implement the policies and programs they already had. Dealing with multiple ways of learning, at this stage, was useless, unless the program was being started in elementary school. So far, there wasn't anything going on in the lower grades. This group wouldn't welcome my observations.

## D) FUND RAISING: *Missing Money*

Someone had taken off with the Band's fund raising money. It was sitting in the teacher's office, and the office had been locked. All indications made it look like an inside job. One of the students had asked for the Band teacher's keys, but he couldn't remember who it was, because he had been conducting the class for a performance at the time. They had returned them, though. The Band teacher had been planning to go to the bank later that day, so the day's receipts had been in the office.

Someone found some of the checks in a trailer court, but any cash was gone. Some of the students had suspicions as to who took the money, but they couldn't prove it. This is another case where sending in payment by check makes more sense than sending in cash.

### E) DIFFERENCES & DISABILITIES: *Disability Versus Disease*

Betty had a conversation with a teacher about Attention Deficit Disorder. She had met the teacher socially. He wasn't one of her son's teachers. She doesn't remember how they started talking about the subject, but she remembers how it ended.

The gist of the conversation was the teacher felt that students who were labeled "Attention Deficit" should be placed on medication, because they needed it.

Betty had the nerve to ask the teacher if ADD was considered to be a disability or a disease. If it was a disability, could it be equated with dyslexia, for instance? The teacher felt that it was a disability, like dyslexia. Betty's next question was posed with precision. If there was a medicine to fix dyslexia today, even if there were terrible side effects, should it be prescribed for the affected students? The teacher's response was shock. He informed her that there were methods to help dyslexics cope with their disability. They didn't need medicine.

Betty asked, "If they can come up with coping methods for dyslexia, why couldn't educators develop coping methods for ADD?" By the time the students who are labeled "ADD" reach High School, they have to be taken off the medicines for a while, to combat toxicity problems. Without some sort of safety net, these students can fail. No one will give them the tools to succeed. They have to depend on a form of "speed" to survive in the world, under the current educational mindset. Wouldn't it be better to look into alternative educational methods rather than condemning a whole section of the population to drug dependency, unnecessarily?

Betty's argument was quite strong. The teacher kept his distance for the rest of the evening. We wondered if the discussion gave him food for thought, or if he just felt threatened.

### *Scotopic Sensitivity Syndrome*

The day Al Gore gave his concession speech, I was watching a local interest show called, "The Norma Goodman Show". I didn't always watch the show, but this day, I was tuned in and watching with intense interest.

There were a couple women talking about a learning disability called, "Scotopic Sensitivity". Before they were done with their subject, there was a news break. I hadn't been able to find out where to get more information on the subject. These women seemed to say that this problem affects reading ability, and colored transparencies can help ease the difficulty. They had gone to a High School to check out a variety of students. They had asked each student if they could read the paper better with any of the transparencies.

One boy, who always seemed to be sleeping in class, said that he could actually read the paper better with several of the transparencies over it. This made it almost black. While he had his head down in class, he was usually reading. The absence of light made it easier for him to read the print on the paper. Black letters on white paper can be difficult for some students to read, and some people perceive the letters as mobile, on the white paper.

I thought of Melissa's classmate who was dyslexic and had the green transparency. If black letters on white paper was a problem, my first thought was, "They're converting all the blackboards in the schools

139

to the white dry erase boards." The move was designed to eliminate the health hazard of chalk dust, but was it making things worse for some students?

Supposedly, symptoms of this ailment are like many other learning disabilities. The child may avoid reading, have varied problems writing, head aches or fatigue while reading, depth perception problems, and their grades won't reflect the child's effort. There are more details on: http://www.irlen.com/sss_main.htm.

Educational Psychologist Helen Irlen isolated this problem in the early 1980's. Scotopic sensitivity can run in conjunction with other disabilities like: ADD, dyslexia, and autism. It's estimated that 10-12% of the population is affected by this. Unlike ADD remedies, transparencies or colored glasses, rather than drugs can help scotopic sensitivity. Finding the color a person needs is like being examined for an eyeglass prescription. The expert will find the right prescription for the affected individual.

There is a book about this syndrome, by Helen Irlen. It's called, "Reading by the Colors".

*A Russian Viewpoint on ADD*

I picked up a book called "Cure Your Cravings" at the library. Supposedly, it was a book about eliminating addictions. Yefim Shubentsov and Barbara Gordon wrote it. Mr. Shubentsov had studied a method of directing the energy in your body, in Russia, and the method could be used to help sick people. He isn't a doctor.

In Russia, there were ideological prisons like people's perception of the government. There were also real brick and mortar prisons. He left Russia to come to America, a land that he thought was free. What he saw here was different ideological prisons. In America, we have individual prisons, where we suffer from various addictions, and act like victims. Our ailments are actually products of an affluent society.

The section of the book which caught my eye concerned ADD. Some parents had a son, who wasn't doing well in school. At the conference, the teacher cheerfully informed them that their son had a disease that could be easily treated with a medicine. The disease was ADD. The parents went to Mr. Shubentsov for a second opinion. He thought the boy was relatively normal. He liked television better than the subjects in school. He could give detailed descriptions of his favorite cartoon characters. With that kind of information storage capability, Mr. Shubentsov considered the boy to be far from being deficient.

Like the psychologist we took Jeff to when he was four, Mr. Shubentsov advised the parents to move the boy away from the cathode ray tube (TV), and have some expectations for him to meet before he got to watch the TV again. So simple, yet few parents think of it.

In April 2004, there would be a study released about the dangers of television exposure to children under 2 years old. Supposedly, the fast images are responsible for ADD in children. Either way one looks at it, television should be a monitored privilege, not a universal right for children.

*Rubber Stamping ADD*

Judy's son was having trouble in school, so she took him to a psychologist. The psychologist gave her the usual papers to fill out about her son's attitude. She was to fill out one form, for what she observed at home. The other form was for his teacher to fill out. She was surprised by the teacher's responses to the survey. If it was a question of negative activity, the teacher indicated that her son ALWAYS did it. If it was a positive question, her son NEVER did it. Sitting quietly in class was a "never" activity. Roaming the room was an "always" activity. Considering there were three other options between Always and Never, none of them was used.

When Judy asked the teacher about this, the teacher's response was, "Well, don't you want him to get the help (medication) he needs?" This made Judy's job, and the psychologist's job, more difficult. It was difficult to diagnose a child if part of the puzzle was skewed. If I were in Judy's shoes, at that moment, I might have asked the principal to have the teacher give a more accurate accounting of my son. Of course, you always run the risk of the teachers and administration "circling their wagons" to repel the aggressive parent.

Judy's son was put on the medicine, but was only on it for a couple years. He finally found a teacher who liked him for who he was, and didn't feel he needed to be drugged.

## F) PROGRAMS: *P.E.R.K.S.*

Matthew obviously wasn't doing well in the normal 8th grade class. He still had some gaps that needed to be filled in. According to the "benefits" of being in a Middle School, the Middle School would provide basic skill repair and extension, but I don't think they could handle this in a regular classroom. Matthew was literally behind everyone else when it came to Math. They needed to repair information gaps that he had since fourth grade.

The counselor suggested that I put Matthew in the PERKS program. PERKS stood for "Pursuing Education with Responsibility for Knowledge and Success". Matthew entered the class at the beginning of the second quarter. He was doing well in the class and he was able to see his friends at lunchtime.

One day, while the Science Fair was set up in the cafeteria, students who wouldn't usually socialize with each other were all crammed into the gym for the lunch period. One of Matthew's PERKS classmates was sitting midway up the bleachers. Below him were some Gs or Gangsters. This was a black clique. Above him were the Preps, or the kids whose parents had money. One of the Preps threw a French fry from lunch, and it hit a Gangster. The Gangster looked up and decided that Matthew's classmate had thrown the French fry, even though he didn't have any.

After lunch, a group of Gangsters beat Matthew's classmate up in the hallway outside the gym. They had him down on the floor and were kicking him. He tried to move his arms around to get himself off the floor and managed to hit one of the Gangsters.

The victim was suspended for fighting. Two of his friends received death threats from the Gangsters. The victim's mother went to the school, to find out from the principal who had attacked her son. The principal refused to release that information. No disciplinary action was taken against the attackers. This was quite suspicious. Was the principal protecting the attackers because, like her, they were black, while the victim was white?

This altercation caused a big shift in the schedule for the PERKS students. Their lunchtime was shifted to the second lunch period. That meant Matthew lost any reason for wanting to be in school. All his friends were in the first lunch period. Besides moving the lunch period, the PERKS students had different passing periods. They weren't allowed to be in the halls at the same time as the other students. When they did use the bathroom or go to their locker for their scheduled passing periods, they were harassed by security for being in the halls without a pass. The students in PERKS had become vilified.

I spoke with the PERKS teacher at conference time. First, I had to find her. The chart showed that she was supposed to be in the gym, but she had been placed in the cafeteria. I was the first, and maybe the only parent this teacher saw during the whole conference time. The school hadn't made it easy to find her. I talked with her about the prison-like atmosphere the class had developed. She said that she had pretty much expected this to happen since the beginning of the year. The principal's original intent had been to move the students outside the school, in a portable classroom, and they would eat their lunches there, too. The plan had been no contact with the regular student population. The teacher had insisted on a regular classroom and had received it. The fight was just the excuse the principal needed to punish these students. They needed actual, short-term, remedial education, not punitive measures.

### The Japanese Club

Jeff had failed twice with his petition for a Japanese class, so he decided to try to have a Japanese Club. The first problem he noticed involved the fact that all the other language clubs were hooked to an actual class, and therefore had a natural advisory teacher. Since Japanese wasn't taught in the school, he would have to look for a teacher who was willing to be the club's advisor.

Picking a time to meet was also a problem. High school kids have jobs, so after school is difficult. They decided to do it during lunchtime. The first time the group met, they had to decide what activities they wanted to do. The classroom was standing room only, because everyone assumed that the club would be watching anime. Jeff was hoping for more culture and language.

The head of the language department had one textbook, which we made copies from for the club, at our expense. We had to have something to work with. Jeff was also given the name of a college student who was studying to be a Japanese teacher. Jeff and his friends could get their Japanese class, and the student teacher could get some practical experience.

We ended up with about two dozen students who came to study Japanese two days a week at lunchtime. The teacher would either catch the bus to school, or call me for a ride. The students had 40 minutes to try to learn something, while eating and being interrupted with announcements. Between our textbook, and some of the teacher's resources, we patched together a very rudimentary class.

We started in November and ended in April. The students had the equivalent of one class per week during that time. That's about 20 lessons. We didn't make much progress into the textbook.

At the time, I thought the students might generate a little more interest in the Japanese language, if they taught some of the words they had learned to their friends. Maybe, if the faculty heard a lot of Japanese being spoken in the halls, they would bring Japanese to the school. When Jeff brought this concept up, they wondered whether it was him talking or me. The idea was shot down, because one of the students mentioned some other kids had made up a language and had been speaking it in the halls. If the school wasn't going to offer a class in that language, why would they offer classes in Japanese?

The word "impossible" ran rampant through this school, and Jeff didn't have enough time left at the school to press harder for the class he wanted.

I drove the teacher back to the university after he taught the kids at our school, so he could make it to his next class. He barely got enough documentation of his progress with the students, to get a grade for the project. He would become a teacher at the University, and Jeff would finally be able to get the Japanese classes he had always wanted, once he graduated.

## G) TRANSPORTATION & FIELD TRIPS: *The Floating Band Tour*

The Band had originally scheduled to have their band tour on a cruise ship. Unfortunately, the cruise company they had chosen seemed to have too much of a party atmosphere. Parents were worried about sending their teens on the ship, because of recent press coverage.

At almost the last minute, the plans were changed to another cruise line. There would be a High School band competition on this cruise. Everything couldn't be that bad. The band would have to fly from Anchorage to Los Angeles, where they would get on the ship. The cruise would take them to Mexico. Of course, the students were advised not to eat or drink anything while they were in Mexico since their performance would take place after the shore visit. Shopping for souvenirs was acceptable, but they had to make allowance for going through customs before getting back on the ship.

As we saw Jeff and his classmates off at the airport, I handed out samples of sun block. I got strange looks, but I thought everyone could use at least one covering of sun block. (Several students did return with sunburns.)

Jeff said that the ship seemed nice enough. It was huge, though. There was an itinerary about what activities were taking place on which deck, at which time. He said that the ship was so big that by the time they found the activity and realized it was meant for adults only, it was too late to make it any place else before having to check in with the chaperons. It would have been nice if they could have had some activities highlighted on the schedule, that were both age appropriate and on decks near where the students had business.

One of the other things Jeff noticed was all the places someone could hide. The ship was technically a chaperone's nightmare. I don't think it was any more difficult to monitor than any of the places I went on band tours, when I was in High School. I still thought Jeff's viewpoint was interesting.

Our Band students had a much earlier curfew than the rest of the schools did on the ship. What a bummer! I think Jeff came back with the least amount of sun exposure of all the students. One of his ears was a little pink. The rest of his skin had little opportunity for exposure, since he wears multiple layers, even in summertime.

## H) HOMEWORK: *Request for Compassion*

Mary's neighbor, Johnny, was going to be attending the Middle School this year. His father had terminal cancer, and there were good days and bad days. As a sixth grader, several of his classmates knew about Johnny's dad's condition. On bad days, someone would remember to bring Johnny's homework to him.

Moving to the Middle School, Johnny's mom requested that his classes be scheduled so at least one of the students from his old school was in each of his classes. She informed the school of Johnny's father's battle with cancer. A familiar face in each class would give a little comfort and provide a conduit for missed class work.

When the school year started, none of Johnny's classes had any of his classmates from the old school. This is a relatively rare occurrence. His mother went back to the school and spoke with the principal. The principal was unsympathetic. If the boy was going to lose his father, he should be able to take it, without any crutches. No accommodations would be made for this unusual situation. I wondered if the principal had ever lost a family member. If she had, how had she handled it?

### *Teach Yourself Creative Writing*

Did Jeff's problem with writing have anything to do with how the concept was presented? I didn't know. Like so many times before, I scoured the bookstores to see if there were any books that could help me teach my son creative writing. I expected a book to jump out at me and say, "Here I am!" The book this section is named after wouldn't nearly jump out at me for almost a year. I found, "Painless Writing", and a couple other books, that I thought might be helpful. I don't know how many hundreds of dollars I spent on supplemental materials to try to teach my kids what the schools were failing to teach them.

Teachers fussed about not having much free time for their families because they had to deal with correcting so much homework and other school related paperwork. Besides my job and any of the kids' extracurricular activities, I was trying unsuccessfully to teach myself how to be a teacher. Trying to work with my children on their homework was becoming a major battle. I couldn't teach Jeff to do something that I, myself, had found so daunting in school. Both Jeff and Melissa had outstripped my Math abilities also, but they spoke different languages. Jeff was unable to lead Melissa through her Math difficulties any better than I was.

No matter the medium, I was failing in my efforts to learn how to help my children. The process was "hit and miss". Sometimes I got lucky, like when I suggested Jeff read, "Rich Dad, Poor Dad". When his Economics teacher referred to the book, Jeff was the only one who had read it already. Unfortunately, "Painless Writing" and "Teach Yourself Creative Writing" came too late in the process, and Jeff had neither the interest, nor the time to absorb the information.

## K) CURRICULUM: *Don't Know Much About Geometry*

When Melissa started her Geometry class, she was still considered to have "gifted" status. Attempts to do Geometry during the year of home schooling had been unsuccessful, so she had a year's gap between her Algebra class and the Geometry class. Even though she was gifted, she struggled with Math. As the year progressed, I would notice the difference between the Geometry class that Jeff had taken, and the class Melissa was currently taking.

Jeff's teacher had required ten proofs per problem. She felt that ten were enough to show that the student understood the concepts. Melissa's teacher required more than twenty proofs. Since I know nothing about Geometry, except for the facts it involves shapes and formulas, I asked around about the requirements. Some of my friends who had taken college were surprised because twenty proofs is closer to a requirement for a college student who is going into a field that requires extensive Math skills. It was almost as if Melissa were in an Advanced Placement class, for those students who are taking the fast track for college. Melissa wasn't proficient enough for Advanced Placement and was visibly struggling.

Melissa tried to get help before school, at lunchtime, and after school. None of these times seemed convenient for the teacher, despite her assurances that she was available to help students with their questions.

At conference time, I spoke with the teacher about Melissa's problem. I explained to the teacher that Melissa had missed a year of Math with the home schooling. Minimal assistance could go a long way toward getting her on track. The teacher told me, she thought Melissa was "gifted", and had been placed in her class because of the certification. This was another teacher who thought being gifted means that a student needs more work. Nothing was done to help Melissa and she continued to struggle through. The final straw was a major exam.

Two weeks before school let out, Melissa had to take a major Geometry test. She was recently back at school after an illness that she hadn't quite recovered from. She picked up her supplies at her locker after lunch and headed towards class. She should have checked her supplies more carefully. The school is known for malfunctioning pencil sharpeners, so students usually carry mechanical pencils.

Melissa arrived at her class ready to take the test, or so she thought. About five minutes into the test, her pencil ran out of lead. Her refill container wasn't in her folder. With nearly 75 minutes left of testing; she needed to find another writing implement. The teacher wouldn't allow them to use a pen on the test. She couldn't go to her locker for another pencil, nor could she ask a classmate for a pencil. The teacher didn't have any pencils either. Nothing could be done to allow this student, who was willing to take the test, to reach the goal.

As soon as Melissa got home, I went to the school to speak with this teacher about the problem. The office paged the teacher, but there was no response. I was told that the teachers only had to be in school for a certain amount of time, due to their contracts. They couldn't be forced to stay any longer. With time being critically short, I asked if there was any way that Melissa could be allowed to retake the test. I was told that I would have to speak with the teacher about it.

Trying to track down the teacher without a major audience was difficult. She arrived at the school just before class started, and left nearly as soon as the students did. I finally reached her at lunchtime. I asked if there was any way that Melissa could retake the test, and was told (in no uncertain terms) that there was no way that it could be done. Melissa should have been more prepared. No allowances could have been made for her to use a pen on the test either. The test would have been marked wrong still. The teacher clearly believed that she was within her rights with her expectations, and there would be no more discussion. With an F on a major test, Melissa failed the second semester of Geometry, and would have to take it again during the second half of the next year.

I think this problem could have been solved in at least two simple ways. I know that a teacher can't afford to give a pencil to every student who needs one. At the beginning of the year, students could be required to bring an extra pencil for each of their teachers. That way, a teacher could have emergency pencils, if needed. In our school, there were at least 30 students per class, and each teacher had five classes. Even if a teacher had to hand out a pencil per day, and not get it back, there would be almost enough pencils.

The second solution would have been for Melissa to take the test in ink, no matter what the teacher said. At least, that way, she could have fought for the credit. If it had been a bubble sheet, the answers could have been transcribed onto a new form quite easily, if a computer couldn't read pen.

There are a variety of reasons this situation could have arisen. In general, students should be expected to be prepared. Sometimes, things just happen. Usually, Melissa was prepared. In fact, she often gave other students a spare pencil when one was needed. This teacher expected her students to be understanding about the difficulties with her pregnancy. It's too bad she couldn't have shown a little compassion for a student who was struggling. I give this teacher an "F" for her competency in doing her job.

## L) CRIMES & PUNISHMENTS: *Pencil Tapping and Detentions*

Matthew was required to take health class. Somewhere along the line, Matthew tapped his pencil in class. I don't know whether it was an accidental tapping, the type you see when kids are thinking while taking a test, or if it was more structured. I had seen Matthew use his pencil like a drumstick. It's unfortunate that he was never able to be in the Band properly. His forays into the music world were full of personality conflicts. He obviously marched to his own beat. I had also seen him use his thumbs to beat on various surfaces. If he was doing a more complicated beat, I could see why the teacher might have had a problem with his tapping. But she let him know that it REALLY bothered her, and that was her mistake. She had given the "Negative Attention Monster" his first snack.

I don't know if other students tapping their pencils bothered her, but she jumped on Matthew whenever he tapped. By the time he was ejected from her class, he had filled his cargo pants with every writing implement he could find around our house, and had tapped them all in class. The teacher looked at us (parents) as enablers. Did she really think I wanted to spend more money on writing implements, just so Matthew could have some fun? I never did get any of the pencils back. Once he had run out of pencils, he used his thumbs. Fingers are a little harder to confiscate.

There were several other ways the teacher could have reacted. One situation could have required him to have a foam rubber ball on the end of his pencil. That would have muffled the noise.

Before he was kicked out of the class, I had asked the principal to speak with the teacher. Matthew's discipline problems usually disappeared when little or no attention was given to them. The principal told me that I had to get Matthew under control because it was bothering this teacher so much. I countered with the fact that the teacher was the adult, and should handle the matter as an intelligent adult. I might have been overly generous with my assessment of the teacher's abilities.

Besides pencils, Matthew had brought fingerboards to class. These are mini skateboards that you maneuver with your finger. The Health teacher had decided that I couldn't do anything to improve the situation with Matthew, so she called my husband's work, about the problem. Often, he would come in on a Friday or Saturday, after being out of town for the week, to hear a message from Matthew's teacher. The teacher wanted to know what to do about the toy situation. It was relatively simple. She could have removed the toy from Matthew's possession. If she had a June box, or just confiscated it until one of us came to retrieve it, either solution would have been acceptable.

Without input from us, Matthew was given repeated detentions, after class. This detention cut into his lunch period. The detention from the Health teacher caused a domino effect. The detention caused him to be late for lunch, which might not be considered a hardship, unless you are forcibly removed from the lunchroom for not being seated.

Matthew would come into the lunchroom and be looking for a seat at the already crowded tables, when security would remove him from the lunchroom. Students were supposed to come into the lunchroom, get their food, and sit down immediately. There was no "looking" for a seat allowed. Matthew wasn't seated ten minutes into lunch; therefore, he must be "looking" for trouble. After my complaint about the situation, Matthew was given morning detentions.

Morning detentions required the student be in the school half an hour before school started. That was the same time my husband had to be at work across town. Unfortunately, we shared a car. I couldn't drop Matthew off earlier, because there weren't any teachers in the school to supervise him. School was too far away to walk. It took at least 45 minutes at a rapid pace. I got him to school, one morning, just as the detention was letting out. It only lasted ten minutes. The other 20 minutes, the students sat in the lunchroom and waited for the first bell to ring.

One morning, I was ready to take Matthew for the morning detention. My husband was out of town, so there would be no problem getting Matthew there on time. I opened the curtains to find a thick fog. I drove towards the school and miscalculated my turn. I was one stop light too early, and had to go around the "block" to get to the school. By the time I pulled into the school's parking lot, detention was over. I wondered how many other students missed the detention that day.

*Caffeine Alert*

The story was on the news that a middle school student had brought some caffeine pills to school. He had given them to his friends, and one friend ended up in the hospital because of an overdose. The principal was on the news vilifying the student for giving his classmates caffeine. While the student shouldn't have brought the pills to the school, the schools push more caffeine than any student does, and they do it for money.

At Matthew's middle school, the soda and snack machines had a time lock on them. As soon as the afternoon bell rang, kids were lined up by the soda machine, with their money ready. I watched two students empty about ten cans from the machine. One fed the machine the money and the other caught the cans as they came out. Supposedly, there were rules against food and drink on the school buses that these children were getting ready to board, but that didn't stop them from buying enough for all their friends.

Sodas may be a major contributor to the Attention Deficit problem. When you're pumped full of caffeine, can you really focus on your work? The schools usually sell the 20 oz bottles. The carbonation decreases the amount of oxygen in your blood. Insufficient oxygen in the blood means you aren't getting much to your brain. Phosphoric acid and citric acid, in the amounts that sodas use, leach calcium out of the bones. Calcium has a calming effect on the nervous system. Besides, kids are now becoming one of the fastest growing segments of the population for osteoporosis. Caffeine and sugar increase the calcium loss and cause dehydration. Without enough moisture, your brain doesn't function properly. Sugar also compromises your immune system. That's great for a petri dish environment like a school. The artificial sweeteners make your liver sluggish. Who was the real "pusher" in this situation? The educated principal, or the misguided student?

## M) DISCRIMINATION, HARASSMENT & ABUSE: *Betty's Quandary*

Betty's son had been doing pretty well in school, when his grades suddenly plummeted, and anger management problems appeared. In most of my experiences, the teachers would start pointing fingers at the parents for abusing the child, or demand the student be checked for substance abuse. Betty noticed the grades drop on her son's report card, and she was pretty sure what was causing the problem. She just didn't know how to deal with it. How could she explain the situation to the teachers? Would there be fallout if she trusted the teachers enough to tell them what was bothering her son?

Her son had recently discovered that a serious crime had been committed against some of his younger cousins and close family friends. The perpetrator was someone he had known all his life, and trusted. There wasn't any tangible evidence, and the victims were young and inarticulate. Without the necessary evidence, there wouldn't be any justice. The perpetrator would get away with the crime. How could anyone explain to a teenager why a criminal can escape punishment? What kind of counseling can you get for a person who isn't considered to be a victim, but is still deeply affected by the crime?

The teachers started calling Betty after the grades had bottomed out for about two months. She asked the teachers if they could tell when the grades started dropping. Every teacher gave a date that was within a week after the crime. This wasn't something that could be discussed over the phone, so Betty arranged her schedule to speak with the teacher she felt was most approachable.

Betty arrived at the school and found the teacher she wanted, in the office. When she told the teacher, "I need to tell you what's going on" she had the teacher's full attention. They found a place where they could talk privately. The teacher listened to what Betty had to say, and commented that she now understood what was causing the angry outbursts. It seemed like he would get upset if a bigger student seemed to be picking on a smaller student. With the missing pieces of the puzzle, the teachers could deal with the situation better.

The rest of the year progressed uneventfully. The teachers managed to deal with the situation without making an issue of it. His grades went up, and he finished the year with respectable grades.

## N) SAFETY & SECURITY: *The Mountain View Slashings*

A half an hour on the morning of May 7 changed the lives of several students at Mountain View Elementary. According to accounts, a man carrying a filleting knife entered the school grounds, about 8:15 AM, and attacked four children, inflicting wounds to their faces and necks as they were preparing to enter the school for breakfast. A twelve-year-old boy on the playground saw a man stabbing kids, and threw himself at the assailant. Then he tried to draw the assailant away from the injured child.

The assailant gained entry to the school. The teachers implemented their lock down procedure, which they had just practiced the week before. A couple members of the Community Patrol were nearby and heard the call for the police. Within minutes they were at the school, helping to contain the assailant.

By 8:43 AM, the assailant was in custody and the school grounds had been checked for other victims or assailants. Students were bused to a neighboring school, where the police were able to question witnesses. School was closed the next day.

Could anything have been done to prevent this situation? Maybe not. How secure can you make a school playground? School employees can't watch it 24 hours a day. During school hours, some adult should be able to supervise students. There was no supervision on this day. Students should be made aware of what to look for in an intruder. Supposedly, this man came from the wooded area along the playground. He wasn't accompanied by any child. Since then, a fence has been installed between the playground and the woods, but children still need to be aware of their surroundings. Students also need to have limited access to the building. Could a child have entered the building in a hurry, or were the doors locked?

The teachers did the right thing by running through their lock down routine. The boy who distracted the assailant was cheered as a hero. He probably saved the other boy's life. Later, authorities would chastise him for putting himself at risk. We all have a mission in life. Who's to say that this action wasn't part of his mission? It's probably easier for him to accept the criticism than to be dealing with survivor's guilt, if he hadn't done anything. He had a brilliant show of compassion, which can seem rare in a neighborhood that's always in the news for its violence.

Everyone did what he or she was supposed to do, and by some miracle, no one died. Increased community involvement and awareness are the only things that can make our schools safer.

## P) POLICIES & PROCEDURES: *No Hats Allowed*

Matthew slipped on the ice and cut his head at the beginning of January. We took him to the emergency room, they trimmed his hair in the affected area, and they glued him together. Head or facial wounds tend to bleed profusely, and Matthew is a normal teenage boy. I thought that a classmate would say something about the little bit of hair that was sticking up with the glue, and he would touch it or they would touch it. If it was disturbed, it could bleed profusely, causing a disruption in school.

I asked the doctor for a note that said Matthew could wear a hat in school for a couple days. The doctor wrote a note that specified 10 days. I figured if Matthew could get past the three remaining days of the week, he would probably be healed enough. We took the note to the nurse. Matthew intended to wear his baseball cap, with the bill curled around the back of his neck.

After I left the school, I went home. Upon my arrival at my house, I got the message from the assistant principal. Matthew wouldn't be allowed to stay in school if he wore a hat. The nurse had a couple options for me, though. Supposedly, the baseball cap was a sign of gang members. Even with the bill down, the principal thought that someone would try to pull the cap off, causing Matthew to be injured. This type of cap was obviously too risky.

The nurse gave me her options. Her first option was a knit cap. While it covered the affected area, in my opinion, it resembled more of the gang hats I had seen. Besides, it would be a lot hotter and itchier than the baseball cap. The other option was a headband. I tried the headband on Matthew's head. It nicely covered his ears, which weren't affected by his injury, but it left the crown of his head exposed. Anyone still had access to the wound. I tried to explain to the nurse the objective of a hat was to protect the wound. It was hard to put a Band-Aid on the area, and sending him to school with a bandage wrapped all around his head just to cover the small area would only draw attention. I begged for them to let him wear the baseball cap through the end of the week. I was told if I insisted he wear the cap, he would be suspended.

He was suspended for three days, and I wasn't allowed to get his homework. He had to be absent three days before I could even ask for it. We went to the woman in charge of Secondary Education, and asked for support for our doctor's note. The woman said that she wouldn't interfere with the school's disciplinary measures. My son had to follow the rules.

Matthew went back to school on Monday morning without his hat. Keeping him out of the school really taught him a lesson. No one wanted to teach him. We had toyed with the idea of sending him to school sooner with a hat that wasn't as closely related to gangs. Maybe he could have attended school wearing a beret, a sailor's cap, a sombrero, or a yarmulke.

### The Book Sneak

Jeff's grades were so low that the teachers knew he wasn't going to graduate if nothing was done. At this point, they're required to contact the parents of any failing students, to apprise them of the situation. Hopefully, the parents can motivate the failing student into completing the work well enough to bring up the grade.

Jeff's composition teacher called me. She said that Jeff wasn't doing much work in her class, but she had seen him reading a lot. I commented on the fact that I used to be a book sneak, when I was younger, so I would speak to him about it. (The book always seemed to be more interesting than the task at hand.)

The teacher told me, while she wasn't against books, Jeff really needed to spend the time working on his homework. I told her I would try to remind him that he needed to budget his time better. The book could wait. He continued to move at a snail's pace for his work, and ended up failing the class. He wouldn't graduate this year.

Q) ALTERNATIVE EDUCATION & GETTING CREDIT: *All Schools Are Not Created Equally*

Jeff's friend Thomas lived in Anchorage as a child, then his family moved to a rural area. While in the rural area, Thomas took his first year of High School by correspondence course. When they came back to Anchorage, Thomas' mother enrolled him into the school system as a sophomore. Unfortunately, his credits from the previous year didn't translate into credits by Anchorage's standards. The Anchorage School District didn't recognize the correspondence school. It didn't matter that the correspondence school was valid, his credits just wouldn't be recognized. He had to take the classes over.

Thomas was a smart kid and being held back for a year, to repeat things he already knew was too much for him. After a year in the High School, he dropped out. What was the point of going to school? His mother enrolled him in Nine Star, and he got his GED.

*Urban Rural Youth Exchange*

The High Schools were advertising an exchange program between rural and urban students. In Alaska, you have the metropolitan, urban areas, and you have the nearly Third World conditions in the isolated villages in the Bush. Some villages didn't have any indoor plumbing yet. People who live in urban areas generally don't have any clues as to how the Native population lives. This program was started to promote understanding, so we can come up with laws that are fair to all of the State's population.

Melissa was interested in the program. My husband worked in the Bush, so she knew a little bit about what to expect. There were orientation classes. Students learned about the language and the culture of the people, as well as the geography. Ground transportation in the area they were going to visit was snow machines.

Melissa took the classes, and went to a village for eleven days. The students were paired up to visit the villages. In the village that Melissa went to, there wasn't any indoor plumbing, but the school had Internet. Students at the school didn't start to formally learn English until they were in the third grade. Before that, they were taught their native language of Yupik. While the students were away, they had to do their own schoolwork, as well as the schoolwork from the school they were visiting. The urban to rural part of the exchange took place around spring break. The rural to urban exchange took place about a month later.

The students came back from their exchange to speak about what they saw. Melissa tried hard, but her village had very little cultural activity. While other students had done handicrafts and learned to dance in their host villages, the culture seemed to have been gutted in her village. It didn't seem like her host family understood why she was there. For the first ten of the eleven days she was there, they thought she was there to convert them somehow. They didn't realize that she was there to learn from them. Nothing she could say would relieve their suspicion. This was an extremely sensitive point.

When Melissa's host sister came to visit us, I felt so sorry for her. I only saw her smile one day. She was extremely homesick, and the city was extremely noisy compared to the Bush. I took her to visit some of her relatives who were in town, at her request, but we weren't welcome to visit with her.

Our experience was quite different from the experiences the other families had. This was the pilot year for this program, so we were questioned about how everything went. When we were called by the independent observers, for the follow-up, I was afraid to speak with them because I didn't want anything I said to jeopardize the program. After making sure who I was supposed to talk to, Melissa and I explained our position.

I had been an exchange student through the American Field Service (AFS). This program didn't have any more problems than I had seen in my AFS experience, and they had been in business nearly 40 years when I went through it! Like AFS, the rules had specified that the exchange students wouldn't be allowed to drive a vehicle or use a firearm. Also, like AFS, sometimes there were misunderstandings.

The people in Melissa's village didn't understand the rules Melissa had to abide by and they didn't understand the mission. It would just have to be made clearer for future exchanges.

During the course of the exchanges, there was a story on the news about the low Native population in our University system. In Anchorage, I think there had only been a very small amount of students from the Bush, in our University over the past four years. It was expected that only 10% of them would complete college. This made me very sad.

After our exchange experience, I realized how difficult it must be for these students to come into town. Our high school had 2000 students in attendance. The village Melissa visited only had 300 residents. Our school alone must have been terrifying for someone coming from a place that small. What must the city of Anchorage seem like for someone from one of the villages? It may be one thing to come into town for a couple days to shop, but it's totally different to have to survive here.

I think the University needs to have a program where several local students adopt a student from the villages, to help them find there way around during their first year. That way, their survival rate in the educational system might be a little better.

*No Prior Authorization*

I met Eddie when Jeff was in summer school. Eddie was epileptic and dyslexic. He was in Jeff's Trigonometry class, but he was only in the eighth grade. When the school year started, he would be a freshman in High School. Eddie was a Math whiz, yet his summer school credits couldn't be allowed in High School. He needed to have the High School know that he was taking these classes during the summer, so they would allow the credits.

He had to accumulate Math credits again, despite respectable grades during summer school for the higher math. Goodness knows we can't give students credit for information they have learned ahead of everyone else.

*Last Minute Calls*

Dolly had checked with her daughter's counselor before the summer vacation to find out if her daughter was any credits short. The counselor told Dolly her daughter would still be half a credit short, if she took a full class load, her senior year. Dolly enrolled her daughter in one class for summer school, to make up the difference.

When the new school year started, Dolly thought everything was fine. Just before second semester, the counselor called her and informed her of her daughter's status. She was still half a credit short, even with the summer school credit. Dolly had to pay for a correspondence course, for her daughter to make up the missing credit. It was nearly $200. The school shouldn't have waited until the last minute to let her know about this problem. If they had told her before the summer that her daughter was a whole credit short, she would have put her in another summer school class. It sure would have cost her less.

In the next school district, Susie was on a romantic trip with her husband when she received the call from the high school counselor, that her daughter was short half a credit. This was really last minute notice. It was the last day that the girl could sign up for a correspondence class. The counselor could make the request. Susie just had to give her permission and she could pay for the class when she got back from her trip. Susie gave her permission, and paid the bill.

Both girls managed to graduate on time, but it's hard to budget for a big bill, on the spur of the moment. It would have been better if the school could have done their job, and noticed the credit problem sooner.

### S) SICKNESS & HEALTH: *Patient Heal Thyself*

Melissa's year had started out like the previous year, with the flu. She would get it about five times during the year. Because of numerous absences, we received letters for attendance probation and threats of withdrawal/failure if she missed any more school. About a month before the end of the first semester, she developed mononucleosis and had to have a doctor's excuse for Gym class.

Melissa found out later, when she had turned her head to look at a friend during lunch, another classmate who was infected had decided she wanted to try Melissa's soda. Melissa had no idea that the classmate had taken a drink of her soda, because she didn't usually share her drinks.

Even though there were only about two weeks left of the semester; the Gym teacher tried to fail her. The teacher who was responsible for issuing the grade was on maternity leave due to a difficult pregnancy. Actively teaching would have been just as hazardous to her health as actively participating in class would have been for Melissa. Yet we had to fight for Melissa's rights and safety. Complications from Mononucleosis could include such dangerous things as an enlarged/ruptured spleen and meningitis. (The next year, a student in another school would die of meningitis as a complication of the mononucleosis virus.)

Whether it was mono or the flu, Melissa's tonsils swelled so big, they obstructed her breathing. I was worried about losing my daughter and the school could only harass me about her absences. If we had her tonsils out, she would miss a lot more school because of recovery time. She also needed to be healthy to have the surgery, so we had to wait until summertime to schedule the surgery.

Doctors' notes didn't carry much weight in this school either. A week before school let out, Melissa injured the ligaments in the top of her foot, and it was extremely painful to walk. The doctor gave her a note stating she wasn't to climb stairs for three weeks. The note was promptly given to the school nurse, who issued her a key for the elevator. Two days later, the nurse asked for the key back. Since Melissa's foot wasn't in a cast, it mustn't be very serious. We had to fight for the key.

It's a difficult situation, having a school aged child who gets sick. If you send a sick child to school, you're a bad parent. If you keep the child home, you're a bad parent. If your child is well enough to go to school, but weak enough to need a doctor's note, school personnel still think your child is considered to be healthy enough to participate in any school activity. It seemed, in our case, that the school didn't concern itself with the student's health and welfare. If students don't matter, what's the school's mission?

## U) CELEBRATIONS: *The Junior-Senior Prom*

Melissa was invited to the Prom this year. Her date was a senior boy who wasn't serious about her. They just thought it would be fun to go to the Prom. After Melissa had accepted the Prom invitation, she found out that her host sister (from the Bush) was going to be staying with us during that time.

Since there were no proms or school dances in the village Melissa had stayed at, she thought it might be nice for her exchange sister to experience one. We had been encouraged to include the exchange siblings in as much of our normal activity as possible. This week, Prom would be a normal activity and her date had no objections, so Melissa set out to buy her a ticket. I wrote a note explaining our situation, and enclosed a check. The school chose not to contact the exchange program coordinator, and informed Melissa, in no uncertain terms, that she couldn't invite another student to the Junior-Senior Prom, because she was neither a junior nor a senior.

I contacted the exchange program coordinator and explained our problem. She contacted the school. The next day, the people who had yelled at Melissa were quite friendly about providing a ticket.

The girls both looked very nice when they were all dressed up. I understand they had a very pleasant evening.

## V) SUPPLIES: *Being Prepared*

Jeff had told me he needed a music book for band class. He had given me the name of the book, but I misplaced the paper I had written it on. I was at the music store when I realized this. The clerk asked if I needed any help. I told him I was looking for a music book, but I wasn't sure if he could help me, since I had lost my note. The clerk asked which school Jeff went to and which hour he had the class.

The Band teacher was good. He had given the information to all the music stores in town, in case a person like me came in and needed help. It also seemed that many other Music teachers in the School District were doing the same thing. I bet that made everyone's job much easier.

## Z) LAST IMPRESSIONS: *Forcible Removal*

Matthew had learned to skip school more often. There was barely anything in the school to make him want to stay. He wasn't able to see his friends at all during school, so he skipped school with them. The city bus ran near the school and it was easy for him to catch the bus back to our neighborhood. He was getting so much attention from the disciplinary staff that it wasn't funny. Towards the end of the school year, I was called and asked if Matthew should be put into in-school or out of school suspension. From Matthew's behavior, I decided out of school might be better.

He was upset when I told him about the suspension, and said that he wanted to have the in-school suspension. We went to the school the next day to see if it could be changed. The office told me that in-school suspension was full, so the suspension couldn't be changed. It didn't matter much either way. I wondered about the sudden interest in school. Maybe his friends had been put into the in-school suspension.

About two weeks before school ended, Matthew was suspended for the last time. I received a call from the counselor late one evening. She told me that Matthew could pick up his homework packet from her the next day. She would go over the packet to tell him what was necessary for him to complete for graduation from the school. After this meeting, he wouldn't be allowed on school property again.

I sent Matthew to school the next morning to pick up the homework packet. I passed by the school on my way home from dropping my husband off at work. I figured that would give Matthew enough time to collect anything he still had at the school and his homework.

When I arrived at the school, the office personnel sternly informed me that Matthew had been suspended and wasn't allowed to be in the building. When I asked where he was, the secretary said she had to locate him. It took fifteen minutes. I tried asking about the homework packet that the counselor had called me about the previous evening, but I was only told that Matthew and I were to vacate the premises immediately, or the police would be called. Matthew still hadn't been located, at this point.

I finally found Matthew in the counselor's office, but he hadn't been able to see the counselor yet. The vice-principal grabbed my arm and propelled me towards the front door. I had bruises for a week from the pressure that was applied. We left the building and went home.

I called the counselor and made an appointment to go over the homework and pick up the packet. In order to see her, I had to sign in at the office. The secretary heaved a loaded garbage bag at me from behind the counter. As it came flying towards me, she said it was Matthew's locker contents. I was glad to be leaving this school. If they did this to the parents, what did they do to the students?

I picked up the locker contents and the homework packet. None of the contents of the bag the secretary had thrown at me belonged to Matthew. He shared a locker with two friends, who had been quite surprised when they went to their locker and found it empty. The bag also contained a few textbooks. In their haste, school employees had discarded school property that could have impacted these boys' grades. No textbook equals no report card. Luckily, Matthew saw these boys outside of school and he returned their property to them.

Matthew completed the homework and I returned it to the school. We got a glowing form letter from the school, congratulating Matthew on graduating from the 8th grade. During the summer, I found a whole pile of textbooks under his bed. I don't understand how he managed to get all these books out of the school. One of them was a library book, which shouldn't have been able to leave the library. It was an encyclopedia. In spite of having several outstanding library and textbooks, his report card wasn't withheld. I returned the errant books to the school district offices. I had been tempted to throw them at the office staff at the Middle School, but that would have just been petty and dangerous.

# Chapter 18
## All Three in High School 2001-02

A) FIRST IMPRESSIONS: *Chaos Incorporated*

I took each of the kids to the school for their registration. They had filled out paperwork the previous year for their class requests. Each grade level had a color-coded class schedule. If there was an error in your schedule, you made the necessary changes and turned it back in. Senior requests had first priority. Jeff was a second year senior. Hopefully, they would be able to give him the right classes, the first time, this year. Last year, his class schedule changed five times in the first two weeks.

Matthew's schedule had the most changes necessary. They had him scheduled for ROTC and French. I doubted that ROTC was what Matthew needed, and he had shown neither aptitude nor interest in a foreign language. We had to request changes, but choosing new classes was near impossible. There wasn't a list of classes that were offered specifically at our school, only the master list from the School District. We would have to play "hit and miss" to find appropriate classes. We were only allowed one alternative to replace the scheduled class. I had Matthew fill in two for each class. I felt that would give us a better chance of getting a class he wanted, without having to endlessly repeat this exercise in futility.

Melissa was scheduled for a computer class that was coveted by much of the student body, but Melissa hadn't requested it. One of her classmates had requested the class, but he was given a Home Economics class that he hadn't asked for. We wondered if they put the electives in a fish bowl and picked them randomly.

Betty was having difficulty. Her son was at the charter school, which had a seven-class schedule with the two rotating afternoon classes. Charter schools don't have the resources to offer a lot of electives, so students wanting a class that is offered elsewhere can take that class at another school. Betty's son wanted Latin. She tried our school, but was told that it would be "impossible" for her son to attend the class at our school. Looking at the logistics later, she discovered this was true, but no one explained to her why it was impossible. She called the School District to find out who was teaching Latin this year. She was told to call each of the schools individually because the School District didn't have that information. The only schools that would fit her travel parameters were our school, and our neighboring high school. Neither schedule was compatible with the charter school's schedule. The quest for Latin (in a school setting) was abandoned.

E) DIFFERENCES & DISABILITIES: *The Aptitude Tests*

We were losing valuable time. Jeff basically had to have his English credits, and the credit he was having the most trouble with was English Composition. After years of trying to figure out how to get Jeff to do his homework, I finally got some answers, but I shouldn't have needed to figure this out. After all, I'm not a "trained professional" like the teachers and the counselors are.

I had Jeff take two tests. One was for the Slingerland Program, to determine if he might have Dysgraphia or another learning disability. I dropped him off at the testing site and ran some errands. The test was to be taken in pen, so the tester could monitor errors. The amount of errors indicated whether or not there was a learning disability. I returned to the testing site, about the time he was supposed to be finished. He was the only "student" still in the classroom. He seemed to be intently listening to the tester. She saw me at the door, and motioned me to come in. I sat in one of the desks and watched their exchange in quiet fascination.

Jeff had one section left on his test. It was an essay section. The tester gave him an impromptu lesson on organizing ideas. I had tried to help Jeff with this concept in the eighth grade but, since I didn't understand it myself, we just couldn't figure it out. The concept was the story web. They picked an arbitrary subject: Halloween. Then she asked Jeff to give her a list of things he associated with the holiday. Next, she talked about grouping them. I was fascinated. It was an outline. They had always plagued me through school, but this one seemed less menacing. After this five-minute lesson, Jeff set to work on his paragraph. Within twenty minutes, we were on our way home. The extra lesson didn't affect Jeff's score. It just loosened him up enough to fill in the required space. I'm sure the tester had places she needed to go, so the five minutes probably saved us all a lot of time.

We got the results of the test back. The tester read Jeff's paragraph to me over the phone. It had to do with being labeled as a gifted student. He didn't have a learning disability, but he did seem to have some noticeable gaps in his writing mechanics. She said it was almost as if he had missed a lot of critical English classes in elementary school. That's exactly what had happened, but we had run out of time to go back for the basics.

I suggested the second test because I thought it would help him figure out what he was suited for once he left High School. It was an aptitude test, through the local Job Center. When we got the results back, I was shocked. I had never seen 25 or 50 percentile on any of my son's tests before. If the test had to do with thinking, he was in the 88-98 percentile range. His fine motor skills (working with fingers) were at 25 percentile, and his gross motor skills (using the whole hand) were at 50 percentile. The fine motor skills problem affects your writing. My son hadn't been lazy (or maybe disorganized) for all these years. He had a physical disability that could have been remedied in elementary school.

About the same time I got the results for the tests, I was reading a book I had around the house, but had never been able to get into. It was a book about being a parent of a gifted child. I had been bogged down by the sections about dealing with underachievers and perfectionists. Both seemed to be Jeff, but I had been overwhelmed by the school system and I couldn't seem to concentrate on the problem. If I had read a little further, I would have reached the section about fine motor skills problems.

Many "gifted" kids have fine motor skills problems because they can think faster than they can actually write, at a young age. Things like playing the piano, working with clay, doing bead work, and knitting, all help with the fine motor skills. If Jeff's fifth grade teacher had encouraged the knitting for more than the required project, we might have had more success with Jeff's writing earlier.

Despite the special label that was supposed to help Jeff, none of the trained professionals ever figured out the problem. It had been like a huge cavity that went through three teeth. Jeff could test well in English, Math, and Science, but writing was the problem. He was the perfect student, except for homework, and the experts had warned us about that. "Gifted" students always had a weakness somewhere. Identifying it was usually the problem. After years of begging for help from teachers, and being told that I was doing something wrong, I was the one who figured out what had been holding Jeff back. It wasn't a mysterious and rare malady like Dysgraphia. It was a simple, fine motor skills problem. The delay in diagnosis had kept him from graduating. Would we be able to make it this year?

*Math Problems*

While we were dealing with "Everyday Math" in Alaska, my friend Laurel was dealing with a different Math program in Minnesota. Math experts in her School District had pored over textbooks until they found a program that fit the needs of their students. They considered the concept of story problems that fit real life situations to be of major importance. The students needed to be able to figure out which information, in the story, was necessary to construct the equations they needed in their own lives.

Laurel was a teacher's aide in an elementary school. Despite the excellent program in the chosen textbooks, Laurel was having problems working with certain students. The program assumes that students of the appropriate age for the level of Math also have the commensurate reading ability. Laurel found two groups that won't do well with this premise. The first group speaks English, but is below grade level in their reading ability. The second group are students who have English as a second language, and may not have had much exposure to it before being required to comprehend it (in written form) at an elevated level.

The School District Laurel worked for might not have as much language diversity as Anchorage does, and some of this problem might be overcome with help from members of the different cultural communities. Anchorage has about 90 different languages in their School District. That means that some of our immigrant communities might be quite small, and not as organized to help with the language problems. Immersion in a language is definitely the best way of learning the desired language, but it's hard to achieve the desired goal if you are only exposed to the language in school. This is one example of how mobility can hinder the education process.

The logical method for teaching Math effectively was being undermined by the lack of language comprehension.

*Underachievers Anonymous*

I have recently heard of at least three cases of early elementary aged children, whose parents were told erroneously that their children were candidates for the "resource" side of the Special Education program. In at least two of the cases, the children in question were found to be working on the "gifted" end of the spectrum.

The first case is a first grade girl. Her parents are well educated, and the girl speaks quite well. The teacher was testing students individually, and this girl failed the testing. Because of the one test, the teacher recommended she be placed in "resource" classes. Any perceptive adult could have seen that the child had no affection for the teacher. The little girl displayed her empowerment by being non-compliant. If someone else might have done the testing, she might have scored better. Her parents moved her out of that class, and her grades went up. This little girl is quite quick to pick up any information around her. I know because I have talked with her.

The second case involved a boy who was entering kindergarten. For a couple years, he's had his mom's undivided attention during the school day. Suddenly, his mom was taking him to a strange place, and leaving him with strange people. There was no time allowed for him to warm up to his testers. They couldn't overcome his feeling of being abandoned and he didn't test very well. The testers perceived his lack of compliance as lack of ability and labeled him as "resource". They might have made a little more progress if they would have started by playing games with him, while his mother was still in the room. She could have left once they were fully involved. Or, they could have had an adjoining room with a small window, so the child knew Mom was still nearby.

The third case was a boy in kindergarten. His mother was a volunteer at the school, so I had talked with her. Before they sent their son to school, they taught him that the teacher's job is to educate him. He wasn't supposed to challenge the teacher's authority and be disrespectful. In other words, the teacher is always right in matters of education. The problem arose as they were learning their numbers.

The students were given a worksheet that displayed a single large piece of fruit in the middle of the frame. The lesson was for the number one. Way down in the corner of the paper, outside of the focus frame, was another miniature piece of the same fruit, and teaching notes for the lesson.

The teacher asked how many pieces of fruit were on the worksheet. Of course, the rest of the class were focused on the big picture and answered in a loud chorus, "ONE". The teacher praised the class, but noticed that the boy in question seemed to be in disagreement. She specifically asked him how many pieces of fruit were on the paper. He saw two, but the teacher was supposed to be right, so he refused to answer. That afternoon, the teacher told his mother that she might want to consider getting him tested for "resource". The mother removed her son from that school and placed him in another school. He was tested for Special Education and was certified "gifted".

156

How many other children are labeled on the basis of a single encounter? If a teacher meets a student on a bad day, the first impression can cling to the student throughout the rest of his school career, unless another teacher decides to judge the student on his own merits, and disregard the label.

*Adventures in Tutoring*

Betty's son was having some problems with his Algebra, so she called me to ask which of my kids would be interested in helping him understand his lessons. Melissa was interested, but she was more visual and needed to see the material they were discussing. Jeff was better suited to deal with the problems over the phone, on an on-call basis. It was the beginning of December, and Betty's son was failing. He had always been quick to pick up Math concepts, but the teacher didn't seem to have the aptitude for teaching the subject. Since he was the only Algebra teacher at the school, Betty's son couldn't change classes. Asking the teacher for help was futile, so Betty's only option was to try to find a tutor.

Jeff struck a deal with Betty. He would tutor her son at least one day a week for two hours per session. What did he need to focus on? The teacher suggested they start at the front of the book and work their way up to the present materials. Within two weeks, Jeff had Betty's son up to speed.

The teacher was unimpressed by the progress. Even though the work might be coming in perfect, the tests were less promising. The teacher decided that Jeff had been giving the boy the answers to his homework. Both Betty and I knew this wasn't true. Jeff made him work for the answers. If Jeff had to tell him an answer was wrong, he asked Betty's son to explain how he got to the answer. By talking it out, he usually found his own mistake. When Jeff was looking over the tests, he noticed that the mistakes were relatively minor, in general. The answer might have been the right number; it was just the wrong polarity. Jeff was great at taking tests, but was lousy on his homework, and Betty's son was the opposite. He did fantastic homework, but he froze up on tests. It wouldn't have taken the teacher too much effort to figure out that he was throwing away a bright student.

When they heard that Betty's son had a tutor, his classmates were so jealous. Many of them were also struggling with the material. Was it a student problem or a teaching problem? Because the tutoring started so late in the semester, Jeff was unable to help Betty's son pull his grade up to passing. Like most of his class, he wasn't promoted to the second semester, since he had failed the first semester.

I suggested they look into alternative routes for getting the credit. Maybe he could test out of the subject or take a GSS type class, if the school offered it. The only option that the charter school had was a challenge, and it involved several steps. The first step involved getting a packet of study materials. When the packet was completed, the teacher would administer a test. Several more packets would follow before the credit was given. The boy's first obstacle was persuading the teacher to give him the first packet. This activity took weeks. After completing the first packet, it took more weeks to get the second one. Betty's son finally gave up on the project. He realized, no matter how quickly he completed the materials; the teacher wasn't really interested in working with him to complete the task by the end of the year. If there wasn't any hope of getting any credit for the work, why do it?

Betty's son ended up taking his Algebra through a correspondence course. He completed all of the required work in less than a month and without additional aid from a tutor. His grade was quite respectable. Jeff, a student himself, spent twenty hours tutoring Betty's son, while the teacher (a trained professional) spent ninety hours teaching a class with a high failure rate. This is how our tax money is being wasted.

*Enlightenment*

Mary's son had some of the same problems Jeff had gone through, but their school had handled it differently. A teacher had suggested that Mary's son might be "resource" material, because of his illegible handwriting. She challenged the teacher to ask her son about any subject that they had covered in class, so far. The boy went into a verbal report that left no doubt in the teacher's mind that he was on the "gifted" end of the spectrum, and not "resource".

Like Jeff, Mary's son had been put into a Study Skills class to help him complete his homework. Unlike Jeff's class, Mary's son received credit for his class. Besides the methods of organization and taking notes that Jeff's class had, this class discussed the different ways people learn. By the time the class ended, each student knew where they would fit, as far as their learning styles.

This teacher who had been teaching the Study Skills class seemed to have compartmentalized the information because the "resource" label was made after the boy had completed the Study Skills class. Many of the current teachers weren't taught how to recognize learning differences before they finished college. They're learning it supplementally, and it's not like a reflex yet. If a teacher is teaching above elementary level, they generally don't look for these learning differences, because they have to concentrate more on the curriculum. I don't consider this a deficiency in the individual teachers. It's more of a flaw in their training.

Once the teacher realized that he hadn't been applying the concepts he had been teaching to students in his Study Skills classes, he changed his teaching style and all of the students benefited. Mary's son was allowed to bring a lap top computer to class, to take notes. In Jeff's schools, the computer wouldn't have been allowed.

If teachers could catch these learning differences when the students are in elementary school, instead of just labeling them as difficult and pushing them forward, the schools would be more successful. I believe it could eliminate much of the time and money we currently allot for disciplinary actions.

## H) HOMEWORK: *Ahead of the Curve*

The tester from the Slingerland test had suggested Jeff write formula papers. If he had to do a writing assignment, he could come up with a general format where he could "plug in" the required information for the current subject. Some writers use formulas when they write. For instance, Barbara Cartland's books had a young heroine, an older hero, a conflict, and a location. Of course, everyone ended up happily ever after. It was the same story, you just dress the characters differently.

Unfortunately, we didn't have time for that. He had composition classes where they required different styles of papers. By this time, he was in two composition classes, and a class about Shakespeare. Sometimes, I was successful at tricking him into writing something, but it wouldn't work if the teachers didn't accept it.

One weekend, Jeff came home with an assignment to write a descriptive paper about the island where "The Tempest" takes place. I knew he hated writing descriptions, so I suggested an alternative style that still fit the parameters of the subject. I figured the teacher would rather get something than nothing. We checked out a copy of "The Tempest" from the library, and rented a copy of "Forbidden Planet" from the video store. I told him that I expected him to write a comparison paper about the two versions of the story. By Sunday night, he had a full typed page, in duplicate. If he was going to write anything, I wanted to make sure his composition teacher had a chance to see it, too. Who knows when he might need a comparison paper?

Monday morning, he sat in his composition class as the teacher gave them their lesson. It was a comparison paper. Minutes later, Jeff handed his completed assignment in to a surprised teacher. He received good marks from both of his teachers, for the assignment.

### The Proper Perspective

Betty said that her son learned that grades for homework were subjective, when he was in the first grade. He did in-school work just fine, but he didn't do very much of his homework. At that age, he didn't need his teacher's approval. He knew what he understood and didn't feel that he needed to prove it to anyone else.

When he got to High School, suddenly, those grades had meaning. If he didn't have good grades, he might not be able to get any scholarships for college. With this realization, he started to do his work more.

My friend Elaine, from work, said that she told her boys that school should be looked at as a game. You must complete the game before you can go on to the rest of your life. This is an interesting perspective. Games have competition, strategies and objectives. This viewpoint might make the education process a little easier to deal with.

My viewpoint was education should be looked at as training for business. In the work place, there will always be paperwork, whether we have technology or not. What would they do if the technology dropped out? We may have to convey a specific message to someone else on paper. It won't help if the message can't be read or understood. I also agree with the game concept. Students taking tests should realize they aren't just competing against each other for the high grade, they are also competing against themselves for improvement. It's like trying to make the best time for a sporting competition. An athlete is always trying to improve his "score".

Melissa dealt with school more along the lines of the game concept. She tried to play by the rules, but they kept changing. Jeff and Matthew had reasoning like Betty's son. "I do well on tests, why should I do any homework?"

Turning in homework is the biggest problem I have seen with the kids I know. It doesn't matter which organizational technique the parents try to implement to get the homework to school. It can go to school and never be turned in. One of my nephews told my sister that the teacher never asks him for his homework. Her reply was, "If I waited for my boss to tell me that he wanted my work, I would be looking for another job, before long."

If students could be challenged to do their work, in a logical manner, and not given so much busy work, I think we would be able to make a lot more progress in our schools.

## K) CURRICULUM: *Geometry Round Two*

After filling some space with a remedial general math class for first semester, Melissa started Geometry class with a new teacher. There was something unusual about this teacher's classes and he noticed it quite early in the semester. Many of his students were taking Geometry for the second time. The first time, they had failed and they had been in the classes Melissa's last teacher taught. Obviously, Melissa wasn't an anomaly.

This teacher required fewer proofs. Melissa seemed to be doing quite well in the class, until she fell on the ice and broke her right arm. The bone that was suspected to be broken was under her thumb, so we had to keep her thumb immobile. Melissa was expected to be in a cast from five weeks up until nine months. If the scaphoid bone was broken, it usually took longer to heal. We were looking at a lot of time that Melissa wouldn't be able to write.

Geometry requires a certain format for its homework. That might not be possible under current conditions. Melissa could still use her other fingers for typing on her computer. I asked the teacher if we could modify her homework to fit the format. He told me that we could. I also asked him to put in a couple prayers that she would get out of her cast sooner. Melissa got out of her cast in five weeks and resumed her work, as usual. She finally passed the Geometry.

*The House on Mango Street*

I decided to try to shadow Matthew for some of his classes. I went to the school and tried to find his math classroom, and his English classroom. I figured, if there was any way I could figure out what was going wrong, besides Matthew missing classes, maybe I could help fix it.

The first class was English class. They were reading a book called, "The House on Mango Street". It's a story about an Hispanic neighborhood. I gather the narrator is describing her neighbors. There is one neighbor per chapter.

I sat in the classroom and waited for Matthew to arrive. I sat where he couldn't see me, until he was well into the classroom. The class sat down and opened their books. The teacher proceeded to read to the class for the next hour, or so. I thought I was going to go to sleep. I don't know how the students felt, but they appeared to be bored. The teacher was relatively young, and there were only enough books to cover the class. Youth may not always be a drawback, but I think it might have been in this particular case. I felt she could have run things a little more efficiently, and involved the students more.

There were references to Santeria, a religion that seems to be a combination of Catholic and voodoo. The religion wasn't named, so the teacher assumed the woman who was described as having these diverse religious articles in her house, was confused. I brought up a point earlier, about a word that no one seemed to understand. It was "tembleque", which is a gelatin/pudding/custard type dessert that can be put into a mold. The description was to the effect that someone was jiggling like Jell-O. I didn't want the teacher to look like an idiot, in front of the students, if I explained what I knew (from educational TV) about Santeria.

With five minutes left of class, the teacher made her big mistake, in my opinion. She gave the students a nearly impossible homework assignment. They were to use a certain size paper, and draw a character from the book. On the back of the paper, they were to write five characteristics of this character. Without books to take home, the students had to try to scramble to pick out one character out of at least a dozen, and get a picture in their mind that they could translate into art. I think the teacher should have given them a little bit of warning, so they could have planned better. Maybe the students would have paid more attention to the characters.

I left the English classroom, and tried unsuccessfully to find my son's math classroom. The room number the office gave me wasn't the right number. His teacher had been on long term medical leave, so no one knew which room belonged to that teacher. I also didn't know the substitute's name, which might have been more help.

I went to the library to see if I could find the book Matthew needed. If there was any chance of getting him to do his homework, I had to have the lesson. The library didn't have the book listed anywhere in their system, and it wasn't at any of the bookstores I called, either. Matthew didn't do the homework.

L) CRIMES & PUNISHMENT: *Do The Students Not Have Feet?*

Matthew and Melissa had both seen the ROTC student as he did his drill practice, during lunch, in the large area in front of the office. This was an area that was suitable for a performance. There were two sets of staircases that lead down to the performance area, and a hallway that overlooked it. Both viewing areas were filled with spectators watching this student.

This drill practice wasn't anything dangerous or disruptive, yet the boy was disciplined for his activity. He was one of Jeff's classmates. When he came into class late, he said that he had been given detention because he was causing a fire hazard. If there was an actual fire, the staircases were considered "obstructed". This is the same area that I have sat in watching evening choir or band performances. Chairs were involved in those performances, yet we weren't cited for being a fire hazard. Within ten feet of either of those "obstructed" staircases were two other sets of stairs that had no view of the staging area.

I told Mary about the absurd punishment. She wondered, out loud, "Do the students have no feet?' If the fire alarm went off, I doubt that the students would continue standing on the steps. There's more traffic in those hallways between classes, than there is during lunchtime.

If the student was doing a ROTC drill, and drawing so much student interest, it seems like it would be considered a positive activity. Logically, one would think that the ROTC would like any positive public relations, but I forgot the fact that this is a military entity within the school system. There is no logic. With so many teens involved in destructive activities, a student was punished for this? Reality check please.

### A Minute and Ten Seconds

I understand that rules and regulations are the glue that holds a civilized establishment together. The school is considered a civilized establishment and has appropriate rules to govern its population. Certain rules should be strictly adhered to, but others should have a little leeway.

This was Matthew's first year in the high school. I hoped that the change of school might mean a change of attitude. After having been misplaced for so many years, he was now expected to conform immediately. He considered most of the Math and Social Studies repetitive. He had been put into a Pre-algebra class, but he lacked some of the basic processes that he should have learned around fourth and fifth grade. According to a test he took at Sylvan, he was up to grade level in about 80% of the skills he was supposed to know. The gaps were all over the spectrum. The school was unable to work with us, and we couldn't afford the tutoring costs. He had to sit through the seemingly repetitive classes until they reached a point he didn't already know, so he felt that he wasn't moving forward.

In Social Studies, he couldn't see why ancient (world) history was relevant today. Personally, I think they could have hooked him with some of the art from the times they were studying. The teachers were dealing with overcrowded classrooms and supply shortages. My son's problems were considered to be low priority in a school of 2000 students. The professional educators were unable to reach him, so he drifted.

The school allowed students ten minutes to change classes. Matthew tended to dawdle. Adding a combination lock to the equation just slowed everything down more. Students were allowed one-minute leeway, after the bell. If they weren't in the classroom by that time, they were given a detention slip. Detention took place during lunchtime.

One day, Matthew came home and told me that he had received a detention slip for being a minute and ten seconds late for class. I couldn't believe it. Supposedly, he had his hand on the doorknob, when the principal called him back down the hallway, to give him a detention slip. Several minutes later, he had the detention slip in his hand and was on his way back to class. The teacher arrived in the classroom right behind Matthew.

The next day, I went to the principal's office with a healthy amount of skepticism, and a definite interest in trying to solve this problem. The principal verified that he had written Matthew up for being a minute and ten seconds late. I thought, maybe Matthew had been stretching some truths. The principal told me he was getting writer's cramp from filling out so many detention slips, but carrying out disciplinary action was more important than the actual class time Matthew was missing during this exercise. I wondered if being ten minutes late was actually less disruptive than being a minute late. I felt that there were other options, but the principal insisted that there could be no exceptions to the rules.

I suggested, if my son (who I was struggling with to even get him to the school in the first place) was actually trying to enter a classroom, security should encourage the action rather than discouraging it. I pleaded with the principal to work with me, because I knew time was rapidly running out. I was a 75% single parent, and my influence on my son was diminishing fast. The principal told me that he couldn't possibly work with me.

He told me I should impress the importance of attending school and the value of education on Matthew. Then, I needed to make sure he came to school and attended all his classes. I wondered how I could possibly accomplish that without attending classes with him. I asked the principal, "How often did YOU listen to YOUR mother when you were 15 or 16 years old?" He quickly changed the subject.

Even if I could have "worked with him", and personally delivered Matthew to the front door of the school, there was very little I could have done to keep him there. For goodness sakes, the school authorities couldn't even keep the students from hemorrhaging from the building before school started. I often saw students pouring out of the school five minutes before class was due to start.

By the end of his first year in High School, Matthew had earned half a credit out of a possible six credits, and had accumulated handfuls of detention slips.

## M) DISCRIMINATION, HARASSMENT & ABUSE: *Damage Control*

It was Melissa's junior year in high school. She had accomplished so much. Between summer school, GSS classes, and being an exchange student, she recovered a lot of the ground she had lost in her first scheduled year of High School. I was very proud of her, but I could see she desperately needed to be recharged. I figured a trip "Outside" where she could get a little sun and warmth would be beneficial. Neither of us had left the State in nearly seven years. I planned the trip around spring vacation. That way, she would only miss a few days of school. If we could work with the teachers on the homework situation, everything would be fine.

Unfortunately, Melissa's health didn't cooperate with us. Melissa was getting a lot of headaches because her wisdom teeth were applying pressure. They had to be removed. Her tonsils kept swelling any time she caught a little bug. We had to have them removed, also, but we tried to hold off until summer. Losing the time for tonsil surgery would definitely put her in the withdraw/fail status.

A couple weeks before we left for vacation, I received a letter from the school stating that Melissa was on attendance probation due to excessive absences. She had missed seven days. None of her absences were showing as "excused" absences. When she had her wisdom teeth pulled, we had tried repeatedly to give the office the doctor's note. Constant battles with the school were starting to take their toll on both of us. I believe I was nearing the point of breakdown, and I still had to be in a protective mom mode. Melissa was a good student and a well-mannered teen, yet she was constantly being harassed for things beyond her control.

Our vacation would cause her to lose five school days. I knew the attendance office would harass her when she turned in her request for homework. If the office felt a student was seriously in danger of failing a class due to the vacation time, the absence would be considered unexcused. That would force the parents to decide whether the vacation was worth the risk. Melissa's anxiety level was as high as her grades, and I was worried about her sanity as well as her health. Being on attendance probation only heightened the anxiety and further impaired her immune system. I wanted her to relax while she was on vacation; otherwise the break was pointless.

I went to speak to the attendance principal personally. I figured a face to face visit would help her know who I was. She assured me that the office wouldn't give Melissa any problems. Maintaining her grades seemed to be no problem, so she didn't see why they would withdraw/ fail her. The School District policy was based on the belief that a student couldn't succeed with chronic absences, so the attendance probation and withdraw/fail letters were sent out automatically. They were meant to warn parents whose children might have been skipping school. Melissa had nothing to worry about. Melissa was to bring her papers directly to the attendance principal, and she would deal with the situation tactfully. She told me that Matthew could also bring her his vacation paperwork. I had to explain to her that Matthew didn't need a vacation, since he was already on his own vacation plan: skipping school at least once a week.

I went home and assured Melissa that she had nothing to worry about, if she turned in her vacation paperwork directly to the attendance principal. Two days later, Melissa dropped her paperwork off with the attendance principal. As Melissa turned to leave, the attendance principal detained her and lectured her on the facts that if she took this vacation she would be put in the withdraw/fail category and her education was at risk. Some tact! Melissa came home in a distressed state and promptly vomited.

I drove to the school and stormed the office with fire in my eyes. If I were less civilized, I would have beaten the woman to a pulp. I asked the woman if she remembered who I was. When she said that she did, I asked her if she remembered our conversation about not unduly upsetting my daughter. She said she remembered that, too. I told her that Melissa had come home in pieces after their encounter. The woman apologized for causing more anxiety, and told me that her intention was to inform my already acutely aware daughter of the consequences of taking the vacation. An apology doesn't fix adrenal exhaustion. I told her that legal action would be taken against her if they harassed my daughter anymore. I wished they had used some of this pressure on Matthew. We rarely heard about his absences. Probably because Matthew didn't care about succeeding in school.

The lesson I learned from this experience is: The rules only apply to you if you are actually conscientious about following the rules.

### Paint Balling and Face Slashing

This year, there were two racially motivated crimes that involved students. One of them caught the attention of the national news programmers. The other was completely ignored.

The first incident involved some high school students paint balling pedestrians (mainly Native Americans), downtown, during the early morning hours. The perpetrators videotaped their activity. When it hit the media circuit, the School District Superintendent made a statement denouncing the hate crime and promising to punish the students through School District channels. This activity didn't happen during school hours or on school district property, yet the Superintendent had to speak up about it.

My friend Annie, told me about the other incident. It happened right after school. A black student was on his way home from school, when he was attacked by a group of white students. His attackers were upset because he had a white girlfriend. His face was slashed and he sustained a great deal of damage around his eyes. The School District was silent on this matter. It didn't even make the local news.

The inequity of treatment for these two hate crimes is unbelievable. There is no consistency from the School District when it comes to enforcing their policies. They say that our children are their responsibility from door-to-door. The boy whose face was slashed was between the doors of the school and the doors of his home; yet nothing was done by the school to condemn this crime. If School District resources were used to help punish the boys with the paint balls, I think the money was misappropriated.

Do we teach our children early enough, that prejudice and intolerance, and the violence that comes from these concepts are unacceptable? Do the people whose care we entrust our children with present a positive face for the diversity of the children they teach? We are all responsible for teaching our children how to behave in society. The lessons shouldn't start in High School.

### N) SAFETY & SECURITY: *September 11*

On the morning of September 11th, we woke up to the news. I only had the TV on for a little while as the kids got ready for school, in an effort to inform them, but not bombard them with the information. All three kids thought that going to school would be better than staying home and sitting in front of the television all day.

We had planned to donate our gerbils to the school that day, so we loaded everyone into the car. That morning, it took nearly forty-five minutes to drive less than three miles. Traffic was backed up because one of the entrances to the military bases is about a mile past the school entrance. With the school starting at the same time as day shift on base, the two-lane road leading into the area quickly turned into a parking lot. It took two weeks to reconfigure the road, to make a third lane.

The hopes my kids had of escaping the television images, for a few hours, was a fantasy. Social Studies teachers all seemed to have televisions in their rooms that day, and were discussing the situation at great lengths. It seemed everywhere they turned there was a television.

Betty's son went to school, as usual. She figured, since their house was really close to the base, the school would probably be safer. In my opinion, the charter school handled the situation much better. They had one room set aside with televisions. Students could go to that room, if they chose to do so. The images weren't forced on them. Otherwise, class went on with relative normalcy. The highlight of their day came when a plane was heard overhead. Betty's son said that you could hear all the students move to one side of the school to see the plane. It was one of our fighters, on its way to intercept a Korean Air Line plane that wasn't responding to hails. When the students recognized that it was one of our planes, there was a near audible sigh of relief.

### Security Breach

Melissa had a lot of friends in ROTC. The head instructor had tried repeatedly, and unsuccessfully, to recruit Melissa into the group. Her first full year at the school was spent trying to make up for lost credits. Since one of her options for receiving the necessary instruction took place only after school, it conflicted with the ROTC schedule. If she finished her class early, she joined other students to watch the drill practices, while she waited for me to pick her up. Melissa seemed to be the only spectator that the instructor objected to. She was always being asked to leave the area, and everyone wondered why. I think it had to do with the clothes she wore. She wore my old fatigue shirts as light jackets, and shunned the military overtures.

In her sophomore year, several of Melissa's ROTC friends had claimed that their instructor had made an insulting comment about her, during practice. She had been hanging around with one of the ROTC boys who didn't like to go to the drill practice. On the day in question, Melissa had one of her after school classes and the boy had skipped practice to pursue his own interests. The instructor noted the boy's absence, and commented that he was probably with his "fat" girlfriend. Her sweatshirt was fat, she wasn't. It didn't matter, because everyone knew whom the instructor was referring to. Besides not having time for ROTC, Melissa had decided she wasn't sure if she wanted to be in a potentially abusive situation.

Near the end of this year, Melissa was on track with her credits. She might possibly have time in her schedule for ROTC, as an elective for her senior year. She was considering the potential of joining the military, like her parents. At this time, one of the "recruiting" instructors approached her about joining ROTC. I refer to him as a recruiting instructor because he had a pleasant personality. Standard operating procedure for recruitment starts with this type of person. Once the recruit is signed up, they get the training instructor from hell. Melissa had already seen the leader in action. She told the recruiter that she was wary of the prospect, since the head instructor was already prejudiced against her.

The recruiter advised Melissa if she was interested in ROTC, and really thought there was a problem, she should confront the instructor. In fact, this afternoon would be a perfect time, since there was no drill practice. She walked into the instructor's office with the recruiter. According to Melissa, the instructor was on the phone for several minutes, while she waited. The recruiter left the room just before the instructor finished his call. Melissa was left alone in a room with a man who allegedly despised her. This wasn't a good situation. The recruiter should have stayed as a mediator or witness. Without a witness, it remains a case of "he said, she said".

I don't know how the conversation started, but the instructor assured Melissa that he had nothing against her. How could he? He didn't even know who she was. Somehow, the conversation turned to the ROTC boy from the previous year. Melissa said that she hadn't brought him up. The instructor brought the boy up, by name, and advised Melissa to stay away from him. This was relatively easy since the boy had graduated and was out of state. What the instructor told her next shocked Melissa. The instructor discussed the boy's personality defects, his grades, and his medical profile. After the tirade was over, Melissa left the instructor's office and came home.

I was angry that Melissa allowed herself to be manipulated by these two men, but if she was considering the military, she could expect harassment. I was disappointed that the recruiter was such a coward, and didn't follow through with his support. His behavior was very ungentlemanly, to put it mildly. The point that offended me most was the disclosure of another student's personal information to my daughter. As the military would put it, "She didn't have the need to know." It didn't matter that the boy had graduated and moved away, the information the instructor had provided wasn't public knowledge.

I requested a meeting with the principal. I told him what I knew of the conversation. I asked if there were rules regarding privacy in the school? The principal said that he would look into the situation.

Two weeks later, I called him to find out what happened. The principal said that he had talked to the ROTC instructor the next day. Basically, the instructor told the principal that he thought Melissa was a nice girl. My concern hadn't been about whether or not the instructor liked my daughter. It was about the privacy issue. Had I been speaking a foreign language? I advised Melissa not to get into ROTC, since the instructor had such loose lips. If he was so blatantly indiscreet about one student to another student he claimed not to know, what else was he saying about his other students? And to whom?

## P) POLICIES & PROCEDURES: *Bathroom Breaks*

Melissa walked into her typing class, and felt it. Her period had decided to start. Why couldn't it have started a few minutes before, when she had time to run to the bathroom? The bell was getting ready to ring, so she would need a pass to be in the hallway.

The teacher told everyone to sit down for attendance. As soon as attendance was taken, she asked her teacher if she could run to the bathroom. Her (female) teacher told her that she should have planned better, and used the restroom before class started. We wonder if the teacher could have planned any better at Melissa's age. Few teenage girls are "regular".

Melissa had to waste time pleading for the pass before the teacher relented. As Melissa headed out the door for the restroom, the fire alarm rang. She was pushed towards one of the exits, and they stood outside for about fifteen minutes. When she was able to return to class, the teacher demanded to know why she was late. Melissa had to remind her that she had been given a bathroom pass. The teacher said that she thought Melissa had gone already, and considered this to be a major infraction. Melissa wondered if she had gone into the Twilight Zone when she left the classroom. Hadn't there been a fire drill? A girl should never have to explain to a teacher, in front of the class, the need to take care of personal hygiene.

Laurel's daughter handled it much better. When her (male) teacher tried to challenge her about a bathroom pass, she got really close to him, and told him, in a low voice, "If I have to explain it to you, you will turn as red as the tie you're wearing." The teacher turned bright red, as he let her run to the bathroom.

Girls aren't the only ones who have problems. Cheryl's grandson attended an elementary school. The bathroom was just across the hall from his classroom. He suddenly had to go and was sitting closer to the door than to the teacher, so he made a run for it. He was stopped in the hallway, on his way back to the classroom, for not having a bathroom pass. He was given detention. Too bad he hadn't had to vomit. He could have gotten out of the detention, if he had been able to unleash sewer breath on them.

Most of the time, teachers have hall passes that are big and unique. One of the Art teachers had her hall pass chained to a mug. Some teachers just have personalized placards that can be hung around a student's neck. Hall passes given by substitute teachers are often rejected by security, because they think the pass is a forgery.

Our High School had 2000 students who had to vie for 50 +/- bathroom stalls per sex, twice a day for ten minute intervals, or wait until lunch time. Many of the stalls had broken or missing doors. It was a zoo trying to use a bathroom during the 10 minute passing period. Jeff said that he had to run back and forth to his locker to drop off and pick up his books if he used the bathroom, so he just held it all day. He also drank very little liquid with breakfast.

Melissa tried to fight the crowds, but often she lost. She seemed to have an endless urinary tract infection from having to hold it all day. The doctor gave her a note to be able to use the bathroom, but it wasn't even honored during the time she had her infection. I went to a principal to get some intervention. This could cause some serious health problems. The principal told me that there were often days when she would forget to use the bathroom. This wasn't a case of being too busy and forgetting to use the bathroom. This was being denied access to the bathrooms. I doubt Melissa was the only one who was having this problem.

## Q) ALTERNATIIVE EDUCATION & GETTING CREDIT: *Credit By Examination-Trigonometry*

Jeff had failed Trigonometry the first time around because he didn't turn in his homework. He understood the material quite well. He just hated doing the writing. Since the homework counted for so much of his grade, he had to have perfect scores on all of his tests to raise the grade to passing.

Since he knew the material and tested well, we decided to try for credit by examination for both semesters. Unfortunately, we had to find a teacher who was willing to administer a test, and wait for the test to be developed. It was the beginning of the year, and we made our request for testing for both semesters. Meanwhile, Jeff had to sit in on the Trigonometry class again while we waited for the test.

In November, he was given the first semester test, and passed. There was no place he could go, since it was already mid-semester, so he sat through the class he had tested out of, waiting for the second test. It never came. We don't know what went wrong. We asked for both tests and had been charged for only one, when all was said and done. I don't know if the Curriculum principal ever passed on the request for the second test, or if it had just been too difficult for the teacher to compose two tests.

Second semester started, and Jeff couldn't get into a class for his second semester credit. His teacher had decided not to teach a second semester of Trigonometry this year. With the scheduling problems of being a senior and taking higher level classes, he wasn't able to move his necessary credits around to accommodate the now non-essential credit during another period.

It would have been nice if the schools, or the District, would be prepared with tests for students who request credit by examination. Waiting until mid-semester to administer a test is a waste of everyone's time.

### *Credit By Examination- CLEP Test*

Social Studies wasn't one of Jeff's favorite subjects. With as far behind as he was with his credits, we decided to have him take a College Level Examination Program (CLEP)test for his American History credit.

We had to clear it with the curriculum principal. Then, we went out to find a book to read that would cover the subject thoroughly. Jeff took the test, but failed to pass by the college standards. He missed by two points. The high school would only give credit, if the college gave credit.

There is a six month waiting period between tests, so Jeff waited and studied. When he took the test the second time, he passed and received both high school and college credits.

*Like Two Peas in a Pod*

My friend Elaine had two adult sons and one who was Matthew's age. She was over at my house one day when Matthew made an appearance. She said that Matthew reminded her of one of her older sons. Same attitudes and interests, and the same hole in their bedroom walls.

When they had moved up here, her son was a little bit older than Matthew was. She and her husband knew that they were having problems with him, but it was probably going to be easier to deal with the problem, after the move.

Once they got her son enrolled in school, they asked the school counselor if he could recommend a psychologist or counselor who worked well with teenagers. Basically, she was told she had to fix her son's problems. Being new to the area, it would have been nice if someone could have given them some insight on reliable assistance. She tried one counselor, and didn't seem to get anywhere. Her son dropped out and got into trouble. He eventually got his GED, and had one of the highest scores in the State.

We tried counseling with Matthew. The counselor told us to save our money. Matthew was unwilling to accept any responsibility for his situation. After five sessions, the counselor knew he couldn't dislodge Matthew from his mindset. I wondered if we would be able to get Matthew through school, or if we would even be lucky enough to have him survive long enough to be a success, like Elaine's son, through an alternate method. By this time, we had tried everything we could think of, short of having him locked up. The prognosis wasn't encouraging.

W) SEX: *Sexual Encounter in the Stairwell*

The school year had started out with a bang. According to the news story, two freshmen at our school had a sexual encounter in a stairwell. The girl had been found vomiting in the bathroom. When adults questioned her about what was wrong she told a story about a certain boy touching her, then he had forced her to submit to oral sex. After that, he forced her to perform oral sex on him. The more I heard the story, the angrier I became, but I wasn't upset because a girl had been sexually assaulted. I was angry that the story seemed to be a lot of hearsay at this point, yet it was all over the news.

At the time of the incident, they didn't say anything about gathering any evidence. Was there any? The sequence of events was always the same. Granted, if the incident happened after school, in certain stairwells, the girl might not have been heard, if she protested or screamed. I have had no problems hearing people in most of the stairwells in that school, and I'm partially deaf. The girl said he forcibly performed oral sex on her first. This is the part that doesn't seem to ring true. I think she would have been able to dispatch him in that position, with a knee to the nose. If he had forced her to perform oral sex on him, were there any bruises? Did he have a weapon? How do you force someone to do that otherwise? None of this information was covered in the news story, so it sounded quite flimsy, to me. It seemed like a case of "He said, she said".

The news said the boy was originally charged with five counts of sexual assault. Everyone in the school knew who he was, so there was a problem with him attending school. I understand he was eventually locked up in the youth facility, here in Anchorage. I don't know the circumstances of his trial. Did they find evidence to lock him up, or did he plead guilty just because his life was ruined by a rumor?

Before Melissa graduated, she overheard a couple of girls talking. One of them was the girl who had made the accusations in the first place. Even though Melissa didn't know who the girl was, the girl's partner in the conversation did. The topic ran to the boy in prison. The accuser told the girl she was talking to that she didn't care if he was locked up, even if her story hadn't been true. She had been angry with him because he wouldn't go out with her. The girls were behind an obstruction, so Melissa couldn't figure out who had been doing the talking. If what Melissa heard was true, this girl ruined a boy's life out of spite, and his reputation can never be repaired. Even if she recanted, it's on his record that he's a sex offender.

The lesson students should learn from this incident: Don't allow yourself to be placed in a compromising position.

### Z) LAST IMPRESSIONS: *Jeff Graduates*

Jeff graduated, finally. At the graduation instruction sessions, they said the students would be given an empty diploma cover when they crossed the stage. If they said more than that, Jeff stopped listening. If he wasn't going to get his diploma at the graduation ceremony, what was the purpose of going to the ceremony at all? He had already played in the band for four graduations. Graduates were never allowed to sit with the band, and he would rather be playing.

By not going to the graduation ceremony, he didn't get his diploma, which they handed the students on their way back to the seats. It took us until the following November to finally get the document. They would changed Registrars at the school, and there wasn't any way to tell where the diplomas were.

# Chapter 19
## End of the Road 2002-03

### A) FIRST IMPRESSIONS: *Last Year for Melissa*

Melissa looked like she had come far enough that she would be able to graduate mid-year, if she wanted. We were very hopeful. I was just hoping she wouldn't become ill any more. I wondered about the ventilation system in the school. Was there something she was allergic to, or had she just had so many antibiotics that her immune system was depleted?

I had very little hope that Matthew would complete high school. He wasn't a morning person, and I was having trouble getting him out of bed. I suspected that he might be taking drugs or alcohol, but I had no proof. He had been into running away all summer. Any control I might have had over him was quickly evaporating. I'm responsible for my son, yet I can't keep him in my back pocket all day long. It would be nice if security would just encourage him to hurry up and get to class. He had been playing his game so long and the adults chose to play with him. While it might be fun to irritate the adults, this behavior could adversely affect his future.

### D) FUND RAISING: *School Funding*

The article in the Daily News said that there would have to be funding cutbacks throughout the School District. In the article, one of the School Board members considered the option of removing funding from the charter schools, since they had income sources independent of the School District money.

I have friends in the charter schools. These schools function on a shoestring, with a lot of creativity and parental involvement. The School District's unofficial view of these schools is: "Run them into the ground". These schools feel like they are unwanted stepchildren. The district gives no "emotional" support, no matter how well they do. I have yet to hear the School District officially comment on how well any of the charter schools are doing.

The translation of "income sources independent of the School District" is "students in charter schools fund raise so intensely, that they're nearly professional fund raisers" These schools run multiple fund raisers during the school year, besides the usual ones the regular schools do. They beg and borrow supplies from anyone who will listen. Just because they are coordinated about their fund raising efforts doesn't mean they should have to rely exclusively on their own resourcefulness. To expect the students to do even more fund raising means education isn't the first priority of the education system. Raising money is.

### E) DIFFERENCES & DISABILITIES: *He Loves His ADD*

I woke up to the 6 AM news one morning, and they were talking about Steven Plog, who had an interesting viewpoint on the problem of Attention Deficit Disorder. I was intrigued, and wrote down the information for his upcoming seminar, "I Love My ADD". I called the number and made arrangements to attend.

The night of the seminar, I paid the fee and sat down near the front, but off to the side. I brought my paper and pencil with me. Before he started his presentation, Mr. Plog asked that the audience not interrupt him with questions, because he wanted to stay on track. His performance was fascinating, and as he talked, I could feel all sorts of information connecting in my brain. The way he described a person with ADD can also describe a student who's labeled "gifted" and someone with Asperger's autism.

He painted the ADD student not as deficient, but as a very quick learner. They can process speech faster than the teacher can usually present it. His main platform is: ADD is promoted by nutritional imbalances. There are many other things that can give ADD symptoms, but nutritional deficiencies make sense. Besides nutritional problems (including iron deficiency), I have also heard that problems with allergies, sleeping problems, enlarged tonsils or adenoids, dehydration, heavy metals, Lyme disease, and chemicals can also give ADD symptoms.

Steven Plog is part of an organization called "The Results Project". They are collecting all sorts of information on nutrition and medicine for Attention Deficit. His approach is quite refreshing. He seems to be out to eradicate the stigma of ADD. These are kids who just think differently. With nutrition, the proper coping skills, and encouragement from the adults around them, this group of kids can actually be an asset to society. I agreed with Mr. Plog about one point he made; that many of the teachers I worked with couldn't seem to understand. He suggested praising the child for their good work rather than wasting time yelling at the child for not excelling in difficult areas. He also had a list of successful people who had Attention Deficit symptoms. They were the kids who thought outside the box and probably got into a lot of trouble in school.

Mr. Plog doesn't advocate discontinuing use of the medicines completely, but medication should be looked at as a last resort. Some people might need medication, but they might need it in smaller doses, if they get the right nutrition. The Results Project has a nutritional program for parents who have children who fit the ADD profile. The program studies these children to see how nutrition affects their "condition". So far, they have at least one school that is Ritalin-free because of good nutrition. It's in Wisconsin.

If you're a parent who's being pressured to drug your child, check out the Results Project. They have more information than anyone does about the subject and ways to get help.

*H.R. Bill 1170*

On May 21, 2003, the House of Representatives passed H.R. 1170. It's short title is the "Child Medication Safety Act of 2003". Teachers and other school personnel may speak with parents about having children evaluated for Special Education programs, but they may not require a child to obtain a prescription for substances covered by section 202 ( c ) of the Controlled Substances Act (21 U.S.C, 812 ( c ) as a condition for attending school or receiving services.

Basically translated, this means, teachers can't coerce a parent to put their children on Ritalin (methylphenidate), so they will be allowed in school. The schools are required to put policies into place to keep employees from applying this pressure. Schools could lose funding, if they fail to comply.

In Australia, students have been prescribed psychotropic drugs for ADD, in epidemic numbers. England's numbers are similarly high. In some places, including the United States, you could be jailed for negligence if the drug was prescribed and you refused to administer it to your child. The tide is turning. Australia is encouraging investigation of alternative causes and treatments for ADD, before the drugs are prescribed. Medication should be the last resort.

F) PROGRAMS: *Sylvan Learning Center Can't Fix "Everyday Math" Problems*

It was only the third week of school, and Kathy's daughter was falling behind in Math. Kathy took her to the Sylvan Learning Center to have her tested. There were several concepts where she was below grade level, but she had understanding in other areas, where she was way above grade level. Kathy's daughter was a second grader!

She was surprised to find out how much it would cost for her daughter to be tutored for the whole year. The other option was that Sylvan could get the girl up to grade level and provide an educational strategy plan for the teacher to follow. Unfortunately, with the School District mandate of, "Everyday Math exclusively (or you will lose your job)", the financially friendly option for parents wasn't feasible.

Granted, Sylvan was in business to make money tutoring students, but this counselor could clearly see how much money was being wasted due to the "Everyday Math" program. Sylvan was making amazing amounts of money because of the School District's weaknesses, but no one would listen to their suggested remedies.

H) HOMEWORK: *The Bitter Pill*

My friend Marion lives in Wisconsin. Her son received his report card at the end of the school year. He was a junior, and had fantastic grades up until now. This was the first time, in high school, that he ever brought home a D on a report card. A single "D" would impact his chances of getting scholarships.

Marion hurriedly called the teacher and asked why her son had earned a D in this class. The teacher told her that the son never turned in the main semester project. She hadn't seen any of it, so his low grade reflected the zero he got on the project. Marion and her husband had both seen their son's paper. It was hard to believe that he hadn't turned it in at all.

During the summer, Marion sorted through the various papers that had collected around the house over the year. While she was cleaning, she found a rough draft of the paper in question. Considering the teacher had claimed not to have seen it at all, there were several proofreading marks and comments in the teacher's handwriting. They weren't ever able to find the final paper. (If it had even been returned to their son.)

At the beginning of the new school year, Marion and her husband confronted the teacher with the paper. The teacher said that the grade stood, because the son hadn't turned the paper in on time. The school supported the teacher.

The lesson we learned from this event is: Keep track of all your papers, and make a copy of any term papers, in case there is any question of completion for report card purposes. After the reporting period, all excess papers may be destroyed.


I) DRUGS & WEAPONS: *Suspected Drug Trafficking on School Property*

Matthew was skipping a lot of school, and he seemed to have a lot of disposable income. Considering I was unaware of any employment, there was lots of money. I had a clue where he was getting money. He swore to me that he wasn't selling drugs. Maybe, and maybe not. It depends on your definition of "selling". Matthew is a gregarious type. He makes friends easily. I had information (on good authority) that he was often seen in the company of someone who was known to sell drugs, on school property. Whether Matthew was actually selling drugs, or directing people to the seller, I was concerned.

It was first semester, and Matthew had been withdrawn/failed. At this point, if he was apprehended on school property, he could be arrested for trespassing. For at least two weeks, he had been going to the school but not attending any classes. I was surprised that he hadn't been picked up. Melissa and Jeff's friends were always spotting him in the hallways.

At this point, I contacted the head of security. I gave him authorization to arrest Matthew, but they said they hadn't seen him. How do you miss a kid who wears a hat and cape in his favorite color, neon orange? Two weeks passed, and there were repeated Matthew sightings, by students.

I was getting tired of this. My son was trespassing, and I wanted the school to press charges. Didn't they think he was a risk? I wrote a letter to the Superintendent. I figured it would be sent to the proper channel. It mentioned my concern that I thought Matthew might be dealing with drugs on school property, and something had to be done.

I received a call from the School District, and Matthew took the message. I returned the call on my cell phone. The question I heard from the School District, and school security was, " What do you want us to do about it, Mrs. McDonald?" When the school called me, the head of security complained that there were only five security people and twenty-two openings in the school. It was easy for a student to evade them.

Matthew was caught two weeks before the end of the semester, and given a warning. I was hoping to have deprived him of his social life a little bit longer than that. Maybe deprivation would make him actually want to attend school.

## K) CURRICULUM: *Curriculum Audit*

The previous spring, the School District had hired an outside auditing team to audit the curriculum. They were very surprised by the team's findings. The team had visited all the schools, and 2,139 classrooms. They focused on five points:

Does the School District have control of its resources, programs, and personnel?
Does the District have clear objectives?
Are District schools in touch with one another?
Is data used for improvement?
Has the District consistently improved?

According to the audit, the answer to most of these was no. The head of the auditing team said that the school system acted more like a system of independent schools. This was reflected in comments by teachers talking on the radio, in the morning.

The teachers said there wasn't any standardization between the schools. If you had a student transfer from another school within the District, they didn't always know the same things your students did. Sometimes, they would have to play catch up.

I wondered how this worked with the Junior High/Middle Schools. How much time was wasted each year to fill in the educational gaps between students from different schools, before the teacher could actually teach the class new material?

The auditing team suggested that the District have a six-year improvement plan. The School Board thought this task was daunting. If they had broken it down, they could have looked into decent textbooks. If there was a good program out there, textbooks could be cycled in over five years. Supposedly, that's the life of a textbook.

The report stated that it wasn't trying to pick on anyone personally, but one of the School Board members had commented that she, "felt very well picked". If she can't take constructive criticism, she shouldn't have applied for the job. Unfortunately, if you don't understand the system well, you can't see the solutions very easily. With so much variety in our District, it probably makes the problem even more difficult.

*Chemistry 2*

Melissa started the school year as the only non-Advanced Placement student in a Chemistry 2 class. With the extremely tenuous grasp she had on the previous year's Chemistry, she wasn't feeling confident. She begged her counselor to change the class to any other Science class, but everything else was full, and she needed the credit to graduate.

The Advanced Placement students were graded for their class performance by different criteria than the regular students. The teacher would give them the assignment, and they would relatively teach themselves. Melissa wasn't at this level of comprehension yet, so by the end of first quarter, she was failing miserably. The teacher's notation on the report card had said he was available to answer questions. Melissa had learned, from past experience, this phrase was usually just lip service to placate parents.

At the conference, I found out that the rules were different for Melissa than for the rest of the class. While the other students weren't allowed to ask questions, Melissa was, but no one had told her. The teacher also told me that the textbook used in the class wasn't written in the user-friendliest format. The teacher suggested a supplemental book that might help boost Melissa's comprehension. The book was called, "College Chemistry". I bought the book and a Standard Deviants video set. I don't know if they were of any help. By the time I got her the help, she was nearly past the point of saving.

During the second quarter, things became more difficult because of confusion. The textbook the class was using had answers in the back, so students would be able to check their answers. While the answers were given, how one arrived at the answer wasn't. Several of the students were checking their answers with increasing trepidation. They weren't coming up with the same answers as the book. The first few times this happened, each student thought they were the only one who wasn't understanding the problem. When it was time to check the answers in class, the teacher started to realize that the textbook was flawed. By then, it was too late to buy new textbooks.

I recently read an article about textbooks. The article said that prominent experts would be given a section of a textbook to "critique". If the expert made any comment about correcting erroneous material, the advice might be ignored, but the expert's name could still be attached to the publication, as a consultant. School Districts can base much of their decision for new textbooks on the reputation of the expert consultants. If the publisher ignores the experts' comments, schools can end up with a mediocre, if not simply bad textbooks.

It will be hard to teach a class that meets the "No Child Left Behind" standards, if the teaching materials are faulty. Melissa ended up failing a class that she had almost no chance of passing in the first place.

*Intensive Studies*

Over the years, I've heard Betty speak so highly of her son's intensive classes. They have these classes each year, the first two weeks, and the last two weeks of each semester. The teachers come up with ideas that will interest the students, and where the teachers may have some expertise. One of the intensives was a bicycling trip that involved camping. The students got together in groups of four to decide which supplies they needed, make meal plans, and decide who would carry what. The trip was a great success. A partial credit was given for each of these intensive classes.

A recent intensive class had a strong impact on the students. The students found out about forensic investigation. I understand we have one of the best labs in the country. The students passed through the area where they study the bodies. A question about a recent, high profile, teen murder naturally came up. Had the girl's body been examined in that room? The medical examiner said, "Yes", and a noticeably contemplative attitude came over the class.

The students learned about what it takes to become a forensic scientist. The amount of education may seem daunting, but the lecturer seemed to think it had been well worth his time. He seemed like a man who loved detective work. The students were told stories of unusual cases that were solved, including one where a man hit a police officer and left the scene. Luckily, they caught the man quickly and were able to find evidence. I believe Betty said it had been a print of the officer's face and badge, in the dust on the car. It hadn't been immediately noticeable, in normal light.

For those kids who like horror movies, the forensics lab has a powerful slide show on what kind of damage can be done to a person when the mold on marijuana is active. The mold eats flesh, and, so far, there's nothing to stop it.

Betty provided transportation for the whole two weeks, because she was interested in the subject of forensics, as much as her son was.

L) CRIMES & PUNISMENT: *Chocolate and Vanilla*

A friend of mine told me that her grandson had been suspended from school for three days, because he called another student "Chocolate Milk". The "victim" had given her grandson a nickname that referred to a physical characteristic. Neither boy had taken offense to what the other boy called him, and no one had made a complaint about harassment.

The grandson was disciplined for using a racial slur. No action was taken against the other boy, who could have been viewed as picking on the grandson for physical difference. The school's principal enforced the policy, without determining if there was even a problem.

Another friend told me that her niece had experienced a similar situation. When the girl had been in first grade, she said that her black classmate wasn't black, she was chocolate. The niece considered herself to be vanilla, rather than white. The statement hadn't been made maliciously, yet the niece was disciplined so harshly that it would take years for her to make friends with any of her other black classmates. In her limited experience, the message had been clear, "Don't talk to black students!" She truly didn't understand what her offense had been. In the world of children, as far as flavorings go, chocolate is usually preferable to vanilla any day.

It would have been better if the adults had found out what the whole situation was, before determining punishments.

*Exhausting the Supply of Detention Slips*

One of Matthew's friends was late for class by a minute and ten seconds. The principal apprehended him and dragged him down to the office for security to deal with him. After sitting in the office for twenty minutes and having no one pay any attention to him, Matthew's friend left the office and headed back to his classroom.

They had been herding students for detention slips. I heard of one incident where the principal had stopped thirty students; to give them detention slips. I thought this was an amazing feat, and extremely stupid. In a school that has a handful of security people, and another handful of principals, I don't think the adults could catch up with all of the students, if they just broke away from the group and ran to their classrooms. I was amazed at the fact that thirty students would stand still, like sheep. If I had been in the group, I probably would have tried to run.

I was finally getting Matthew to go to his classes. He had collected quite a few tardies, but they showed up as absences on the attendance report. Attendance sheets are usually filled out in the first five minutes that the teacher is in the classroom. Detainees can arrive in the classroom 10-15 minutes after attendance has been taken.

Matthew was finally picked up by security for being late to class, and taken to the office. The Security Guard talked to him about his absences and tardies. He asked Matthew what he thought they should do about his situation. Matthew's reply was, "Change the current detention policy." Their current policy was very time consuming and the school had run out of detention slips. They were currently using a form that was twice as big, so they were wasting paper. The Security Guard said that he couldn't change the policy, only the principal could. Matthew and I both know that, "Getting to class sooner" was the response the Security Guard wanted.

The charge against Matthew was "Excessive Absences", so his punishment was suspension. Hurray, Matthew gets more days off from school! One of my friends thought that the school might have a detention quota they have to fill each quarter. Betty suggested if they were more efficient about encouraging the students to go to class, dozens of people throughout the School District might lose their jobs. The goal of this exercise can't possibly be educating the children, because they are failing miserably.

M) DISCRIMINATION, ABUSE & HARASSMENT: *Big Brother is Alive and Well*

Annie had a busy schedule. She was a single parent, trying to keep her family together, while working two jobs. The loss of her husband had hit them hard. Her son's school didn't make her job any easier. It was nearing the end of the school year when she received a call from the Middle School that her son attended.  The woman on the other end of the phone delivered her message in a hostile tone.  There was a disciplinary problem with Annie's son, and Annie would be allowed half an hour to get to the school to collect him.  If she wasn't there by that time, the school would contact Social Services.  Annie arrived at the school, and the secretary greeted her with a comment about being ready to contact Social Services.  Annie removed her son from the school grounds.

Two weeks later, Annie was home with her children, and she received a call from a social worker.  He gave her a choice.  Would she bring her family to his office, or would she allow him to make a home visit?  Annie chose a home visit.  She requested that the social worker not identify himself.  She wanted the children to behave as normally as possible.

The social worker arrived at the house and interviewed the children individually, while they did their chores.  The school had recommended counseling for the Middle School son.  They were obviously unaware that the whole family had been in counseling since the recent loss of their father.  The social worker was confused as to why the school had reported Annie to Social Services.  She seemed to have everything pretty well under control, considering the circumstances.  There were no grounds for State intervention.

Through the counseling with her son, Annie found out why he had lost his temper.  He looked white and his mother was black.  His classmates had found this out and had started harassing him about being black.  He had told the school officials about the problem, and they had asked if he was in counseling.  If you were a kid who was considered to have a mark against you because you were black, in a predominantly white school, would you admit to being "crazy" too? Besides, does a student who's black always need counseling, or should the school's "zero tolerance policy against racism" be implemented? No one from the school had spoken to Annie about the situation during the school year.  He was moved to a different school for the next year.

Did the school administration apply excessive pressure to Annie because she was black?  Who knows? We only know that the mandatory reporting system is in perfect working order, at this school.

*Two Peas in a Pod*

My sister lives in Texas.  After having heard about all the difficulty I had putting my children through the public school system, and hearing all the stories of corruption in her local public school system, she had enrolled her children in a parochial school.  She thought, "You get what you pay for", therefore, a private school will provide a better quality education.  Her sons were midway through the sixth grade when she figured out she was wrong.

Both of her sons ended up having the same teacher.  They were both given a writing assignment.  The assignment was to write an extra chapter for one of the books the teacher had chosen.  My sister had the boys choose one of the books.  It was much easier to teach one lesson than two.  They discussed the book, and brainstormed about ideas that they could write about.  The boys had come up with three introductory sentences as starting points.  With that much of a start, she let them choose which of the three directions they wanted to go with their story.  Being twins, both boys picked the same introductory sentence.  By the second paragraph, they were obviously on different routes.

My sister thought the stories were pretty good, so she was understandably upset when the papers came back with Fs on them and a notation about copying.  Hadn't the teacher read the stories?  She confronted the teacher, and asked her why she had given the boys failing marks?  The teacher insisted that the stories were the same.  My sister asked her if she read past the first paragraph?  The teacher refused to reconsider the grade. My sister immediately removed her boys and her financial support, from the school.

*Descent into Hell*

The beginning of the second semester had started off dismally, for Melissa. She had trouble getting the classes she needed to meet the credit requirements, and she was supposed to graduate in June. She had worked so hard to get this far, and I was proud of her. She barely got into the Food Science class before the first two weeks were up. The teacher threw a textbook at her and told her she needed to pay a fee for class. She had a week to turn in the money. Unfortunately, we were between paydays. The cutoff for turning in the fee was our next payday. Usually, she put important papers where I would see them, but there was no paper this time.

The day the payment was due, the roads and the parking lot were extremely icy. Matthew had missed the bus and Melissa had offered to drive him. His dawdling made them run really late, so she had to park at the far end of the skating rink that was referred to as the parking lot. She slowly walked across the sheet of ice, just as the bell was ringing. Should she go to the office to get the receipt she needed for the check I gave her, or should she head directly to class? She opted for the latter.

When she got into the classroom, she pulled out her homework to hand it in, and realized she had forgotten to put her name on it. The teacher passed her while she was doing this and Melissa had to walk up to the desk to turn in her paper. Her teacher cheerfully commented that Melissa would be getting a zero on the paper because it was late. Melissa was incredulous and she threw her paper in the trash.

Since she didn't have a receipt for the check I had sent with her, she wasn't going to be allowed to participate in the lab project, either, and would get a zero for that. Going to the office for the receipt would have made no difference. Another classmate had come in late because she had passed by the office to get a receipt for her fee. She was also denied the credit for the lab project.

Melissa came home quite upset. When she explained the situation, Jeff said he had the same teacher for a day. She had announced that day, "If you come into the classroom with a backpack, it will be confiscated for the remainder of the day." It didn't matter whether you brought your backpack in voluntarily, or not. Often, if the bus was late, security directed you towards your classroom, and didn't allow you to run to a locker first.

I went to the school to speak with the teacher. She said she thought her discipline was appropriate, because the students had been in class for three weeks. I countered that Melissa had attended three days out of a possible four, because she got in late and had been ill during the second day. The teacher said she might consider accepting the late paper, if Melissa's work proved to be as good as I said. I wish I had known that the paper was in the wastebasket in that room. I would have retrieved it. I didn't know it, and left a message with the office for the janitors to retrieve it, if possible. I don't know if they did.

Melissa went to work that night, depressed. On her way home, she was rear-ended. While it left no visible physical marks on her, the damage was considerable. I went to the school on Monday to find out about getting homework for her. I didn't know if she would be missing one week or two. Medications would make it nearly impossible for her to attend a full day of school. She didn't want the teachers to know what was wrong with her, because they seemed to take explanation as excuses.

Tuesday, she attended two morning classes because of testing, but she was nearly screaming in pain by the time I got her home. I tried to collect the homework requests, Tuesday after school. I received two out of the six. The Food Science teacher sent one with a happy face on it and the notation, "She was in class today". We got most of the homework about a month after our request. How timely!

N). SAFETY & SECURITY: *Too Easy Access*

I accompanied Betty to her polling place. After parking in the parking lot, we headed towards the nearest door. At first it was locked, but the hallway was filled with students waiting to get back into their classrooms, after lunch.

The voting booths are set up near the main entrance of the school, to minimize adult interaction with the students. We turned to head towards the main door when a helpful student opened the locked door. We went in and proceeded directly towards the voting booths.

A teacher tried to stop us by telling us that we weren't allowed to enter the building through that door. We were halfway down the hall, so we just kept walking. The teacher had been present when the student had opened the door. Why hadn't she stopped us from entering? If we had been a threat, gaining entry is half the battle. I hope the teachers impressed the seriousness of this action upon their students.

## O). POLITICS: *The Superintendent Wants to Hear From You*

When I received the bright yellow postcard in the mail, I was jaded enough to realize that the invitation wasn't meant for me (personally), just the resident of my address. Thousands of these had been sent out, and I knew that maybe a couple hundred people might attend any of the four Town Meetings, to discuss the School District.

Like a moth to a flame, I couldn't resist going to this meeting. I knew it wasn't going to do much good and I was proved right. At the meeting, I met my friend Average Joe and his wife. Joe was upset about the recent art additions to the school. What good was art going to do if the students needed more classrooms? I was there about the "Everyday Math" Program.

The suits from the School District sat in the left side of the seating. Average citizens sat on the right side. The Superintendent gave a Power Point presentation on how many students were in the school district (55,000), how many schools we had (81), and how many languages were spoken in the district (90). She moaned and complained about how there were financial shortages and we would need cutbacks. Then, she talked about "No Child Left Behind" and how there wasn't a lot of money to fund this program, so money would have to be cut elsewhere. She couldn't see any solutions. At this point, I wanted to stand up and scream, "Stop taking the Federal money and you don't have to meet the Federal mandates that cost two dollars of our money for every dollar we get from the Federal Government!" Of course, I would have been ejected from the meeting immediately.

The Superintendent opened the floor to questions. I was the third person in line. I commented about the failure of "Everyday Math", how it had been revised at least twice in my calculations (and still might have been flawed), and whether teachers were supplementing it with other materials. I also pointed out that Sylvan Learning Center was making lots of money off parents whose children were failing, because teachers couldn't implement Sylvan's suggestions to keep the student on track.

The suits claimed that the Math scores were all high, thanks to "Everyday Math" being taught exclusively, in classes. I knew this was either a bald-faced lie, or simply ignorance. The program didn't have enough rote and repetition in the earlier grades. Most children can't grasp the algebraic concepts that were being introduced in early elementary, until they were at least 13 or 14. I knew at least six teachers, in six different schools who were supplementing, to keep their class on track, but I couldn't mention them. Saying their names would only cost them their jobs. The Superintendent brushed off my comments as invalid. People around me wondered why I couldn't get a straight answer about my valid concern.

Three seats further down the row was a father. He had attended his son's Math class once a week for the past year. He mentioned some of the flaws with the program, but the Superintendent asked for his name and number, so she could contact him after the meeting. The difference between the two of us, I wasn't involved in my child's class, and maybe… I was a woman.

Average Joe stood up and spoke against building all the new schools. Buying land and building new schools cost a lot of money. Why couldn't the schools be built up, instead of out? Anchorage was running out of empty lots. When Anchorage started building up, where will we be building the schools? Basically, he was told that the foundations of most of the schools weren't strong enough to support additional floors. This would have been a perfectly acceptable answer, except it took the experts ten minutes to get to that point. The solution was obvious. If a new school was going to be built, the District should plan for the foundation to be sturdy enough that the building could be added on to. The focus should have been on future building projects, not past deficiencies.

While I thought the meeting was quite informative, I felt like the Superintendent was so far removed from the people who came to speak with her. I know her job is difficult. When she accepted the job a few years before, she inherited a lot of serious problems with it. The situation we are in isn't totally her fault, but she gives parents lip service. There might be some valid ideas in the Anchorage population, but unless you have educator's credentials, you won't be heard. It was abundantly clear that the discussion portion of the meeting was only a formality. Because of the abysmal turnout, it was even easier to ignore us. I would be willing to bet if the topic of discussion was, "Plans to Impose Year-Round Education", we would have had standing room only in any auditorium the School District could have booked. If nobody really cares, will anything ever get done? Whether or not one has children in the schools, we all have to pay for the spending decisions of the School District.

After the meeting, Joe, his wife, and I were all pretty much in agreement. We wouldn't be able to make much of a dent in the School District rhetoric, but thank goodness, our kids would all be out of the system within a couple years, complete with all their battle scars.

*The Fur Ball*

During a winter festival called, "Fur Rendezvous", here in Anchorage, they have a teen dance called, "The Fur Ball". This dance was open to 14-19 year old High School students. This is not considered to be an all-school dance. It's a citywide dance, because the School District has nothing to do with it.

This year, the dance became dangerous. Supposedly, some rival gang members caused some trouble before the dance was scheduled to end, near midnight. The dance was evacuated and about 1000 students forced out onto the street. I heard they weren't even allowed to collect their coats. Police arrived and started disciplining anyone who tried to stay in the area of the dance.

It was freezing outside and kids were being directed blocks away from the parking garage, or where their parents were expecting to pick them up. If my kids had been there, they wouldn't have had a cell phone, so I wouldn't have known where to find them in the chaos. If a teen didn't have a cell phone, they were just out of luck, for contacting anyone. At midnight, the only businesses that were open and could have provided any warmth or telephone access were bars.

In the aftermath of the chaos, the Superintendent was loudly critical of the situation. She denounced the Fur Ball and said that the School District didn't support the concept of "all-school dances". The School District had nothing to do with this dance in the first place, so the outrage was confusing. I wondered, if there are five high schools in our District, was the city supposed to have five different Fur Balls, so we could keep students segregated?

The other popular complaints had to do with the fact that 14-19 year olds were in an unnatural situation. This age span should never have been placed together, because it's dangerous. The people who made this complaint should consider the age of students attending our four-year high schools. The age range is generally 14-19. Personally, I thought the late hour was something that should have been changed, for the age range.

After all the complaints, the Fur Ball was modified. The next year would see shorter hours and only 15-17 year olds would be allowed to attend. I understand the attendance was dismal.

Q) ALTERNATIVE EDUCATION & GETTING CREDIT: *Credit By Examination-Astronomy*

Melissa had been struggling with the Chemistry class, and knew that she might not make the credit she needed. Since it was the first semester, she still had a few options. The option she chose was Credit By

Examination. We asked the Curriculum principal about any classes, besides chemistry, that would fit a science credit for her.

The principal found a teacher who would be willing to administer an exam. Since this is usually a way to test out of a class where the student is well versed in the subject, Melissa really needed to study for it. Melissa asked what the teaching material was, and if there was a course syllabus. The teacher suggested a book called, "Astronomy", which was probably in it's fifth printing, but she didn't know who the author was. I spent about a month looking at bookstores for the nebulous book, before I found it. Melissa had about a month to study the whole book, because the teacher never provided a syllabus about what was covered in one semester of her class.

Unlike Jeff's test, where he was allowed 80 minutes (a class period) to take the test, after school, Melissa was given her test at lunchtime. She was allowed less than 40 minutes to take an oral test that was constantly being interrupted by students coming in to ask the teacher questions, because they didn't realize she was testing someone.

A couple days later, the teacher cheerfully announced that Melissa got a "C" on the test. It would have been a respectable grade under any other circumstances, and it was quite a good showing considering the conditions the test was taken under, but it wasn't good enough to get the credit for the semester. When the teacher couldn't understand why Melissa wasn't happy about the grade, Melissa explained to her that the grade had to be an "A" for her to get the credit. The teacher hadn't known, because no one told her.

Getting credits by alternative methods is a relatively gray area to most teachers, and even some counselors. I received a compliment from Melissa's counselor. He said that I was probably more qualified to do his job, when it came to knowing the details about alternatives for getting credits, because I had all sorts of personal experience.

Melissa lost the time and $50, when she didn't make the grade. It would have been different if it had been her fault for not passing the test. The lack of standard operating procedures for alternative credits made us feel like the money had been stolen from us. With the amount of turnover in administration, it was often difficult to maintain any continuity. Principals and counselors played musical chairs, and moved around inside and out of the school. Just when I would get a principal or counselor who had the right information, they would play the "Administration Shuffle", and be shipped away to another school.

*Choosing a Candidate*

One of the ways charter schools were giving credit towards Government classes was volunteering as a campaign worker, during an election. The students picked out a candidate whose campaign they wanted to work for. The students had to document their hours and write a report when they were done. Students could get a quarter of a credit for participation.

After a recent election, I was listening to a local talk radio program. A School Board member was the guest for that hour. A caller complained about the campaign work that was done by the students. He whined that students who were doing this volunteer work, weren't divided evenly among the candidates. The School District "needed" to do something about this (horrible) situation. The School Board member assured the caller that she would make sure the schools would distribute their student volunteers more evenly, during the next election.

I don't see how she could make this promise. Campaign workers choose the candidate they want to work for because they share the same beliefs. If a volunteer is assigned to a candidate, against their will, it isn't considered to be volunteering anymore. How many candidates would be happy having a resentful volunteer working for them? Also, how many volunteers do their best work for someone they don't particularly agree with?

*AVAIL Graduate*

One of Melissa's classmates graduated from AVAIL this year. AVAIL is the Anchorage Vocational Academic Institute of Learning. Students qualify for this program if they have drug, alcohol, pregnancy, or lingering health problems. You must also be at least 16 years old. Melissa's friend fell into the last category. She had one of those intermittent ailments. It showed up often enough for her to miss a lot of school. The ailment ended up being appendicitis, and she had the offending organ removed. The surgery kept her out of school even longer. By the time she had the surgery, she was well past the Withdraw/Fail criteria.

Her progress in school was so messed up, she needed to start her classes from the beginning, but this was mid-year. She started attending AVAIL and managed to get everything straightened out. She graduated a year later than anticipated, but she graduated. I knew she had been struggling, and I was glad to see her successful, and happy.

This program is part of the Anchorage School District, but it has very limited resources.

*Cutting Melissa Off at the Knees*

I had gone to the third quarter conferences. Melissa had two classes she was failing. One class was Food Sciences, with the rigid teacher. The teacher expected perfection, but she had to be excused for not providing enough supplies for the whole class (despite the student fees). The other class, she had a teacher who was relatively flaky. I asked both of these women if there was anything they could do to work with Melissa, to help her bring up her grades. Both teachers said Melissa only had to request the extra work. I gave them the benefit of the doubt. It was Wednesday. I told Melissa what the teachers had said. She said she had tried, but the first teacher had refused and the other was absent-minded.

On Thursday, Melissa came home in pieces. With two months left before graduation, she had been called down to the counselor's office. It was bad enough to be called down, but she was called down during her 39% class and spent 45 minutes in the counselor's waiting, while the rest of the class watched a video. How would she pass the test on Monday, if she hadn't even seen the video?

The counselor finally called her into her office, and asked if she knew why she had been summoned. Melissa told her that she thought, maybe, she was going to be withdrawn/failed. The counselor told her that was exactly the reason, and sent her back to class. This was the first hour of the day. By the second hour, two of her "A" teachers were asking her why they got withdraw/fail recommendations in their boxes. Melissa blanched as they told her to try not to be absent anymore. Melissa couldn't see any reason to live, if her best wasn't good enough. I told her I would speak to the teachers, in the morning. She was doubtful, because Friday was an in-service day. The teachers might not even be at our school. I prayed for the best and planned my strategy.

On Friday, I went to the school early and headed towards the office. I had a book with me, because I knew I might have to wait. I contacted the counselor first. I told her that I needed an emergency conference with all of Melissa's teachers. She tried to pump me for information, but I only told her that my daughter was contemplating ending her life. The counselor was shocked and hurriedly told me that I needed to get Melissa help. I told her that was what I was at the school for.

I settled in a comfortable chair until the teachers were assembled. We went into a conference room and I told them that I needed ten or fifteen minutes, at the most, if I was uninterrupted. My message shocked the teachers. I started with the inhumanity of the rigid teacher and spoke of Melissa's car accident and the absences associated with it. I also covered her food poisoning absences from the Food Science class, because the other members in her group couldn't read the timer or the temperature for proper cooking of the food that Melissa was required to eat. The final straw had been the counselor telling her she was going to be withdrawn/failed. The counselor denied saying it, but her actions spoke so loudly. All the teachers knew when the paper had shown up in their boxes.

I pleaded for them to work with Melissa. After all, there were eight weeks left of school. Wasn't it possible for her to raise her grades to Ds, at least? I also requested that they not mention absences. The anxiety was killing my daughter. If we didn't get her graduated this year, she would lose all hope. Her endurance was nearly at breaking point, and I feared I was going to lose my daughter. I would take legal action, if necessary.

Melissa graduated with her Fs transformed into a C and a D. Her situation isn't unusual. Betty saw a story on Dr. Phil's show that was similar. The senior in question had missed school due to respiratory illness and was late sometimes, because she had to get two small siblings to school. Her absences weren't any more than they had been the previous year, but the school withdrew/failed the girl. Her mother sued the school district and lost. They had no other way for the girl to get her diploma.

Dr. Phil had criticized the mother's work schedule, which caused the daughter to be late for school. He also said that he thought the family could have planned better, to minimize the girl's absences. I thought this was quite thoughtless, on his part. I don't think that Dr. Phil has ever been a single mother who has to accept any decent paying job to make ends meet, and that has medical insurance. Sending a sick student to school too soon only lengthens the duration of the illness and possibly even the number of missed school days.

In some schools, it just depends on who you are, as to whether your school will work with you. Our two girls worked hard to make the grade, and were bashed by their schools. It just proves that hard work doesn't count in the school system.

## S) SICKNESS & HEALTH: *Vanquishing the Vegetables*

The previous year, I had seen several students eating chef salads. I heard that they were so popular that students had to get in line early, in order to get a salad. This year, Melissa couldn't find a salad in the cafeteria to save her life. The closest the cafeteria had to a salad was a slice of tomato and a leaf of lettuce that would otherwise be put on hamburgers. There was also no milk. The cafeteria had dwindled down to fast foods like hamburgers, pizza, and tacos. If you bought a drink at the school, they had high fructose fruit juices, sodas, and bottled water.

In spite of the interest in salads, fruits, and vegetables, the cafeteria refused to offer them. We were never able to figure out the logic behind the refusal.

## U) CELEBRATIONS: *(Mean) Spirit Days*

Every year, the high school has Spirit Week. The week includes days like: Hat Day, School Color Day, and Pajama Day. Students put in suggestions, and the Student Council chooses the best suggestions. Of course, the Student Council is subject to the judgment of the school's administration.

This year, themes of two of the Spirit Days included "Nerd Day" and "Hillbilly Day". It was Friday afternoon, and next week was Spirit Week. Melissa had a problem with these two days being on the list. She was concerned that one student's perception of a "nerd" or a "hillbilly" might be what another student regularly wore to school. It could be extremely embarrassing.

Just before the end of the school day, there was an announcement. The themes for the Spirit Days were to be revised by the faculty. Hillbilly Day was replaced by Western Day. Nerd Day was replaced by something more socially acceptable.

## V) SUPPLIES: *Missing Books*

In order to collect Melissa's third quarter report card, I had to pay a fine for a missing library book. Of course, I found this out at the conferences. Without the report card, I had trouble remembering which teachers Melissa had. I would have checked the school library, to see if the book was truly missing, but the library was closed. I stood in the long line at the office to pay the required $25 for the missing book.

After conferences, I went home and pinned the receipt to my bulletin board. Melissa told me that she was sure she had returned the book, but she would check her room again. It might have fallen behind something. Melissa didn't have much time to think about the book because the next day, pressure was applied to her in an effort to force her out of school. After fighting to keep her in school, the library book was forgotten.

Just before graduation, Melissa received another fine slip for the same missing book. At lunchtime, she went to the library to look for the book on the shelf. Lo and behold, it was right there. Melissa took the book up to the librarian and explained that we had paid a fine on a book that had been sitting on the shelf, all this time. She took the receipt to the school the next day, and collected the refund. Obviously, the school's computerized collection system doesn't have any place to annotate payment of a fine for a particular book.

When I ended up pulling Matthew out of school, I hadn't been able to find any of his textbooks around the house. His locker at school had been empty, because he couldn't remember the combination to get into it. I offered to pay for the missing books. It seemed like it was a very difficult operation, to look for the prices of these two textbooks. Between the two books, I spent $107 and collected the receipt. Closer to the end of the year, I tried to find out if the books had ever shown up. I was told that they probably wouldn't have all the books in until the last day of school.

I allowed for a little more time to organize all the books, and two days after school ended, I called the school to see if Matthew's books had shown up, yet. The woman on the other end said we had just shown up in the paperwork that morning. I asked if that meant that the textbook was in? She said that it meant that the textbook was still missing and we owed money on it. I informed her that we had paid the fines two months earlier. Even though the woman seemed to be speaking perfect English, she couldn't seem to comprehend my request. I spoke very slowly, and carefully, and repeated my situation. Now, she told me that I was cleared for the books. I gathered that meant that some sort of notation had finally been made on the computer about the payment.

A couple days later, we received another request for payment of the missing textbooks. It came in an envelope that had first class postage on it. I wondered how many other parents had paid the fines and were being asked to pay again. The system didn't seem very efficient to me. I sincerely doubt that I would ever get the money back from the school, even if they did find the books. If they weren't aware that I had already paid, how would they know to contact me to refund my money? Hopefully, they will improve their record keeping system sometime soon.

X) SUMMER SCHOOL: *Wow, Enrollments Doubled!*

One of Betty's friends worked for the School District. In an elated tone, she told Betty that summer school enrollment was doubled. This meant that the students were finally getting the supplemental education they needed to pass the High School Qualifying Exit exam. Betty sort of wondered how her normally logical friend could be viewing this as a positive point. What was wrong with this picture? If the education system is working fine, why do the students need supplemental education?

When I heard this news, I thought having a retention problem would be a great argument for year-round education. After all, what good is there to say that the children need their summer, when they are spending half of it in school still? When is a family supposed to take their vacation, if a vacation during school time is considered to be an unexcused absence?

Sally's reaction was similar to mine. If the summer school methods are so much more successful for reaching the difficult students, why isn't the School District looking into implementing these methods during the regular school year?

The thing that troubles most of my friends who have children older than 10th grade (the age for taking the test) is, "Why are so many children failing?" All of our children passed the test in the 10th grade, easily, with the exception of my son Matthew. He passed the parts he took, but skipped school the day the Math section was administered.

What are WE doing right that OUR children are passing? It's too bad the schools can't figure it out. Everyone would have a lot more free time if they could figure it out.

(By 2006, the Superintendent was touting Summer School as a social activity. Supposedly, many students were in summer school to stay in contact with their friends from school. So much for the concept of the students needing the whole summer for a vacation.)

## Z) LAST IMPRESSIONS: *Expulsion is the Only Answer*

I had put Matthew back in school for the second semester. He said that he really wanted to be there. Looking back, it had to have been mainly for his social life, but there was something else going on. Matthew was talking about Science. It seemed like this was the class he was most interested in. If there was Science that day, he was heading to school. By the time we got the Withdraw/Fail notice, I noticed that he had a "B" in Science class. If he was making progress, should I fight for him?

I decided to poll the teachers. I asked if the days marked absent on the Withdraw/Fail Notice were really absences, or if they were just tardies. According to all the teachers, except his Science teacher, they were all absences. Three of the teachers said that he was a great student to have in class and pulling him out would probably be counterproductive. The other three said that he wasn't even trying in their classes. The latter three teachers taught core classes: Math, Social Studies, and English. The Science teacher asked if he was being pulled out of school for being late to her class, so much? If so, couldn't she just give him extra work, to make up for being late? Removing him from the school seemed like such a drastic action.

I went to talk to the Science teacher, personally. I explained that I had tried to work with the principal on alternative methods, but he wouldn't work with me. He wrote up the last detention slip and Matthew had argued with him. This had resulted in an immediate three-day suspension that could only be appealed in writing. My appeal had been unsuccessful, since the rules said that I had to appeal to the principal. I had tried calling, since the suspension was already underway. Appealing in writing could have taken the three days.

The principal couldn't remember who Matthew was and asked me to refresh his memory about the circumstances. How many other students had been sent home with suspension papers in the previous eighteen hours?

Matthew's Science teacher wondered how she was supposed to teach students if they couldn't get into the classroom. She understood that Matthew seemed to run on his own time, but he had been getting better about getting to her class on time. She had been unaware that the last time she saw him would be his last day, and said she would miss him. It's interesting to note that the most sympathetic teachers for my children either had experienced difficulty getting through the regular system themselves, or had a family member who was also marching to the beat of a different drummer.

I left the school with tears in my eyes. We had been lucky enough to find a teacher who understood Matthew, but it had been too late.

## *Melissa's Graduation*

Melissa's graduation was the first graduation I had attended in Anchorage. I had dropped Jeff off four times to play at graduations, and he chose not to cross the stage. The venue was huge. It was much bigger than the football field I had graduated in. The acoustics were much worse also. If I heard the principal right, he was thrilled that our High School had a graduation rate of about 60%. If that was right, over a third of the students were lost along the way. With people, that's too high a failure rate.

Melissa came up to the podium and gave the announcer her name.  They only got it two-thirds right. They skipped her first name.  The students had to come around the corner to get back to their seats, but the path really didn't get close enough to take pictures.

We took Melissa and a handful of her friends out to dinner to celebrate her graduation.  She graduated, but it had been a battle that had worn out both of us.

# Chapter 20
## Out of the Danger Zone 2003-04

A) FIRST IMPRESSIONS: *The Madness Continues*

All of my children were safely out of the school system. Matthew, the unteachable child, had completed his GED testing, on September 9th, with quite respectable scores. A score of 410 is passing in each area, and his lowest score was 580 out of a possible 800. Melissa enrolled at the University of Alaska in Fairbanks, and Jeff was taking some classes at the University of Alaska in Anchorage. Matthew had applied for Job Corps, but we made too much money. Unless Matthew suddenly became homeless or self-sufficient, the momentum we had worked so hard to generate would dissipate quickly.

The Superintendent of the Anchorage School District is disappointed when parents remove their children from the system, because it shows a lack of faith in our education system. My children were considered undesirable and un-teachable by the schools they attended. The school system had no faith in them. My battle for my children's rights is over. They are adults now. We are no longer in the battle zone, but so many others still are.

B) BUILDINGS & GROUNDS: *The Cost of Buildings in the School District*

There was discussion about building a new administrative building for the School District. A new building would supposedly cost about $42 million, while converting an existing building would only cost $30 million. One of the morning disc jockeys works in construction. He said that building a new building should only cost about $18 million. Of course, his calculations were considered invalid. After all, he was a high school drop out. What did he know?

During the discussion, another man got into the conversation. He said that he had been in construction for over 30 years. He said the disc jockey's calculations were quite accurate. He also added a little more light on the situation. The calculation was accurate for a basic administration building, but the price could be doubled or tripled by using more expensive materials. He cited two recently built schools that were quite beautiful, as examples of extravagant supplies. I wonder how many of us were paying the bill for expensive woods and marble, in these schools. Why do we need this in a school? After all, our children are meant to learn there, and more expensive wood won't improve the educational process. If it did, why aren't we embellishing our Title I schools?

*The Voters Say "No"*

A bond measure for $30 million was placed on the ballot, in April, for voter consideration. It was meant to cover conversion of an existing building into a new administration building. The ads for the ballot measure specified a building, but the ballot measure itself didn't make any specifications. It seemed like there was a large loophole for the "bait and switch" tactic. Voters felt they would be giving the School District carte blanche if they voted for the measure, so they voted against it.

Just before the election, the School District had sent out "educational" information about the bond measure, because voters were (supposedly) uninformed. After the election, the Superintendent said that we needed to have a special election, or the measure needed to be put on the next ballot, because voters had made a mistake.

I think the problem is all in the presentation. The School District seems to think that the voters are all children and communicate with us, as such. If I were a small business person trying to get a loan, and used the arguments the School District did to persuade investors to give me money, I would be turned away. The argument wasn't strong enough.

The premise of the School District's argument is: School District administration is scattered all over town, so it needs to be consolidated. The figure mentioned for employees, who needed to be consolidated, or could be housed in the new building, was 600. Personally, I didn't think the building in question had enough parking for 600 employees.

The current building had been rented for the past 30 years. In that time, rent has obviously gone up due to rising property values. Someone should have bought a building long ago. The lease on the current building was scheduled to run out the next year, so that's why the School District was scrambling.

The Superintendent said that they could reduce the number of employees, if they consolidated the work sites. Of course, no figure was given for how much the savings could be. I guess the voters didn't have the need to know. If the School District could come up with a feasible plan, maybe I would vote for it. Attacking my intelligence isn't the way to get my vote.

(By 2006, the School District would be using a lot of empty mall space to house their employees and some of the charter schools. If the price was right, the spaces fit the bill perfectly.)

*Combating Summertime Vandalism*

The school had completed its second year of its program to fight vandalism. During the summertime, they allowed tourists with campers to stay in the school parking lots. This required at least two campers each day. One group could go shopping or sight seeing, while the other watched the school. Parking, water, and electricity were free. I gather it's been successful, because they are planning to do it again, this year, for the third year in a row. It's an imaginative way to combat the problem. I wonder how much money it saves each year. I think it's too soon to tell yet.

C) PARENT-TEACHER ENTITY: *Affordable Health Insurance*

In Hillary Clinton's book, "It Takes a Village"; she laments the fact that there isn't any way to get decent health care coverage for all of our children. She made some valid points, but I'm not sure if the government is the entity to solve this problem.

In the "Catholic Anchor", I read an article about how so many people can't afford medical care. I wrote a letter to the editor for an idea I thought was radical. Maybe the major churches could have "card carrying members". If you donated at least a certain amount to a church, you could be a card-carrying member of the church. Some churches have such big populations; they could have the same bargaining power as some of the union groups, and could help their members get a better rate on insurance premiums.

I told my idea to my friend Daisie, who's a senior citizen, and member of AARP. She said, by being a member of that group she can get discounted insurance from participating companies. Seniors can fit under the AARP umbrella, but we needed an umbrella for a younger group. There is only one group in the country, that everyone is eligible to join (unless, maybe you're a pedophile), and it's also a child advocacy organization. It should be the perfect group to be able to get some bargaining power for health insurance for families. At the last count, membership for a family was only about $10. That's cheaper than union dues. Of course, the group I'm referring to is the PTA.

I e-mailed my idea to the National PTA. They already have a committee that reviews companies offering products and services that would benefit members. I gather that means this is something they possibly offer, but no one's advertising it.

I was referred to my state's PTA, for more state-specific information, pertaining to my request. Translated, I think that means that the National PTA doesn't offer a list of nationwide insurance companies that offer discounted health coverage for members, but individual states might.

I sent an e-mail to my state's PTA and asked if there was any program like this in place for our state. I sent my e-mail out on October 10, and have yet to receive an answer. Right now, I have friends who are paying $700 per month to cover themselves and one child. Half of their month's pay is going towards the health insurance and their apartment payment. They almost can't afford to be sick, because they have to

186

meet the deductible. Families without health insurance aren't just the poor families. They are families like mine where the husband makes over $50,000 a year. If the PTA is looking into health insurance for its members, I wish they would advertise a little louder. Maybe membership would start going up again.

### E) DIFFERENCES & DISABILITIES: *Ruling Out ADD*

One of my sister's sons had been failing in school for a long time. She had paid for tutoring for him in the summer time, but he still fell behind during the year. He seemed to not be paying attention and sometimes he seemed not to hear her. He had been diagnosed with allergies, and had been prescribed Claritin for nearly two years, so allergies didn't seem to be the problem. She took both sons to a psychologist, and the psychologist said that the one who was succeeding in school had ADD. He didn't find any problems with the one who was failing.

Her family doctor checked the boy out again and requested an MRI of the boy's sinuses, because something seemed to be wrong. They suspected polyps in his sinuses, so he was sent to an ear, nose, and throat specialist. The ear, nose and throat specialist said that my sister's son definitely had some severe allergies. When she told the doctor he had been on Claritin for the past two years, the doctor informed her that Claritin wouldn't touch this problem. He suctioned out her son's sinuses and prescribed a different medicine. He said he wanted to see the MRI results when they came back.

My sister had to fight her family doctor to get the test results sent to the specialist. The medicine helped the grades some. Instead of snoring like a freight train at night, her son's breathing was barely audible. He was more alert and the dark circles went away from under his eyes. He is actually getting some oxygen to his brain, for the first time in years. Unfortunately, he had lost valuable education time before the problem was diagnosed.

### The Bad Boy

While I was having trouble getting Matthew through school, my friend Karen was having a similar problem with her son. Both boys had reached the age where they were flexing their muscles against authority, so it was harder to implement solutions. Karen's family had a history of depression. Some of her relatives had been nearly incapacitated by the ailment. Her son was diagnosed with depression and ADD. It took years for them to figure this out. Depression and ADD can be treated with the same medicine like Ritalin or Tofrinol, but a doctor has to be very lucky to find the right medicine and the right dosage on the first try. It took a while to get the medicines right. Meanwhile, Karen's son was labeled a bad boy. By this time, it didn't matter how well he was doing. If he made any minor mistake, it was magnified way out of proportion because of the label.

By the end of his sophomore year, Karen had very little hope that her son would graduate. He was talking about dropping out and she couldn't prop him up. He didn't want to hear anything his parents had to say. What was the point?

Karen lived in a suburb, and there was only one high school in their district. To get a change of scenery, they would have had to move out of the district, but how far would they have to move him, to get away from the label? At this point, Karen's brother-in-law got involved with the situation. He felt Karen's son was redeemable. Maybe he could help get the boy on track. If Karen's son was agreeable, he could move out to his uncle's farm. There would be plenty of regular exercise to help with the effects of depression, and he would be starting a new school with a clean slate.

Karen's son is scheduled to graduate this year. He has good grades, and is looking forward to higher education. While not all parents can move their children to relatives' houses, this success story might not have happened without supportive extended family.

*Encourage the Progress*

Laurel's younger daughter had been struggling with Math ever since Laurel could remember. She seemed to have a lot of comprehension and retention problems when it came to the subject. Her daughter had been getting grades that were barely passing. It was as if she were holding onto the information by her fingernails.

This year was different. When Laurel and her husband went to conferences with their daughter, they found out that she had a high C grade for the class. They were elated, but the teacher was disturbed by their reaction. He told them that their daughter was A student material, and she wasn't trying hard enough. They needed to do something about this unacceptable situation. Laurel and her husband were just so relieved that their daughter was finally grasping the subject. They told the teacher not to pressure their daughter, and see where she went with a little encouragement. At the time of this writing, I understand the girl's grades are still rising.

Sometimes it isn't laziness that keeps the student from reaching their potential. It might be how the teacher teaches. When a student understands, you can watch it "click" in their minds. You see it in their eyes. With thirty students, it's hard to notice when individual students don't "click". This teacher didn't realize that he was reaching a previously unreachable student.

*Bad Medicine*

Jane is a friend of mine, who is black. Her son had been diagnosed with ADD when he was in the fourth grade. Of course, at the same time, his parents were in the midst of a volatile divorce. The unrest in the house would drive nearly anyone to distraction. Jane and her son actually had to flee the house and live with a variety of relatives, until she could support herself.

Jane's son was labeled a problem child and his grades continued to stay low, despite being on medication. Now her son was in Junior High, and he was complaining about not feeling well. He had no energy. He begged his mom to take him off the medicine, so she did.

The school tried to accuse her of child neglect, since they knew he wasn't taking the medicine any longer. She came to me for advice, before she went to the conference. I gave her all the paperwork I had about the latest legislation and the abuses of the medicines. I also gave her information about alternative methods for dealing with ADD.

In the end, she was able to move him to a school where he gets more individualized attention. His grades, which had been Ds and Fs, are now As, Bs, or Cs. He has more self-esteem and more energy, since his treatment was changed, and he's no longer taking the unnecessary medication.

F) PROGRAMS: *No Child Left Behind (95%)*

I had been listening to the radio, and reading the paper, about the "No Child Left Behind" policies. All of our mainstream high schools failed. The only two who passed were charter schools. They are running without much financial or "emotional" support from the School District. They are considered to be the unwanted stepchildren. One of the reasons these schools passed is that they don't have any resources for Special Education to deal with students who have special needs. Without this segment of the population, their scores would always be higher.

Our neighborhood elementary school had a sudden rise in average test scores when the trailer court that fed into the school was closed. Eliminating the students from the trailer court also eliminated most of the learning difficulties the school had been dealing with.

When I found out how the schools failed, I was amazed. The system can't last or be repaired in the allotted time with the current requirements. The mandates include, but are not limited to:

1) At least 95% of the specified population must take the exit exam each year

2) All ethnic groups must meet the minimum required standards, in all core subjects.
3) All standards must be met now. There's no allowance for time to improve, no matter how large the gap.

If any of these standards aren't met, the whole school fails. In my opinion, one of the contributing factors for our High School failing was less than 95% of the required population probably took the exit exam. Matthew was one of the students who didn't complete this test, because he skipped at least one day of the testing. I think the time wasted filling out detention slips could have been better invested in encouraging the students to attend classes. Since so much effort was concentrated on warehousing a hostile population, there was little incentive for students to take the test.

In the past, my children had been an asset to their schools when it came to raising school test averages. Their abilities have no meaning in this new world of education standards. We only reflected the school's success in educating white students. If we had been black, Hispanic, or Native American, their contribution would have been considered more valuable.

One of our elementary schools failed because it's in a low-income neighborhood. Much of the population is black, Hispanic, or Native American. This school has made great progress over the past two years, but they were so far behind that it wasn't enough. This school had to offer parents the option of placing their children in another "successful" school, and providing transportation. The schools chosen may have room, but do they really want the extra students, who can help drag down their shining scores? Are the special programs, like Title I, offered at the more successful schools? What happens to the failing school if all the parents opt to send their children elsewhere?

After more than 150 years of compulsory education in the United States, one would think that the education system would have a better idea how their students learn and what works to educate them. It shouldn't take an educational expert long to troubleshoot a classroom or a school, to help them get on the right track. Why aren't they tapping the ethnic communities, for help? Not everyone thinks like an affluent white person.

If the school system were any other business, they would have been shut down long before they reached this sorry point.

*No Child Left Behind: A Cheechako Viewpoint*
I have only been in Alaska for 12 years. I still consider myself a cheechako, or newcomer, when it comes to some political issues. Alaska has a few issues that maybe the other states might not have in common with us. I can see certain problems with Natives meeting the "No Child Left Behind" criteria. The first problem I can see is the mandate that all teachers have Master's degrees in every subject they teach. In the villages, because there are smaller schools, and fewer students, the available teachers have to be able to teach a wide variety of subjects to students of various ages. A teacher can be certified to teach at an elementary level, and be fine for a variety of subjects. In High School, teachers usually specialize in one subject or another. It may be necessary for a teacher to be able to teach two subjects in an urban high school, but teachers in the villages need to be able to teach more than two subjects.

The other problems have to do with the history and culture of the Native people. When the Christian churches came into the area, they did what they have done for hundreds of years. They tried to eradicate the pagan culture of the people and replace it with European wisdom. Without a culture, there's a void. Alcoholism helped fill that void. If the new religions and the alcoholism didn't destroy the people enough, after World War II the government told the Alaskan Natives that their children needed to be sent to faraway boarding schools for the proper education. I understand that parents were given the choice of voluntarily sending their children, or being imprisoned, then having their children removed. These boarding schools were basically only accessible by plane, from the villages.

The most notorious of the boarding schools was the Wrangell Institute, which closed its doors in 1975. From the time students entered this school until the school was closed, the people who were supposed to be protecting and educating these children had license to abuse the children however they chose. Who was going to tell on them? The adults who survived this situation are at least my age. Abuse spawns abuse, and the cycle continues. Any teacher can tell you that it's more difficult to teach a child who comes from a dysfunctional family.

Looking at stories written by Natives about their culture and experiences, there are areas where I know I don't have any reference points to understand. I have never been to any village to see how they have to live. There has to be some sort of bridge built by understanding where your student is coming from. This is the same for any cultural difference, especially if it isn't influenced by Western Europe. If the schools can't do it on their own, they should work with the members of the various ethnic communities to find solutions.

### Illegal Lotteries

When Betty originally entered her son in the lottery for the charter school, she had been told that they might have to wait a year for admission. About a week before school started, they received a call to come in for an interview. Betty thought this was a little premature. After all, weren't they so far down on the list that they wouldn't consider him yet?

There was one thing that Betty hadn't considered. When they had filled out the application, she had put her son's ethnic background as Caucasian and Native American. This section had been considered optional, and parents didn't know that the lottery was weighted due to ethnic background. Betty's son was soon third on the list, for his grade level, due to this criterion.

This year, School District policy for weighting the lottery to have a more ethnically diverse population is now considered to be illegal. I don't know if the idea behind the policy was to have a population in the school that reflected more of the city's diversity. If they were doing it to try to monitor test scores of a diverse population for a specified period of time, I think six years should have been plenty of time to collect pertinent data.

The question of favoritism and quotas came up this year. If anyone looked at all the schools around our District, they aren't all racially/ethnically balanced. Charter schools shouldn't be encouraged to weight their lotteries for any reason. Anchorage School District would have to abide by the laws that discourage such favoritism.

As far as I know, there hasn't been any information released to prove whether or not various ethnic students perform better in charter schools. I think this would have been an interesting avenue for exploration.

### 1% Art in Schools

I have heard about the 1% For Art in Schools concept. This seems to mean more about bringing artwork into the schools rather than bringing artists into the school to interact with the students. It doesn't mean much to have a beautiful piece of artwork outside the school if it has no connection with the students inside the building. In our schools, they are contemplating elimination of the arts programs. They are considered non-essential electives. I think that the money should go towards the programs, not just the props.

## L) CRIMES & PUNISHMENTS: *Baiting and Kicking*

Betty received a call from the school. Her son was being suspended, and the teacher wanted to tell Betty her version of the story (as if Betty's son's story would be different). The teacher's story went this way:

Several younger high school students were in the hallway, throwing bottle caps back and forth. Sometimes, they tried to hit people. These boys tried to hit Betty's son with a bottle cap. Then, the ringleader suggested they target his guitar. When they hit his guitar, Betty's son kicked the ringleader. He was suspended.

Betty's son's story went like this:

The teacher was watching the activity. He had ignored having his body hit by the bottle caps, but they messed with his guitar, so he kicked the ringleader. He had been suspended and everyone else involved had been sent back to class. The teacher had done nothing to try to diffuse a situation she knew would escalate. School policy prohibited unauthorized projectiles (i.e. bottle cap throwing). He knew he deserved to be suspended for kicking the other boy, but the other boy should have been punished, too.

The key to stopping the harassment is to be consistent about what isn't allowed. Not punishing the victims. They are the ones who will be bringing the guns to school, in the future.

## M) DISCRIMINATION, HARASSMENT & ABUSE: *The Novel Concept*

Betty had a friend whose son was being beaten up on the playground. The little guy was in the first grade and his assailants seemed to be sixth graders. Despite the presence of a Security Guard, and the school's zero tolerance policy, the child was still in danger. The mother thought of pulling her son from the school.

Betty mentioned the problem to her son, since he attended the same school. The concept of the school involved younger students interacting positively with the older students. Betty's son had an idea to stop the attacks, without causing more violence. The idea was brilliant, but not within the limited mindset of the Security Guard.

At lunchtime, Betty's son asked the Security Guard to point the boy out. The Security Guard gave Betty's son a visual inspection. Long hair, dark glasses and trench coat. Must be trouble. He suspiciously asked why Betty's son wanted to know. The reply was, "I understand he's being picked on." The Security Guard wanted to know what Betty's son intended to do about the situation. I loved the response. "We want to make him the coolest kid on the playground."

Betty's son had decided if he and some of his high school classmates showed that this little boy was of some value to them, the other kids might stop picking on him. Not one punch needed to be thrown. They were just going to be a group of guardian angels.

The Security Guard refused to point the boy out. It took Betty's son a few more days to figure it out himself. I don't know whether the plan worked or not, but I think the concept was neat.

## N) SAFETY & SECURITY: *Harassment Policies Are Working Well*

At the beginning of the school year, the School District received a grant to have two police officers in each junior high and high school. This is a measure to reduce the amount of violence in schools. The addition of police officers to our schools suggests there's a reason for them to be there. After all, the school and the government don't just waste money on programs that aren't necessary, do they?

On February 8, the headline on the Anchorage Daily News reads, "Bullied boy brain-damaged after suicide attempt." The incident happened five years before, but the case was finally settled. The parents won an undisclosed amount. School employees knew or suspected that he was being harassed, but they volleyed between doing nothing and punishing the victim for defending himself. Important school records have since been destroyed, per standard operating procedure, so no one will know what really happened. One of the biggest problems was the lack of communication between the school, his parents, and his psychologist. The school refused to work with the parents or the psychologist, without the proper paperwork. Neither the parents nor the psychologist were informed of this requirement. The school dropped the ball.

Secondary Education and the Superintendent both were quoted that they felt their harassment policies have been handling bullying issues appropriately for years. I beg to differ.

In June, there was an anti-bullying conference in town. The School District was asked to endorse the activity, but they refused to do so because it was outside of the school year (translation = outside the school's jurisdiction). They can refuse to officially endorse this activity, yet the Superintendent officially condemned the Fur Ball and the paint ball incident. Neither of these activities was under the School District's jurisdiction.

In Barbara Coloroso's book, "The Bully, the Bullied, and the Bystander", she pointed out that the three roles are fluid, up to a certain point. Up to that point, the roles can be changed. After that, you deal with a host of social ills that will end up costing our society dearly. She has checklists for parents and teachers to consult, so they can recognize these students. Most of the students fall into the bystander category. Bystanders range from disinterested to actively supporting the victim or the bully. Ms Coloroso pointed out that the people who brought guns into Bethel and Columbine were actually victims who used the most extreme method to fight back.

Has the escalating violence in our schools been stemmed by the police intervention? If our system was working so well before, why were violent incidences rising in the schools?

*Life and Death Situation*

As I mentioned in the previous section, there are police officers in the High Schools. Near the beginning of the year, the police moved into action to stop a fight that had started during a passing period. One of the police officers felt threatened and rather than just pointing his pepper spray at the suspected assailant, he made a wide arc with it, spraying several students in the area.

The fight was stopped and a bystander with asthma was taken to the hospital. He happened to be at his locker when the fight broke out. My friend Lisa worked with this young man. Every day he had to go to school became a potentially life-threatening endurance test. If he was afraid of students before, he also became fearful of the police who were there to protect him. The anxiety can be a killer. In "The Bully, the Bullied, and the Bystander", Barbara Coloroso said that it doesn't matter how much security you have if the students still feel threatened.

Adding the police will not help the situation, if there isn't a code of conduct in place from elementary school. The system has dropped the ball, and it's costing a lot of money in the later stages of education. In my experience, by the time students reach High School here, they are treated more like children than like the responsible young adults they are supposed to be. If this is supposed to prepare them for how they are supposed to interact in the "real world", then responsibility and accountability aren't necessary requirements in the "real world".

*Rules About Dances*

Whenever a school has a dance, they sell tickets for it. Sometimes, students have friends from other schools who they want to invite to the dance. Unlike the Fur Ball, there are rules about bringing students from other schools to your school's dance.

When you want to invite a student from another school to your dance, you have to put in a request. The guest in question must be 19 or under, or attending school. This process screens out undesirable guests.

Matthew's girlfriend went to another school, across town. She put in a request to invite him to the dance. A week before the dance, they went out to buy clothes, but they hadn't received the permission slip yet. The day before the dance, they received denial of permission. He was denied permission, because the principal from his old school and the new principal from his girlfriend's school, had personal problems with him.

While this process may seem unfair, I guess it can go a long way towards reducing problems between students. Matthew wasn't the only one turned away from a school dance this year, as a guest. At least two other students Matthew knew were turned away from dances. These students had good grades and fit the required criteria, but I may have overlooked something in stating the criteria. It seems that the student may have to be attending a School District school. The other students who were turned away were not part of the system. They were being home schooled.

Since there is no "qualified and unbiased" adult who can vouch for their character, such as a principal or teacher, they can't attend the dances either. I understand that there have to be rules, but sometimes the rules don't fit every situation.

O) POLITICS: *Community Task Force*

Anchorage had a major budget deficit. I remember hearing somewhere that the School District budget either equaled two-thirds of the city's budget, or accounted for two-thirds of the city's budget. Either way, that is a lot of money. Both Anchorage and the School District had to look for ways to tighten their belts. The School District Superintendent had the brilliant idea to form a community task force to help find ways to cut the budget.

I spoke with a woman whose husband had been a member of a previous task force. He had made several realistic suggestions that could have saved the District money. Unfortunately, he was picking at all the District's sacred cows. How dare he suggest cuts in those areas! About 85% of the School District's budget is spent on salaries and employee benefits, but the emphasis for cutting costs is placed on areas like music and sports programs. The man on the task force quit in exasperation. I know how he felt.

When I started making suggestions on how we could reduce consumption of supplies in the schools, I was shunned. Individual schools didn't want to hear how much paper was being wasted due to inefficiency. It wasn't completely the teachers' fault that they were being inefficient. They were so busy trying to teach the students and conform to the varied government mandates that paper was a minor issue in their big picture.

The Superintendent inherited a nearly insurmountable task when she got the job. She isn't necessarily a bad person. I think she just can't think outside the box and doesn't like/understand anyone else who can.

*A Teacher's Viewpoint*

Laurel's uncle has been a teacher for decades, in the Midwest. Over the years, he has seen the expectations for his job change. He recently realized that the main objective for his job is to try to achieve "C" status for every student. There isn't much support or encouragement for the teachers to exceed that expectation. No matter how many A and B students the teacher has, he has failed if the rest of the students haven't achieved at least Cs. Matthew or Jeff would have made this teacher's life hell. They both had knowledge but not the paperwork, to back it up.

The other problem Laurel's uncle noticed was that if you have two sets of economically opposite parents whose children are in your class, and they both have educational problems, the more affluent parents will disregard the "lowly" teacher's expertise. Conversely, the family who might be struggling financially will do everything they can, to help their child reach a better life.

These are two of the best illustrations I can think of to show how difficult it can be for a teacher to excel in his vocation.

## P) POLICIES & PROCEDURES: *Sorry, We Dropped the Ball, But Nothing Can be Done About It*

Jimmy had been one of Matthew's classmates. He was an average size boy, but his voice hadn't caught up with his size. Ever since elementary school, he had been teased about that. No teacher ever intervened or told his tormentors that the behavior was unacceptable, so he became a fighter, and was labeled a "bad boy".

This year, he was in the tenth grade. It didn't matter that his voice had changed; he had been a favorite target for so long that school was the last place he wanted to be. Even though he caught the bus to school every morning, he wasn't attending very often.

By the time parent-teacher conference came around, school had been in session for nine weeks, and he had missed three consecutive weeks. Jimmy's parents were shocked when all the teachers told them that Jimmy had been withdrawn/failed for excessive absences. They hadn't heard a word about this before conference time.

School policy specified a process of parent notification, in the case of absences. First, the parent is either called or e-mailed, when their child misses school. If it's suspected that the student may be intercepting the messages, the parent's work phone number is called. At seven days of absence, in any class, a parent is notified by mail, that their student is on attendance probation. At eleven absences, the teachers are asked to fill out a withdraw/fail form, if they feel the student isn't making any effort. The withdraw/fail notice is mailed to the parents, and the student will be arrested if they set foot on school property, during the school day, for the remainder of the semester.

Jimmy's parents went to see the principal and the counselor. Both school employees said the same thing, "We're sorry. We dropped the ball, but there's nothing we can do about it now." Basically, their son was being expelled for the rest of the year.

The parents figured out that Jimmy had been spending his free time at a local department store. Supposedly, Anchorage has no truancy policy, so he couldn't be arrested for truancy. If he had been misbehaving at the store, the store could have removed him and ticketed him for loitering. The school viewed his chronic lack of attendance as his parents' fault. Jimmy's mother wondered about the policy of parents and teachers as partners in education. It's hard to be in a partnership if your partner won't communicate with you.

Jimmy's parents moved him to a private school, where he's bringing in good grades again. Another failure of our wonderful public school system.

## Q) ALTERNATIVE EDUCATION & GETTING CREDIT: *Expelled for Epilepsy*

Eddie had been epileptic for years. He had also been severely dyslexic. Epilepsy, being a health concern took precedence over the learning disability. By the time he was a senior in High School, he had made up all his math credits, but his English credits were eluding him. He wasn't able to do the work, the way the school wanted it, with his dyslexia. The letters wouldn't stay still in the books he had to read. There were no accommodations.

Stress aggravated his epilepsy to the point that the school looked at him as being a liability. They expelled him. His father tried to find a way to finish his son's education, and the School District wasn't very helpful, until the father used the word "lawsuit". That got some immediate action.

Despite the school year already being in progress, Eddie was able to enroll in one of the charter schools and work on getting his credits on-line. The charter school had assured Eddie and his father that the late enrollment wouldn't be a problem. They should have required that promise in writing.

Unfortunately, about six weeks before school was scheduled to end, Eddie received notification from the school he was getting his classes from. None of his work would be given any credit due to his late enrollment. He was told he could start again the next year, and probably graduate mid-year. This amounted to a wasted year with a mass of busy work.

Eddie's father fought the school district to get his son's credits. Even though Eddie had started late, he had finished his work in a timely manner. Eddie received his diploma for the 2004 graduation year.

*Cutting Electives*

The School District has started cutting electives. One of Melissa's friends said they had started cutting the art and music programs. He wondered if these cuts were making them stupider, and if "stupider" was even a word.

I read a book called, "Riches For the Poor", by Earl Shorris. He is involved in a project called the Clemente Humanities program. He feels that many of the poor people don't learn about humanities. Things like the works of Socrates and Plato, which deal with politics, and other works in arts and literature. In the case of minorities, our White Anglo-Saxon Protestant (Western European) cultural influences have no bearing on their realities. Much of the art, literature, and music that are taught in the schools don't reflect the cultural diversity of our population. Our minorities don't have any identity, and therefore they have no voice.

The classes that help us express ourselves in society are being cut, and nothing is there to fill the void, but hopelessness. The Clemente Program is reaching out to the hopeless people, but wouldn't it be great if we could help our children to find their voices before they become hopeless?

Susie's son asked her when he was in the fourth grade if there was a place in society for him. Being Athabaskan, Susie didn't know what to tell her son. Current trends seemed to be unfavorable for Native men. She told him that she hoped things would be better by the time he graduated. If he completed school, he would have a much better chance of success.

*Abuse of Funding?*

This year, charter schools were investigated for how their students spent their "education" money. This money is provided by taxpayers. Money was spent on various activities that can be questionably considered as educational. According to the Anchorage Daily News, on December 29, 2003, families enrolled in some of these programs used money for a family pass to a local water park and activities on cruise ships. A child's membership to a local health club or music lessons would have been considered more reasonable.

Many of the students getting funding for charter school activities are also attending private schools full-time. They are using the charter school money to pay for extra-curricular activities. Students in the traditional schools are required to pay fees for after school activities. Why do charter school families feel entitled to the money? If a student is enrolled in Personal Alternative Choices in Education (PACE), and chooses educational materials from religious programs, the materials aren't covered because of the separation of church and state. These parents may pay for the curriculum and use their "allowance" for extra-curricular activities.

The tide is turning to cut out coverage for elective options for students in charter schools. This is following right along with the diminished electives offered through the traditional schools. If the charter school is part of the School District, allowances should be able to be made for students in these charter schools to receive the electives from a traditional school, if the electives are still available.

This controversy is ongoing as of the writing of this book. We will see if our State can standardize expenses in our charter schools, and still have a viable program.

V) SUPPLIES: *Obsolete Books and Dead Piglets*

My friend Bill used to work for a school. Textbooks are a valid expenditure for a school, but he told me something that really opened my eyes. It was something that can easily be hidden in a school's budget, unless you know what you're looking for.

If you are a first grade teacher, and your textbooks are getting ragged, you might order a new set at the end of the school year, for the next year. The books arrive just before school starts, and they are stamped with the school's name. For some reason, you are moved to second grade, for the next year. Because of the lack of standardization in the curriculum, the teacher who replaces you in the first grade decides she doesn't like the books you have chosen, so she makes an emergency request for different textbooks.

The life span of a textbook is only about five years. Then, they are considered obsolete. At this point, the textbooks are all destroyed, even if they haven't been used by any students. How often does this happen in schools around the country?

Another hidden expenditure is supplies that were wasted. One case involved some piglets for a dissection lesson. They arrived, from out of state, in formaldehyde. The container had to be topped off, since some of the preservative had evaporated. The teacher was informed that his piglets had arrived and were in the storage room. Near the end of the school year, the teacher remembered them. By that time, the preservative had evaporated enough that the piglets were no longer any good. Unless someone oversaw all the waste in the schools, no one would notice it.

Z) LAST IMPRESSIONS: *How Far Have We Really Come?*

In a recent political ad by a candidate running for our School Board, she said that our School District budget has gone up 46% in the past 10 years, and enrollment has only gone up 6%. I know we have gone from 55 schools to 81 schools in that same time frame. That's over 50% increase in school buildings. We have also replaced at least three existing school buildings due to age or damage. We currently spend $377,417,071.00 on 50,000 students per year, yet it isn't enough money. Why not?

Teachers have been given incentives to retire early, before the 20-year mark, in an effort to save money. I don't think teachers should get full retirement benefits at 20 years. I think it should be more like the military, where you don't qualify for full benefits until 30 years. A two-tiered approach might save some money. We keep getting rid of good, experienced teachers, so we can hire two new teachers, fresh out of college, to replace each of them. We act like a tree that keeps cutting off our root system, and we can't grow under those conditions.

Our schools have become more interested in warehousing and punishment, than actually educating the students. Some of my friends say that the students almost seem to be considered an inconvenient nuisance in the educational process. It would be great if the schools were open only to those who wanted to learn. We would have a lot fewer disciplinary problems if the students actually wanted to be there. Most children are interested in learning something, even if it isn't required. It's the nature of being human. If our children can't be productive members of society, then we've failed. Throwing money at the problem won't fix it. Community involvement might, because education is a problem that affects us all, even if we don't have any children.

I wonder how the education system will look ten years from now.

# Chapter 21

## 2004-2006 Small Wheels Moving

### A) FIRST IMPRESSIONS: *A "Lost Cause"*

I thought I had finished my book when my kids left the school system. Even though I was still active in local politics, education seemed to be more of a money pit. Then, I started hearing quiet movement.

### E) DISABILITIES AND DIFFERENCES: *Autism: The Genetic Epidemic*

In 2005, autism was in the news a lot. The Today Show had an expert come and speak about the fact that they are realizing symptoms of autism as early as 6 months. Unfortunately, it's a hindsight approach. After taping several children interacting with their parents, they have noticed lack of eye contact as early as 6 months. While this could also be an indicator of a hearing problem, there are ways to figure out whether it is a hearing problem or not.

Autism is a medical problem that has gone from 1 in 10,000 in 1980 to 1 in 250 by 2000. Currently, it affects children at a rate of 1 in 166. The government may claim that it is a genetic problem, but it has increased 40 fold in 20 years! That is epidemic. In some states, a parent can't get aid for a child with autism, unless the child was diagnosed with autism before age 3. Most often, the symptoms start becoming noticeable between 18 and 24 months, and seem to coincide with the childhood vaccine schedule.

In David Kirby's book, "Evidence of Harm", he addresses the issue of mercury in vaccines. In 1991 and 1992, more vaccines containing thimerisol (mercury) were added to the childhood vaccination schedule and autism expanded. The mercury in the vaccines is supposed to be a preservative, but it's better at killing healthy brain cells than the bacterial meningitis that may be contaminating the vaccines. This book has the stories of several frustrated parents of autistic children and their experiences trying to get some answers. The government won't release information about the vaccines, nor do any studies that can prove whether or not the vaccines cause the autism. Parents who are trying to get information are treated as greedy fanatics.

Symptoms of autism are amazingly similar to symptoms of acrodynia (pink's disease), Mad Hatter's disease, and Gulf War Syndrome. They are all neurological ailments that respond favorably to treatment for mercury poisoning. "Evidence of Harm" puts forth some possible cures for autism. Of course, despite favorable results, there is no FDA approval.

How much of the education problem is possibly caused by mercury laden vaccines that the government and the schools require us to have injected into our children? If a child had neurological damage, and can't function properly, his parents are told they need to work on their parenting skills. If a parent chooses to not give the child the vaccinations and has a healthy, well-behaved child, the parents can still get friction from the powers that be. Parents can be charged with medical neglect for not giving their children the shots. Military members already have no choice in vaccinating their children. Disciplinary action can be taken against the parents.

At what point do we reach the point of no return? Maybe we have passed it already.

### *The CDC Decides Autism is an Epidemic*

At the end of the first week in May 2006, the morning shows and the news started having segments about autism and the fact that the CDC is considering it an epidemic. Now they are going to start looking into causes. Despite unrelenting efforts from parents of autistic children to get the CDC to investigate the cause of this epidemic, the CDC dragged their feet. During this delay any existing data could have possibly been corrupted, destroyed, or even reclassified. Will they start from scratch, or will they consider investigating the information the parents of autistic children are concerned about?

On May 15, Time magazine had an article, "Inside the Autistic Mind", about the various types of autism and how pervasive it is, in our society. The article says that it's been 60 years since American psychiatrist Leo Kanner defined the ailment. As you can see from the previous section, incidence of autism has nearly doubled in the past 10 years and is nearly 10 times more prevalent than it was nearly 30 years ago. The United States isn't the only country showing rapidly rising cases of autism. Japan, England, Denmark and France are also experiencing it.

A second article in the same issue of Time, "A Tale of Two Schools", highlighted two schools that have had high success rates educating autistic children. Claudia Wallis wrote both articles.

*Deaths from ADHD Medicines*

On February 10, 2006, Reuters News Service released a story about a study of deaths of patients who took various ADHD medicines. The study took place between 1999 and 2003. Fifty-one patients died during the specified time frame. Sixteen of the dead patients had been prescribed Ritalin; twenty-four had been prescribed Adderall; and the other eleven had been prescribed other amphetamines.

According to the article, "Health Canada had suspended sales of Adderall in 2005, after twenty reports of sudden death in people who took it." It was allowed back on the market after Health Canada decided there was no proof it (Adderall) was riskier than any other therapy.

The FDA said, "Conclusions about the relative safety of these two stimulant therapies (Ritalin and Adderall) cannot be made on the basis of this analysis."

I find it interesting that the FDA is studying ADHD medicines to see if they may be related to psychiatric problems. The makers of Ritalin said patients who used methylphenidate didn't have any more risk of sudden death, high blood pressure, heart attacks, or strokes than the "general population".

I may not know a whole lot about drugs, but when I was in school (and when my kids were in school), we were warned about the hazards of taking drugs like amphetamines because they made your heart beat faster. It was stressed heavily that these drugs could kill you. If patients who take these medicines aren't at a higher risk, why are they monitored more than the "general population"?

*Treatment Without Side Effects*

According to Roman Bystrianyk's article, "Flax Seed Oil and Vitamin C Improve ADHD", in the January 8, 2006 issue of "Health Sentinel", there was a three month study of sixty children to determine the effects of a natural remedy for ADHD. The results of the study had been published in the January 2006 journal, "Prostaglandins".

Thirty of the subjects had been diagnosed with ADHD. The other thirty children were considered to be healthy control subjects. All sixty children were given flaxseed oil supplements, which contained 200 mg of alpha linolenic acid (ALA) and 25 mg of Vitamin C, twice a day for three months. None of the children suffered any side effects, and none of them dropped out of the study. Blood tests were also done during the study. There was a noticeable improvement in social and learning problems.

*The Trouble With Boys*

In the January 30, 2006 Newsweek, there was an article about boys falling behind in school. The article said that elementary school boys were twice as likely to be diagnosed with learning disabilities and placed in special education classes. When Matthew was taking the ADD medicine, out of six students in his class taking the medicine, only one was a girl. That meant one third of Matthew's class was medicated, and it was five boys to one girl. It might have been the luck of the draw as far as the teacher getting a higher percentage of kids with ADD. I was too busy trying to deal with my own son, that I wasn't figuring out the ratio for his whole grade level. It was a privacy issue, so I might not have gotten very far, unless I had parked myself outside the office at lunchtime, and watched how many kids were medicated. The 30% medication rate in Matthew's class seems to indicate more of a learning difference than a disability. If the school only allows for 15% of their students to have Special Education, what happens to the rest of the students under this label?

The article states that 30 years ago, girls were lagging behind, so in 1972, federal law Title IX forced schools to give girls and boys equal opportunities. Emphasis on girls. Even with the attention from books like Mary Pipher's, "Reviving Ophelia", are girls really doing better today? Or, are they just doing better in comparison to the boys who are failing?

The article points out that boys who don't have fathers or other positive adult role models tend to do worse in school, and according to psychologists, "A boy without a father is like an explorer without a map." In one middle school, in Pueblo, Colorado, they have tried separating the girls from the boys, to see if teaching same sex will improve test scores. After all, boys and girls do think differently. Boys tend to be more spatial and girls more verbal. The school seems to be seeing some early positive results. Only time will tell if it will be a successful experiment.

Another point that was brought up in the article was the reading curriculum. In her example, author Peg Tyer mentions "Memoirs of a Geisha" and "The Secret Life of Bees" as let's say "chick books", which a particular boy didn't score so well on. When I was a junior high student, we were offered five books to choose from, to do a presentation. This way, the class learned about five books in about the same time they would have learned about one. The teacher had a list of projects we had to do as a group. They included: making a bulletin board, acting out a scene, doing a newspaper article based on an event in the book, and presenting a book report.

Books that were cited in the article were "Raising Cain", by Michael Thompson; "Real Boys", by William Pollack; and "The Minds of Boys", by Michael Gurian. It seems that how a child learns is one of the keys that teachers need to be taught. Boys and girls definitely think differently.

In an article in Esquire's July 2006 issue, Tom Chiaurella wrote the moving article, "The Problem with Boys". As a college teacher and father, he's "a little worried" about what he's seeing. According to the statistics in his article, boys are twice as likely to score below basic standards in the 12th grade, be threatened with a weapon on school property, and abuse alcohol as young adults, than their female peers. Boys between 15 and 24 are five times more likely to commit suicide than their female counterparts. Their dropout rate is increasing, as is the number of boys who are testing below grade level. According to the Department of Justice, 95% of the inmates under 25 in state and federal prisons are male. Current statistics show there are 42 men for every 58 women in college. Where are the guys going? Alternatives seem to be maybe trade schools, suicide, military, or just drifting aimlessly.

Fathers need to be involved in the school system. They need to attend meetings, volunteer in class, or get involved with the after school programs. If 34% of children in this country are raised without a biological father in the household, men have to make their presence known in a positive manner somehow.

*I Am Not Alone*

I wrote a letter to the editor about flaws in the gifted education program. It had taken me a long time to figure out what my children had really gone through. Gifted kids had to do twice as much work as "average" students to get the same grade. Jeff chose not to play that game, and it cost him potential scholarships. Melissa gave it everything she had; yet twice as much was never enough. The stress and lack of sufficient sleep has contributed to depression, a weakened immune system, and possibly even extra weight. I looked around at the carnage that my friends and I lovingly call our children. All that potential laid to waste made me angry. In less than 225 words I expressed my frustration. The letter showed up in the Anchorage Daily News the Friday before the 2006 Super Bowl.

On Super Bowl Sunday, I got a most interesting phone call. The woman on the other end of the phone had read my letter and it excited her. She said I was describing her situation, exactly. In her case, they had found the fine motor skills in her child before the 7$^{th}$ grade, yet they expected him to write more. She was given sheaves of parenting skills paperwork and her child had been given lots of study skills information. She said she had told the teachers the paperwork was about as helpful as telling Stevie Wonder that pink lenses could fix his vision problems. Her child was counting the days until legal dropout age: 365+ days.

We spoke for an hour. She said the homework sessions past midnight were unacceptable and had removed her child from the "gifted" program for relief. I believe I was speaking to a white woman. Her color doesn't matter, but the treatment of the student does. If teachers complain about doing more than the 6 or 7 hours per day their contract requires, what do they think they are doing to their students? I thought child labor had been abolished. These kids put in more hours than the teachers did.

In sales, there is a concept about getting a letter from a customer. If the company gets one letter from a customer, it equals so many customers. I think one equals 100. That means for every customer who writes a letter, there are 99 others out there who feel the same, but don't follow through with the thought. It's one thing for my friends to like my writing. They are supposed to. It's another thing to get a call from a stranger. I wonder how many others are out there who feel the same, but don't know how to be heard.

## F) PROGRAMS: *Oprah's Show and Drop Out Nation*

April 11& 12, 2006, Oprah Winfrey's show was called, "Oprah's Special Report: American Schools in Crisis". I was traveling the first day, but I caught it the second show. The second day, they spoke about the Knowledge is Power Program for schools which prepare students for college, and the high tech high schools supported by the efforts of Bill Gates and his wife. The concepts were exciting and they were successful. The show I saw indicated there was actually hope out there. Unfortunately, the options aren't very widespread yet.

The KIPP program started inside a Houston inner-city elementary school, in 1994. It made enough progress in its first year to gain charter school status. At this time, there are only 45 KIPP schools in 15 states and the District of Columbia. For more information on this program, check out:
http://www.kippschools.org.

In the April 17, 2006 issue of Time magazine, the article is, "Drop Out Nation". It spotlights Shelbyville High School. Shelbyville is a small town outside of Indianapolis, IN. It's basically a snapshot of what is going on across our whole country. Students in the article dropped out because there was nothing to hold them in the system. One girl dropped out because school was an endurance test, which seemed to be so much busy work. Another girl dropped out because she was repeatedly told that she was bad due to her name. She wasn't like her relative, who had problems, yet she was judged on that basis. When given the option of just dropping out of school by an administrator when she was 15, she jumped at it. She didn't have the life experience to understand what she was throwing away. Another young man found trouble before he figured out education was a better route. By that time, they almost didn't let him back in school. Again, there wasn't anything positive to attract his attention from negative activities at a young age.

Considering we now have the "No Child Left Behind Program" our dropout rate is currently 1 in 3. If you're Latino or Negro, it's closer to 50%. Almost half of dropouts between 16 and 24 are unemployed. We are losing potential at an alarming rate.

The sidebar to the article illuminated the benefits of vocational or career education programs. President Bush has proposed eliminating spending in vocational education to pay for "No Child Left Behind" high school initiatives, which are geared more towards college-bound education. In California, Arnold Schwarzenegger is pushing for increased funding for vocational/career education, because many students don't want to go to college. As one of my friends said, "Society can't function without garbage men and repairmen. We can't all be brain surgeons." In the article, it stated, "According to a 1998 University of Michigan study, high-risk students are 8-10 times less likely to drop out if they enter a career-tech program". High-risk can end up in suicide, or as a drain on society as a prison inmate or a welfare recipient, if there is no positive outlet.

M) DISCRIMINATION, HARASSMENT & ABUSE: *Natives Demand Equal Rights*

The September 17, 2005 the Anchorage Daily News and the September 23 Catholic Anchor gave accounts of a historic meeting between 300 Native Alaskan citizens and the Anchorage School District. This meeting had been long overdue. This large group of Native Alaskans were demanding accountability from the School District because their children were being grossly discriminated against. The stories these people told were inexcusable. Native students comprise 12% of Anchorage School District's population in 7th-12th grade, but they are 30% of the dropouts.

According to the article, the Superintendent said she had been warned that there was a lot of anger and pain, and that she had known about the situation intuitively. This is a woman who prides herself on the fact that she reached her current employment position by rising through the ranks, from starting as a noon duty. I have been in this state for 14 years and volunteered in the schools for a fraction of that. Despite the "Zero Tolerance Policy" for discrimination, it seemed like many teachers and administrators never got the memo. I saw the teachers treating minority children differently. Their parents were treated sub humanly. If one was employed by the system for as long as the Superintendent was, and didn't consciously realize the magnitude of this situation, one had to be both blind and deaf.

With the advent of the "No Child Left Behind" policy and the exit exam requirements, Native children from the villages moved into the city, for education. They found it very unwelcoming and exclusive. The people in the villages have a different way of thinking, just as Hispanics, Orientals, and Negroes have different ways of thinking than white Europeans do. There was no allowance for this. If the scores for Native students weren't improving, something needed to be done sooner than now. As a minimum effort, the School District should have contacted the Native corporations to see if they could figure out what needed to be done.

By the end of the meeting, the Superintendent had agreed to set up a pilot program in one elementary school that fed into one middle school. The program will include cross-cultural training to improve communication techniques, and outreach to Native parents to make them feel more welcome in the schools. Training the staff to deal with the Native students better won't help if the "Zero Tolerance Policy" about racial discrimination isn't fixed as far as the student population is concerned. If students are still unwelcoming, the program will only be half formed.

This program will only help a small part of the minority population. The Native population is broken down into five tribes who speak basically five different languages. The Anchorage School District currently has over 100 languages spoken. If the parent doesn't speak English fluently, the child is often the interpreter. This may not be a problem in other business situations, but the child may not be the best interpreter when it comes to trying to solve a school problem. If there are 95+ languages that may not have interpreters through the School District, it's a major gap to have to fill. In areas with a higher population base, you might be able to go to the next town to find an interpreter in the language you need. Anchorage's problem is somewhat unique and our kids don't have the luxury of time. Parents and ethnic communities will have to be more committed to becoming involved in improving the situation.

O) POLITICS: *School Bonds*

In September 2004, the Anchorage Assembly put the question of some previously vetoed school bonds on their agenda. The Superintendent and a School Board member spent half an hour trying to present their case for putting the bonds on the upcoming ballot. The major part of their case involved the concept of 'debt reimbursement' from the State. This meant that the State would pay for part of the bond money the voters voted for.

Granted, the money was needed in some projects. For one reason or another, the voters had voted against these bonds. Voters may vote against bonds because they don't live in the area affected by a certain bond. The projects in a bond are usually in groups, to help them pass, because a variety of projects tend to get more votes when they affect more people. This strategy can be counterproductive if there is a widely unpopular project in the mix. Personally, I voted against the bonds on the principle that I felt the School District didn't spend the money they received, wisely.

This meeting was open for public testimony. I am part of the public, so I put together a 3-minute speech. Mostly everyone else who testified that night was in favor of the bonds. Sometimes, you felt the small town attitude that Anchorage has, when Assembly members interacted with the people testifying.

I approached the microphone, took a deep breath, and emptied both barrels. The looks on the Assembly members' faces were priceless. The Superintendent had chastised the voters for not keeping faith with the School District by not voting for the bonds. I chastised the School District for not keeping faith with the parents and failing to educate at least a third of the students who came through their doors. What good are beautiful schools if the main mission isn't being accomplished?

Of course, there were no comments from the Assembly on my speech. The bonds were placed on the next ballot, and some of them passed.

*Stupid in America*

On January 13, 2006, ABC's program 20/20 aired an eye-opening show about our education system, in general. It was called, "Stupid in America". In the program, author Jay Greene ("Educational Myths") said that educational spending per student has doubled over the past 30 years, yet the return on the investment has been less than would be expected.

Ben Chavis, principal for an alternative charter school in Oakland, California was spotlighted as an administrator who was getting good results with less money. His school has gone from the bottom of the barrel to the top of the heap in the four years he's been there. It seemed to me the kids had a feeling of ownership of the school, and the principal was accessible. In our High School, there were 5 principals. After Jeff had been in High School for the first year, he was given a survey to rate the principal and four vice principals in the school. He barely knew who he was supposed to rate, because he had only basically seen them from a distance. There was no personal interaction. I bet Mr. Chavis didn't need police officers in his school, to keep kids in line, either.

The American students were compared to their Belgian counterparts. They think we are stupid. In European school systems, the funding is tied to the student. Where the student goes, the money goes. Schools don't want to lose the funding, so they have to have results that satisfy the parents. A dissatisfied parent will move their student. Also, if the student is disruptive, the school can kick him out of their school. Eliminating the disruptive student is more financially advantageous than losing more students due to an intolerable learning environment. In the US, we don't have school choice unless we want to pay extra for it. The money is tied to the schools, and there is no requirement for standardization, accountability, competition, or imagination.

According to one New York principal, it's exceedingly difficult to fire a teacher who's a member of the NEA. Some procedures are so time consuming and costly. Whether the teacher is a bad teacher or a sexual predator, sometimes school districts still have to pay the salaries, even if they aren't allowed to be around children. It's sort of like the problems with the Catholic Church. The costs continue rising because of people who aren't doing their job properly. How many teachers are we paying for who aren't really teaching?

S) SICKNESS & HEALTH: *The Naked Chef's Crusade*

In the spring of 2005, Chef Jamie Oliver presented a petition to 10 Downing Street in London, to improve the nutritional value of school lunches in England. He decided that England's kids were the unhealthiest in Europe. It took six months for him to get school kids trained to eat the more nutritious lunches. Once they got started though, the kids really liked the more nutritious meals.

This 30-year old man's quest was so successful that he was in the US in September to discuss the concept for US schools. If England's kids were in the worst shape in Europe; American kids were in the worst shape in the world. We lead the world in obesity and Type-2 diabetes. Mr. Oliver was chosen ABC News' Person of the Week on September 30, 2005.

*Obesity and Vending Machines in Anchorage*

In spring of 2006, the Anchorage School District focused on the problem of obesity and the vending machines in the schools. The new policy for the Anchorage School District is that there will be no sodas in elementary or middle/junior high schools. Diet sodas will be available in the High School. They will try to change the products in the vending machines to more nutritious snacks, but it will take time.

According to the Superintendent, the obesity problem isn't the School District's problem, since eating habits start at home. While parents are responsible for teaching their children how to eat properly, if vegetables are eradicated from the lunch menus by high school, a student has very little choice other than to bring their own lunch to school. If your student is average, you allow 8-11 hours for sleeping, 6 hours of sitting still in school, maybe an hour of riding the bus, and 2-3 hours of homework. Unless you have military precision scheduling, there is very little extra time for actually exercising.

The School District is being pressured to provide more physical education to combat the obesity. The District estimate for upgrading physical education space is ten years! By then, the students who are currently in school will be almost all gone.

Z) LAST IMPRESSIONS: *A Walk in Their Shoes*

In my experience, the more unconventional teachers tend to reach the students. Being a relatively unconventional teacher can also be dangerous. I know because I had a glimpse of it as a Sunday School teacher. With any teaching, materials have to be approved of by the administration and the parents. Then you have to watch out for language in explanations or descriptions.

Teaching a religion class, one is dealing with people who hold the same beliefs on the one subject. In my experience, I was chastised for using the phrase "collective conscious" when describing why Catholics get together in church to pray, and I tried to use a school analogy to describe making a petition to a higher source in terms elementary students could understand. You get better results in Heaven or Earth if a bigger group is asking. I was told to read only what the textbook said without commentary or explanation. Anything I said could be used against me.

My class was only for one hour a week, and about 30 weeks a year. What kind of minefields must the regular teachers face? They have to deal with 36 solid weeks, and not say anything that anyone can object to on a variety of subjects. It's a wonder many of them last at all.

It seems we have the tools for education if we can keep the politics out of the equation. There doesn't seem to be any centralized organization that can evaluate the success of various educational programs for mass distribution. Therefore, individual schools are doomed to have to keep reinventing the wheel if they are going to have a successful school. Not every student fits into a sedate mold and all teachers don't need to be sensational. We need to keep the students interested in the dialog, so they will become educated enough to ask meaningful questions. Maybe some of the concepts in this chapter will make education easier on the teachers. Let's hope so.

# CONCLUSION

I wrote this book because the subject fascinated me. It was sort of like watching a car accident. No matter how much I wanted to turn away and shut my eyes, I just couldn't. For whatever reason, I was supposed to be a witness. People ask me what I hoped to accomplish with this work, because I can't change the system. I think it's supposed to make people aware, and give some parents hope. There were so many ways I could have received help for my children, but I didn't know where to go, who to talk to, or how to ask for help. Maybe other parents will be able to find help sooner.

In my experience, our educational system is like a monster that's eating itself. With all the resources available to us in this country, our education system is supposedly in crisis. We keep throwing money at the problems. Yet it almost seems like the more we spend on public education, the worse the quality.

Education has become so polarized, sanitized, and modernized, that nothing anyone says about improving the quality can be put into practice. Teachers have to be careful about how they say anything, because anything they say or do can be used against them. Everyone can take offense to something.

There are a variety of reasons why our schools are failing, here in the United States. One of the biggest problems we have is lack of standardization. The materials we use and the subjects we cover vary from state to state, as well as from school to school in some districts. We can't be sure the information in our textbooks is even accurate. Even though the list of consultants can look like a "Who's Who List" for the field of study, that only means these people were consulted, not that any of their input was actually accepted.

There are no requirements or expectations of civilized behavior in the schools. People may argue that the real world isn't civilized, but how much of that lack of civility was accepted in our schools? Students come into the school with bad manners and the adults in the school can actually aggravate the existing condition. I have seen the adults at the school abuse and ridicule children, without any restraints. Many of these students need a model to follow, or encouragement. Instead, they can learn that bad behavior is acceptable and a child is considered to be worthless. If a child is being abused, the parents are more likely to move the child without comment, than to confront the teacher. Proof of abuse in schools is hard to prove without witnesses. If we don't start with the expectations of civilized behavior, from all parties involved as soon as the student walks into the school, and follow through with the concept, we are participating in a losing game.

The flaw we have, as we compete against foreign countries is that our system is egalitarian. Everyone has equal rights to a basic education, no matter what your disability. In other countries, they start moving students who are unsuccessful out of the mainstream education system, and start teaching them trades that can make them productive members of society. We are comparing the scores of our whole population, in an age range, to maybe the top third or two-thirds of the same population in other countries.

Inclusion means that teachers have to teach to the lowest student. Excellence isn't the goal. Students aren't allowed to learn at their own level, and we must be "age appropriate" at all times. Students aren't encouraged to compete against themselves. In fact, competition and teamwork are looked upon as bad concepts. In a society where there is only one winner, therefore all the others must be losers; we don't want our delicate children to have their feelings hurt by being in second place. The improvement or potential isn't celebrated, because the inadequacy is the focal point. "Teamwork" conjures up visions of gang activity, rather than a cohesive society. Wouldn't it be great if our gangs weren't as popular because there were more positive groups where kids could feel valued? Gangs exist to fill voids.

Teachers are overwhelmed with federal mandates and the latest programs. They are supposed to be entertainers, psychologists, mandatory reporting officials (in matters of abuse and neglect), and disciplinarians, besides doing the job they were trained to do. The casualties in the teaching profession are enormous. We lose good teachers because they have too much experience and cost too much to keep. Other teachers are lost when they are assimilated into a mindless education machine mindset. If they disagree with the school's politics, they can be bulldozed by the system, and ostracized. We lose good teachers, while mediocre teachers (who cost less) fill the spaces. We obviously aren't looking for educational excellence. How much does it cost in remedial education because we have lost the teachers who might have been able to reach the students the first time around?

Parents and teachers are no longer partners in the education of the children. Teachers either patronize or ignore the parents who know how to achieve the desired results from their child. (I have seen better results if the father gets proactively involved with the situation.) Parents disrespect the teachers because of perceived lack of action or communication. Many administrators have unrealistic expectations of teachers. With mutual disrespect between the adults, who are the children supposed to respect? Besides, children almost seem to be a hindrance in the education process.

"Labeling" is rampant in our school system. It's so much easier for teachers to say that they can't teach this child because of his limitations, rather than looking at the child's potential. So many children limp through the system with problems the "professional educators" should have been able to identify in the elementary grades. We do need to figure out what the obstacles are that are keeping our children from getting a basic education earlier. Things like fine motor skills problems and dyslexia can be less crippling, if a diagnosis is made early enough. Medication should be considered as a last resort to remedy a learning disability. Parents are expected to identify their child's learning difference or disability. How do they know their child has a disability? A child can't tell you he has an ear infection or an ulcer, but they can tell where the pain is. The doctor can diagnose the ailment by the symptoms. We need to recognize the symptoms, to figure out why our children aren't succeeding. Teachers with years of experience should be more adept at this than parents.

Children are being told more often, what is impossible rather than being encouraged to explore the possibilities. Considering that our country is known for its accomplishments, and our "can do" attitude, "Impossible" is the word I heard most in our school systems. How can our children be successful in the real world if they have been shot down in school, any time they have had an original idea? Exploring possibilities can be dangerous, because you can be given more negative labels for actually thinking. People say that abortions may have deprived our society of brilliant minds. Our education system may be stunting potentially brilliant minds. Imagine the productivity if we only allowed our children to explore the possibilities.

We live in a country that is richer than any other country in the world. Besides monetary wealth, we have cultural wealth. Because of our "melting pot" population, we have a wealth of access to foreign cultures, foreign languages, varied hobbies, varied occupations, and varied viewpoints. Every person has a strength that we have yet to tap. If we gave a little bit of ourselves to the schools, just think how much more meaning there could be in a social studies lesson about a far away place, or how this math principle is necessary in this (particular) type of work.

We keep throwing money at the education system. If the education system had to work like any other business, it would have gone under years ago. There is so much waste, yet the people who know about it are unwilling or unable to stem the tide. This book wasn't meant to bash teachers. If there were some sort of neat, ideology bomb that could blow the unproductive educational process away, yet not destroy any property or injure any people, I would be all for it. We almost have to start from scratch, but that is expensive, so we limp on as we have been, for years.

If we don't get involved in solving our educational problems soon, we could be in big trouble. The effectiveness of our socialized education system has a heavy impact on the future of our society. Not having children in the system doesn't excuse us from being involved. How the children are taught now will affect everyone later. We (adults) will be the "frog in the cooking pot" before we realize that we are there, and we are responsible for turning up the heat that is cooking us.

# APPENDIX A
## Roll Call

The following is the status of the children I wrote about, at the time I finished the original manuscript:

Jeff barely graduated from the traditional high school after his second year of being a senior. He graduated from the Alaska Vocational Technical School in June of 2006. (AK)

Melissa graduated the traditional school on schedule, and a wasted year. She is currently attending University of Alaska in Fairbanks (AK)

Matthew dropped out and got his GED. He is gainfully employed in a job he loves.(AK)

Betty's son graduated on time through a charter school, and is attending college (AK)

Mary's daughter graduated from a charter school, on schedule. Her current job is wife and new mom. (AK)

Mary's son graduated on schedule from the same charter school, and is considering college. (AK)

Sally's son graduated from a correspondence school. (AK)

Linda's older son graduated from a traditional school after five years spent in a charter school. He is attending college. (OH)

Laurel's older daughter graduated from a traditional school on schedule, and is nearly finished with college. (MN)

Laurel's younger daughter graduated on schedule at the same school, and is attending college. (MN)

Karen's son graduated half a year late from a traditional school. (WI)

Susie's daughter graduated on schedule from a traditional school, after a last minute correspondence credit. She completed a course at Job Corps and is gainfully employed. (AK)

Susie's son graduated from an alternative program. (AK)

Marion's son graduated on schedule from a traditional school, and is attending college. (WI)

Dolly's daughter graduated on schedule from a traditional school, after a last minute correspondence credit. (AK)

Thomas dropped out and got his GED. (AK)

Eddie finished his class work through a charter school and had to fight to get credit for his work. He graduated on time. Because of his epilepsy, he's hard to employ and is currently considered disabled. (AK)

Lauren's sons are happily being home schooled. Her older son reached the status of Eagle Scout in 2003. He will be taking college courses for both high school and college credits, this year.

## APPENDIX B
## Ten Reasons Not to Homeschool

I got an e-mail from a friend who home schools her sons. I don't know who wrote the clever original, but I've tried to abbreviate the form some. I love what the original author did with a tongue in cheek look at reasons why parents shouldn't homeschool.

Ten Reasons Not to Homeschool

10. Children need to learn to sit still and do mindless tasks, because actually using your brain isn't a quality that's in high demand, in today's workforce.

9. I couldn't possibly teach my own child, because I don't have the right credentials.

8. Children can't live without the school—based health clinics that provide them with birth control supplies.

7. Only the schools can provide our children with the most current and accurate version of the subjects they need to know.

6. Everyone needs to stay on the same schedule, so we can all take vacations during peak seasons.

5. Children need to make a variety of friends whose values differ from the family as much as possible, since our family's values aren't acceptable

4. The longer my kids are under the state's control, the less I have to worry about the church's harmful influence on them.

3. Children learn how to function in society best when they're around their peers, and the child sitting next to my child is the best example to follow.

2. You can't learn efficiently in a group of less than twenty-five.

1. Our children need to learn at the proper pace, because learning something at the wrong speed will only confuse them.

# APPENDIX C
## PROPOSAL FOR YEAR ROUND EDUCATION IN THE ANCHORAGE SCHOOL DISTRICT

(I sent this to the school board early in 1996. It is unadulterated, except for a few commas.)

I am trying to get the idea of year-round education promoted in the Anchorage School District. I presented the idea to the Anchorage Assembly, in an effort to get it on the ballot for the next election. I provided a brief outline of the pros and cons of the system. Since there is sufficient ignorance and opposition to the concept, I will try to clarify the concept.

Year-round education is being practiced all over the world. The United States has the shortest school year in the world and it is quite inefficient. While other schools around the world may have all their students on the same schedule, I am trying to promote the idea of a multi-track system. This means all the children will not be in the school at the same time, but the school building will be in use all year round. It also means the school year will have the same number of days as the students currently attend. Thirty-nine states currently have some form of year-round education.

The plan I have observed and participated in works best with three classrooms per grade in elementary school. There are four groups of students, or "tracks". Let's say that Track A starts school July 2. Track B will start school three weeks later. Track C comes in three weeks after that. By the time Track D is ready to start school, Track A is ready for their first vacation break. Track D moves into the classroom vacated by Track A. The only times the school was empty was during Christmas vacation and spring break. Any major maintenance was done during these breaks

In the system we participated in while we were in Sacramento, parents were asked to rank the tracks in order of preference. All efforts were made to give parents the first track they requested. Unless parents specifically requested, all siblings would be put on the same track. This pattern would follow through to high school, if the plan was implemented district-wide.

Using the plan described above, Anchorage could either get 1/3 more students through each participating school, per year, or reduce class sizes by 1/3 (depending on current student fluctuations). If the schools are overcrowded and more schools are needed to compensate for the overcrowding, this plan would mean that fewer new bonds need to be voted for the building of new schools, and purchasing durable supplies. Durable supplies include textbooks, library books, gym equipment, playground equipment, desks, and other supplies that each school has, which don't have to be bought each year. Each school has to have a certain quantity of these items. Think about how many thousands of dollars worth of books are in each elementary school library. Think about how much gym equipment is required to outfit an elementary school, and how much it all costs. If three schools were converted to year-round education, the cost of all these supplies to outfit ONE NEW SCHOOL could be saved. Of course, money would have to be spent on more teachers and support staff, but that money would have to be spent anyhow, if a new school was built.

When we were in California, the state would not allow individual schools to have more money unless they had shown that they had made every effort to utilize all existing classroom space to its fullest potential. Efforts included double-sessioning, year-round education, and use of portable classrooms. At the time, it cost $5 Million to build a new elementary school. I think that was for your basic unfurnished building. That was the year that California needed $17 billion for building new schools to accommodate the increase of students, and to upgrade existing buildings. Experience had shown that a bond would not pass on the ballot, if it were a billion dollars or more. That means it would have taken EIGHTEEN elections to raise the money that was needed at the moment. I think Alaskans are innovative and adaptable. With year-round education, we could conserve our resources and use them to the best advantage. On January 1 of this year, an article appeared in the daily News, about the sad state of the technology program in our schools. Money saved by converting some of our schools to year-round could be used towards furthering our technology programs. This would not only mean that fewer computers would have to be bought, but they could also cover a larger percentage of students.

Attached to this paperwork is some information that I sent for from the California Department of Education. Some of the savings also include savings in insurance costs and the school would incur fewer capital costs. I'm not exactly sure what that means, but it does seem important. As I said earlier, it lowers the cost per student, as also shown in the California paperwork. The savings are quite a large percentage. Starting up the system may have an initial increase in expense, but after that, the saving starts.

Between the three week vacations and being in the same class throughout their education (unless a student were to move away or be held back), the get acquainted time at the beginning of the year is reduced. The class would work together, more like a team. A possible side benefit to the team idea is that a teacher can tune into the personalities of their students and pass their observations on to the next teacher as a whole package. It could possibly minimize disciplinary problems. The shorter vacations could also help students retain the information they learned before the vacation. This would be especially beneficial for students with learning disabilities. With the level of technology that our children have to deal with to compete in the real world, it is a waste for them to go three months without working on their education. How many of our children will have jobs when they graduate from high school, where they will get full summers off? After three solid months of vacation, we (parents) have to fight the children back into a regimented learning mindset. Teachers would not have to waste the first two months trying to re-teach the students everything that was taught to them the year before, and they wouldn't have to try so hard to cram in tons of new information during the last month of the year, to try to prepare them for the next year. This is not efficient.

I think the shorter vacations spread out over the year could be beneficial for the teachers. I think the teachers could be getting burned out trying to push so hard for 8 months of the year. If they are getting burned out, the quality of their teaching could suffer. Our children deserve better. Studies have shown that smaller breaks over a longer period of time are more beneficial and can increase productivity better than a long vacation. I understand that teachers consider the shorter vacation breaks to be more of an inconvenience. Yet their argument that they need the three months vacation time to take classes, doesn't necessarily hold up. How many other people have to take classes to keep up their profession? How many of these people have large chunks of time off to take these classes? Most of the people I know have to take evening classes, or take leave/vacation time if their schedule is not a straight, one-shift schedule. I even had one teacher tell me that the number of classes she needed to take per year was laughably low. It didn't seem like too much of a hardship, to me, compared to what I had been led to believe at an earlier time. If there is a year-round schedule, the teachers can have the option of taking the time off for vacation, taking needed classes, or being a substitute teacher or tutor. One thing many teachers aren't thinking about, is that if they (only) teach until they are 65, they won't have enough Social Security quarters to retire and get any decent benefits.

A side benefit of the school being occupied year round (with the exception of Christmas vacation and spring break), is the fact that occupation is a bigger deterrent to vandalism. With three months of continuous vacation, there is only one custodian keeping an eye on the building, sometimes. Potential vandals would know this. Vandalism costs money. Less vandalism costs less money. Of course, the breaks mentioned above could still allow for an occupied school. It would be a great time for major maintenance to be done at the school.

Arguments against year-round education come from both parents and teachers. The first has to do with the shortness of Alaskan summers. One teacher I heard from complained that Alaska's climate is hostile for teaching year-round. After all, we don't have great weather like California or Arizona, where they already have year-round programs. Several parents complained that children need the sun in the summertime. I am from Minnesota, which has a similar climate to Alaska, yet it has year-round programs also. Montana and North Dakota are two similar states, as far as weather patterns are concerned, but they do not have year-round. I think it might be because they are more sparsely populated and rural, not because of climate conditions. My first summer was the year Mt Spurr erupted. There was very little sunshine that summer because it kept raining. My children were as housebound as they would have been if we were in the middle of a blizzard. I doubt that children save up enough sunlight from the summertime to last the whole winter. If summertime is so short, then winter is SOOOO long. Since I have been in Alaska (December 21, 1991), I have seen several of my children's classmates leave on vacations for two or three weeks at a time. I don't think this can really be beneficial for their education. With year-round education, the vacation could be built in for that time, instead of sacrificing the book learning.

There are a lot of parents who can't get the time off in the summer for vacation, due to a high concentration of co-workers competing for the same twelve-week period. This situation can lead to parents having to choose between going on a family vacation during the school year, or their children's education. If there were a year-round program in Anchorage, a family would have four three-week vacations in a year. With a vacation in each season, a family has a better chance of finding a vacation time without having to take their children out of school. Having all these vacation windows open can also be beneficial to Anchorage's non-summer daytime economy. An example of this would be families who would be able to go skiing in the middle of the week, during school vacation, when they otherwise would not be able to do it.

One parental argument that I heard quite loudly was the problem of providing childcare for their children during the year-round schedule. One parent claimed that she couldn't possibly take twelve weeks off during the year to take care of her children. That makes me wonder how she managed during the twelve weeks of summertime. Childcare providers, who take care of school-aged children during the summer, could probably use some of that income throughout the year. There are regulations on how many children that a childcare provider can have on-site, for certain age groups. They are allowed to provide care for a higher number of school-aged children than preschoolers. If the daycare centers had year-round business, they would have a more level income. This does not impact the school district nor the municipality directly, but it negates this argument against year-round education.

At least one teacher complained that nine weeks at a time is not enough time to really get into teaching the students, and that she, and several of her colleagues, rarely get home from work at a decent hour, to see their families. In her opinion, if year-round were implemented, she would never see her children. If there were a nine-week learning period, with a three-week breather, there would be more continuity with the education. Right now, her children are orphans (in her opinion) for nine months at a time, instead of only nine weeks at a time. I think she would have been smart enough to see that her argument had holes in it. As far as not seeing their families, I think the problem is a case of working harder, not smarter. I think the teachers should look at how they manage their time. They should use their students to their best potential, as partners in the education process, instead of thinking of them as someone to lecture to.

A somewhat valid argument teachers have, is the fact that they have to pack up their classroom at the end of the nine weeks, if there is a four-track rotation. The bright side, is the fact that they only have to bring nine weeks' supply of materials to class, instead of carting in a whole year's supplies. I can understand this problem, if there are no on-site storage facilities. The school I dealt with was built specifically with year-round education in mind, so storage facilities were built in for the teachers.

Parents will complain that, if their children are in sports or music programs, that the year-round plan will not allow for vacations. Every sports program has a season. Unless your child is in every sport of the year, there should be some time during the year to take a family vacation. Just because your child is not in school, due to a vacation break, doesn't mean that he can't participate in the programs of their choice. Sports programs, and choral programs are usually extracurricular activities, so school attendance would have no affect on them. When I was growing up, there were summertime programs for band and orchestra, to keep us up on our instruments for the school year. I am sure that interested children could sit in on band and orchestra classes, even if they are on vacation. Since these classes would be at a specific time, vacationing students would check in and out at the office. This way, there would not be students all over the school without reason.

The two reasons that seem to make a difference, in Anchorage, and may be specific to Alaska, are subsistence and custody. Supposedly, many Anchorage residents participate in summertime subsistence programs. If they participate in summertime subsistence, do they participate in hunting also? Possibly, year-round education could be beneficial to these people also, because they could have a vacation window to fish, and another window for the hunting season. Since I am not familiar with SUBSISTENCE, and how it works, I don't know exactly how it would be affected, or who would be affected.

The other problem was, that Alaska is a high custody state. One custodial parent told me that, if she enrolled her daughter in a year-round school, she would be breaking the law, because then her daughter wouldn't be able to see her father without financial hardship (the price of 4 plane tickets to the Lower 48 per year) to fulfill the visitation contract. Since I am not in this legal position, I am not sure how it would work.

I know that year-round school may not be able to be implemented district-wide. If even ¼ of the school district, K-12, were able to be put on a year-round program, I think it would result in a substantial savings. In the 1991-92 school year, I filled out a questionnaire that was passed out at Chester Valley Elementary, about year-round education.

They were distributed through the PTA. The PTA president, at the time, tried very heavily, to influence me to fill it out with a negative opinion. I didn't give in to the pressure, and I don't know what ever became of that survey. I thought year-round was a good idea. Was this survey sent out by the school district? If so, what were the results of the survey?

Rochelle McDonald

# APPENDIX D
## The Results Project and Mannatech

In the book I mention Steven Plog, in the section called "He Loves His ADD". About 14 years ago, at the age of 39, Mr. Plog was diagnosed with ADD. A friend introduced him to Mannatech nutritional supplements, and he saw visible results. He made the nutrition connection to ADD and started speaking about it.

People started telling him that he should spread his message to the world. In 1997, a Chicago public school was involved in a pilot program for nutrition and ADD. It was a success. The Results Project soon followed.

The Results Project has access to all sorts of health information. They also have tests to determine physical causes for Attention Deficit, such as allergies, heavy metals, and hormonal imbalances. Lab testing is more tangible than the customary evaluations and checklists.

For more information on the Results Project or Mannatech, go to http://www.resultsproject.net . Mannatech is under Glyconutrients on their home page.

Through the Results Project, I found out about a web site called, "Raising Small Souls". My introduction to this inspirational web site was their video, "Animal School". It shows the different learning styles of the animals, and they can be compared to how children learn. The woman who runs the site is Ellen C. Braun, and she has information on the parenting side of education. The web site is: http://www.raisingsmallsouls.com.

214

# APPENDIX E
## Masonic Philanthropies

I bet you have heard about the Shriners' Hospital, for burn victims. The Shriners are part of the Masonic Philanthropies. Since finishing this book, I found two others that are related to education.

The first is the Scottish Rite Clinics, Centers, and Programs for Childhood Language Disorders. This group deals with children who are having trouble speaking, reading, or understanding the spoken word. There may be problems with attention, memory, word retrieval, or processing auditory information. Dyslexia and Aphasia are the two most common conditions they work with.

As of 1996, almost every state had a facility or was in the planning stages. You can probably find them in the phone book, under Scottish Rite, or you can contact a local Mason Lodge, to find out where there is a facility near you.

Services are available regardless of race, creed, Masonic affiliation, or ability to pay. They will work with families about payment.

The second group I heard of is called, "Job's Daughters". Job's Daughters are females ranging from ages 11 to 20, who are relatives of Masons. They have a philanthropy called HIKE, or Hearing-Impaired Kids Endowment Fund. They raise money for kids who need hearing aids, but their families can't afford them. Being able to hear makes a major difference in education

# Bibliography

Canfield, Jack; Hansen, Mark Victor & Kirberger, Kimberly, "Chicken Soup for the Teenage Soul", Florida: Health Communications, Inc., 1997.

Clinton, Hillary Rodham, "It Takes a Village", New York: Simon & Schuster, 1996.

Coloroso, Barbara, "The Bully, the Bullied, and the Bystander: From Preschool to High School – How Parents Can Help Break the Cycle of Violence", New York: Harper Collins Publisher, Inc., 2003.

Hirsch, E.D. Jr., "The Schools We Need and Why We Don't Have Them", New York: Doubleday, 1996.

Kirby, David, "Evidence of Harm", New York: St. Martin's Press, 2005.

Shaywitz, Sally E., "Overcoming Dyslexia: A New and Complete Science-Based Program for Reading Problems at Any Level", New York: Alfred A. Knopf, 2003.

Shorris, Earl, "Riches for the Poor: The Clemente Course in the Humanities", New York: W. W. Norton & Company, Inc., 1997 & 2000.

Shubentsov, Yefim & Gordon, Barbara, "Cure Your Cravings: Learn to use this revolutionary system to conquer compulsion", New York: G. P. Putnam's & Sons, 1998.

Walker, Sally Yahnke, "The Survival Guide for Parents of Gifted Kids: How to Understand, Live With, and Stick Up for Your Gifted Child", Minnesota: Free Spirit Publishing, Inc., 1991.

CPSIA information can be obtained
at www.ICGtesting.com
Printed in the USA
BVHW011306130521
607276BV00013B/173